THE NEW YORK
STOCK EXCHANGE

RESEARCH AND INFORMATION
GUIDES IN BUSINESS, INDUSTRY, AND
ECONOMIC INSTITUTIONS
(VOL. 6)

GARLAND REFERENCE LIBRARY
OF SOCIAL SCIENCE
(VOL. 759)

Research and Information Guides in Business, Industry, and Economic Institutions

General Editor: Wahib Nasrallah

1. Franchising in Business: A Guide to Information Sources
   by Lucy Heckman

2. The Informal Economy: A Research Guide
   by Abol Hassan Danesh

3. Staff Training: An Annotated Review of the Literature
   by William Crimando and T.F. Riggar

4. The World Bank Group: A Guide to Information Sources
   by Carol R. Wilson

5. Global Countertrade: An Annotated Bibliography
   by Leon Zurawicki and Louis Suichmezian

6. The New York Stock Exchange: A Guide to Information Sources
   by Lucy Heckman

THE NEW YORK
STOCK EXCHANGE
A *Guide to*
Information Sources

Lucy Heckman

GARLAND PUBLISHING, INC. • NEW YORK & LONDON
1992

Library of Congress Cataloging-in-Publication Data

Heckman, Lucy, 1954–
    The New York Stock Exchange : a guide to information sources /
Lucy Heckman.
        p.   cm. — (Research and information guides in business,
industry, and economic institutions ; vol. 6)   (Garland reference
library of social science ; vol. 759)
    Includes bibliographical references and indexes.
    ISBN 0–8240–3328–0
    1. New York Stock Exchange—Bibliography. I. Title. II. Series.
III. Series: Research and information guides in business, industry,
and economic institutions ; 6. IV. Series: Garland reference
library of social science ; v. 759.
Z7164.F5H43   1992
[HG4572]
016.33264'273—dc20   92–118
                                                                CIP

Printed on acid-free, 250-year-life paper
Manufactured in the United States of America

SERIES FOREWORD

The new information society has exceeded everyone's expectations in providing new and exciting media for the collection and dissemination of data. Such proliferation has been matched by a similar increase in the number of providers of business literature. Furthermore, many emerging technologies, financial fields, and management processes have amassed an amazing body of knowledge in a short period of time. Indicators are that packaging of information will continue its trend of diversification, confounding even the experienced researcher. How then will information seekers identify and assess the adequacy and relevancy of various packages to their research needs?

It is my hope that Garland's *Research and Information Guides in Business, Industry, and Economic Institutions* series will bridge the gap between classical forms of literature and new alternative formats. Each guide will be devoted to an industry, a profession, a managerial process, an economic institution, or a field of study. Organization of the guides will emphasize subject access to formats such as bibliographic and numeric databases on-line, distributed databases, CD-ROM products, loose-leaf services, government publications and books, and periodical articles. Although most of the guides will serve as locators and bridges to bodies of knowledge, some may be reference books with self-contained information.

Since compiling such guides requires substantial knowledge in the organization of information or the field of study, authors are selected on the basis of their expertise as information professionals or subject specialists. Inquiries about the series and its content should be addressed to the Series Editor.

Wahib Nasrallah
Langsam Library
University of Cincinnati

Photograph courtesy of The New York Stock Exchange.

CONTENTS

ACKNOWLEDGEMENTS

I would like to thank Sister Marie Melton, Dean of St. John's University Libraries for her generous support. Thanks to my colleagues on the faculty, staff, and administration at St. John's University Library for their assistance. Thanks to all those in the Interlibrary Loan Department for their help in tracking down those often hard to find materials.

I wish to thank the administrators, faculty, and staff of the following libraries:

St. John's University Law Library

New York Public Library

Brooklyn Public Library

Queens Borough Public Library

The New-York Historical Society Library

Hofstra University Library

Adelphi University Library

The Library of Congress

C.W. Post Center for Business Research

Special thanks are due to Steven Wheeler, Archivist of the New York Stock Exchange who allowed me access to the Archives and answered my questions about the NYSE and its publications. Thanks also to Richard Bryant of the NYSE Communications Department.

vii

INTRODUCTION

The New York Stock Exchange or the NYSE is almost as old as the United States itself. On May 17, 1792, twenty-four brokers signed the Buttonwood Agreement which established the first organized exchange, later to be called the New York Stock Exchange.

In the year of its two hundredth anniversary, developments at the NYSE have profound implications for the financial community and the nation's economy. A review of trading activity at the NYSE is a part of evening news broadcasts, daily newspapers, and magazines. The NYSE has been over the years the subject of numerous books, newspaper and magazine articles, dissertations, and government reports.

The New York Stock Exchange: A Guide to Information Sources gathers together selected materials concerning the NYSE: histories; biographies and autobiographies; studies of a time period or a particular event such as the Stock Market Crashes of 1929 and 1987; statistical sources; bibliographies; introductory guides; directories; and dictionaries. Formats of these materials represented are: books, journal articles, government documents, newspaper articles, pamphlets, videocassettes, dissertations, archival material, motion pictures, and serial publications. Appendixes list and describe: information services at the NYSE; periodicals; indexes and abstracts; online databases; and CD-ROM products.

This book consists of English language primary and secondary sources on the Exchange. Dates of materials covered range from May 17, 1792, to Fall 1991. It is a selective bibliography of sources about the NYSE; a complete listing of materials by and about the NYSE would fill a great many volumes of books. Materials selected were located through scanning separately published bibliographies; bibliographic citations in NYSE histories and other works; online and CD-ROM databases; printed periodical and newspaper indexes; and consulting lists of materials at the NYSE Archives. Copies of material were examined at the NYSE Archives and at local academic, research, and public libraries. Those materials not available in the area were sent for through the St. John's University Interlibrary Loan Department.

Each annotated item has been assigned an entry number and items are indexed according to these numbers by author, title, and subject. Since some sources fall into several categories and/or time periods, cross-references are provided. For example, biographies have been included in one chapter and cross-references link the biographies with specific time periods. Appendixes containing lists of indexes and abstracts, serial publications, as well as online and CD-ROM databases are arranged alphabetically.

The New York Stock Exchange: A Guide to Information Sources is not designed to provide a detailed history of the Exchange. Chapter I provides an overview of the history of the New York Stock Exchange and a description of its present organization. Also included in Appendixes I and II are names of NYSE Presidents and Chairmen as well as a Chronology of the NYSE's history. A brief overview of historical events and key documents for specific time periods have been included with each time period covered in chapters. To understand the NYSE's present and make projections for its future, it is important to learn about its past. This source is designed to be a starting point for locating sources about the NYSE, including historical materials.

The New York
Stock Exchange

CHAPTER I
ORGANIZATION AND HISTORY

I. Organization

The New York Stock Exchange is a not-for-profit organization governed by a Board of Directors, with a full-time salaried Chairman and an Executive Vice-Chairman and President. It is the Board of Directors who is responsible for guiding the NYSE's programs and policies. The NYSE staff have responsibility for carrying out these programs and policies. Additionally, thirteen Advisory Committees are appointed by the Chairman and approved by the Board of Directors. Each Committee has a charter that is renewed annually. These Committees are: the Listed Company Advisory Committee, Individual Investors Advisory Committee, Pension Managers Advisory Committee, Institutional Traders Advisory Committee, Exchange Traders Advisory Committee, Committee of Upstairs Traders, Regional Firms Advisory Committee, Specialty Firms Advisory Committee, Regulatory Advisory Committee, Advisory Committee on International Capital Markets, European Advisory Committee, Japan Advisory Committee, and Legal Advisory Committee.

By the end of 1990, there were 1408 members of the Exchange, including 1366 members who own seats and have full distributive rights in NYSE net assets. Members of the NYSE may buy, sell, and lease seats on the Exchange. Prices for seats vary but generally are in the approximate range of $250,000 to over $430,000, according to 1990 data. In 1876, however, the price of a seat was $4,000 and in 1987 another sold for $1.1 million. Leased seats ranged, in 1990, from between $48,000 to over $85,000.

Prices of securities traded at the Exchange are not set by the

NYSE. They are determined by decisions of individual and institutional investors where buyers and sellers of securities meet and agree upon a price in an auction environment. Securities traded at the NYSE are: common stock, preferred stock, bonds, options, warrants, shares of beneficial interest, and American Depository shares. The New York Futures Exchange, a wholly-owned subsidiary of the NYSE, specializes in financial futures. Major indexes of securities traded include the NYSE Composite Index, the Dow Jones Averages, and the S & P 500 Index.

Those participating in the New York Stock Exchange market include: listed companies from the U.S. and other parts of the world, individual investors, securities dealers, institutional investors, and specialists. The New York Stock Exchange market is governed by set rules and regulations as set forth in their Constitution and By-Laws. All NYSE rules and regulations are, however, subject to approval by the Securities and Exchange Commission. The first Constitution for the NYSE, then called the New York Stock and Exchange Board, was published in 1817 and has undergone revisions throughout the Exchange's history.

The NYSE's 1990 survey of shareholders indicated that approximately 51 million individual investors owned stock in a publicly traded company or in a stock mutual fund. NYSE Services to the investing public include: materials published and distributed at the NYSE Publications Department; a visitors' center where individuals have the opportunity to watch activities on the trading floor, see a film about the Exchange, and view exhibits about the NYSE; and the Archives, available by appointment, which house historical materials concerning the NYSE. Further information about these services is contained in Appendix III.

Throughout the past decades, the NYSE has expanded its automated trading systems. The NYSE's SuperDot is an electronic order-routing system that enables member firms to transmit market and limit orders in all NYSE-listed securities directly to the NYSE trading floor where the order is routed to the specialist assigned to the securities or to the member firms' booth. Information concerning the order is then reported back to the member firm through the SuperDot system. Other electronic systems include the Intermarket Trading System or ITS which links the markets: the New York, American, Boston, Cincinnati, Midwest, Pacific, and Philadelphia Stock Exchanges and the NASD. The NYSE's Consolidated Tape lists and reports transactions in NYSE-listed securities which were executed on other markets, including seven stock exchanges and two over-the-counter markets.

II. History

On May 17, 1992, the NYSE marks its two hundredth anniversary. During the late 1700s, Wall Street was the center of government and finance. New York City was the United States' first capital, from 1785 to 1790 and Federal Hall, located in the Wall Street area, served as Congress' headquarters. George Washington was inaugurated at Federal Hall as the nation's first president on April 30, 1789. Throughout the late 1700s, merchants and brokers met to buy and sell securities, including bank stocks and government bonds. These securities were bought and sold through competitive bidding at auctions. The founding of the New York Stock Exchange is traced back to when twenty-four New York brokers and merchants, who did not want auctioneers to gain control, signed an agreement. This agreement, known as the Buttonwood Agreement or Buttonwood Tree Agreement was signed on May 17, 1792.

The Agreement was named for a buttonwood tree on Wall Street under which the brokers met to conduct business. The Agreement stated: "We the Subscribers, Brokers for the Purchase and Sale of Public Stock, do hereby solemnly promise and pledge ourselves to each other, that we will not buy or sell from this day for any person whatsoever any kind of Public Stock, at a less rate than one-quarter of one percent percent on the specie value, and that we will give preference to each other in our negotiations. Whereof we have set our hands this 17th day of May at New York, 1792."

Among early meeting places for the brokers was the Tontine Coffee House, which opened in 1794 on the northwest corner of Wall and William Streets. Funding for the Tontine Coffee House was through Private subscription, with a total of 203 shares selling for $200 each.

The year 1817 marked the establishment of a more formal organization of brokers: the New York Stock and Exchange Board (NYS & EB). A constitution, adopted on March 8, 1817, set rules for: selection of a President; membership; sales procedures; commission rates; and contracts for delivery. Forbidden by the rules were fictitious sales or contracts. The NYS & EB's first location was a rented room at 40 Wall Street. The Constitution of the NYS & EB, and later, the NYSE, was to undergo continuous revisions throughout its history.

During the following decades, trading increased in: government securities; state and municipal bonds; and stocks of banks and private companies. In one example of trading, over $8 million worth of New York State bonds were issued to fund construction of the Erie Canal, which opened in October 1825. The Mohawk & Hudson Railroad in 1830 became the first railroad stock to be traded on the Exchange. Railroad building expanded to bring about a proliferation of railroad stocks traded among which were the New York Central Railroad, the Chesapeake & Ohio Steam Transportation and Mining Company, and the Marine Railroad.

The Panics of 1819, 1837, and 1857 were early crises which affected the financial community. Wall Street, however, survived these crises, maintaining and solidifying its status as the nation's financial center. By the conclusion of the 1850s, prices of securities traded on the NYS & EB were telegraphed to major U.S. cities.

At the outset of the Civil War, the members of the NYS & EB, formally pledged not to trade in Confederate bonds. The early years of the Civil War saw the beginning of a depressed period on Wall Street, due to losses on money owed to New York brokers by their customers from the South. The market rallied after a series of Northern military victories over the Confederacy. Jay Cooke, founder of Jay Cooke & Co. was a major financier of the Northern cause; his biographers called him, "Financier of the Civil War."

In 1863, the New York Stock and Exchange Board changed its name to the New York Stock Exchange (NYSE). After moving to various rented spaces, the NYSE established its first permanent headquarters at 10-12 Broad Street, located just south of Wall Street. In 1867 membership in the NYSE increased to over 1000 when the Exchange merged with a competitor, the Open Board of Brokers, and also added members of the NYSE's Government Bond Department. 1867 was, in addition, the year that the stock ticker was first used on the Exchange. The practice of selling memberships or "seats" on the NYSE was introduced in 1868.

During the 1869s, financiers who had great influence on Exchange activity were Jay Gould, Daniel Drew, Cornelius Vanderbilt, and Jim Fisk, Jr. These individuals were at the center of the Erie Railroad Wars, a struggle for control over this railroad. As a result of Erie stock price manipulation, the NYSE instituted stricter registration standards for its securities. In 1869, Gould and Fisk attempted to corner the gold market through a series of intrigues and precipitated the "Black Friday" panic of September 24. Hearings investigating the "Gold Corner" were conducted by the Committee on Banking and Currency in January-February 1870.

In 1873, the renowned Philadelphia banking house of Jay Cooke & Co. failed due to overspeculation in railroad stocks. The collapse of Jay Cooke & Co. caused other bank closings, a major decline in stock prices, and the subsequent closing of the NYSE for ten days. After the Panic of 1873, a severe depression followed, lasting for six years.

Among notable developments at the NYSE during the 1870s were: continuous trading replaced calls of stock at set times; the role of the specialist began when brokers who dealt in a particular stock or type of stock stayed at one location on the trading floor; and the first telephone was at the NYSE was installed in 1878.

During the 1880s and 1890s, "trusts" or giant conglomerates dominated U.S. industry and had a great impact on stock trading. The first million share trading day at the NYSE took place in 1886, due to increase in shares issued by the trusts. During this time period, the financier J.P. Morgan, Sr. gained international recognition and prominence. Other developments during these decades included: the publication of the first issue of the *Wall Street Journal* in 1889; the creation of the first major industrial stock index, the Dow Jones Industrial Average; and the increase in issues on the NYSE to 1000. The securities markets suffered major setbacks during the Panics of 1884, 1893, and 1907.

In 1903, the NYSE moved into new headquarters, where it remains today. The building, styled in classical-revival manner, was designed by the noted architect and engineer, George B. Post. The pediment statues were designed by sculptor, John Quincy Adams Ward.

The NYSE was investigated during the early part of the 20th century by the Governor Charles E. Hughes Committee and in the Pujo Committee or Money Trust Hearings. Reports by the Hughes and Pujo Committees, issued in 1909 and 1913, respectively, studied NYSE organization and practices and called for reforms.

At the outset of World War I, the NYSE was closed to forestall a major panic and market collapse. The NYSE was closed in July 1914, reopened in December 1914, and was only able to resume trading without restrictions in April 1915.

During the first World War, the NYSE traded issues of United States Liberty Bonds. The issues were in such large quantities that the NYSE installed a separate ticker symbol for bonds. After the War ended in 1918, the market experienced a period of decline. The market, however, recovered by the early 1920s and the subsequent years were a time of a bull market. On September 17, 1920, a bomb, which was placed by an anarchist, exploded on Wall Street causing thirty deaths and injuring hundreds of individuals.

From 1925 to 1929, the market value of NYSE listed stocks increased from $27 billion to $90 billion and market volume grew from 450 million shares to approximately one billion shares. More Americans had decided to invest in securities due to: people buying Liberty Bonds had become familiar with the market and continued to purchase securities; individuals could buy on margin, a process of purchasing securities by putting up between 10 to 25 percent of the price and borrowing the rest from brokers; personal income had increased giving investors available capital for investing; and dividends were now being paid on a regular basis. Events at the end of October 1929 would abruptly end this decade of the bull market.

Events of the 1929 Crash or "Great Crash" began on October 24, 1929 when the market fell. Crowds gathered on Wall Street and bankers met to attempt to deal with the crisis. Despite efforts by the bankers and officers of the NYSE, the market did not recover but, rather, conditions worsened, and on October 29, the market crashed. On October 29 or Black Tuesday, the market lost $14 billion of value, and a record 16,410,000 shares were traded. The market was not to recover fully for several years and the early thirties became a time of significant declines in stock prices. The state of the country changed from a time of great prosperity to the years of depression in the 1930s.

After the Crash, the securities markets, banks, and brokerage houses became the subjects of Congressional investigations and subsequent legislation. From 1932-1934, a Subcommittee of the Senate Committee on Banking and Currency held hearings which studied events of the Crash, manipulative activities at the Exchange, and practices, including margin buying. The Counsel for the investigation was Ferdinand Pecora and the Subcommittee conducting the study became known as the "Pecora Committee." Among key witnesses at the hearings were: Richard Whitney, President of the NYSE; Michael Meehan, of M.J. Meehan & Co.; Charles E. Mitchell, Chairman of the National City Bank of New York; and Fiorello H. LaGuardia, a Representative from the Twentieth District of New York.

Key legislation resulting from these hearings were the Securities Act of 1933 and the Securities Exchange Act of 1934. The Securities

Exchange Act of 1933 requires registration of new securities issues and full disclosure to the public regarding these issues. The Securities Exchange Act of 1934 established the Securities and Exchange Commission and gave the Federal Reserve Board the authority to regulate margin requirements. Other legislation during this time period included the Glass-Steagall Act or the Banking Act of 1933 which established the Federal Deposit Insurance Corporation (FDIC) and required complete separation of investment banking and commercial banking.

The year 1938 was an important year for changes at the New York Stock Exchange. Two major events led to a major revision in the NYSE's organizational structure. The first catalyst for change was pressure from the Chairman of the Securities and Exchange Commission, William O. Douglas. After a market break in 1937, Douglas indicated that the NYSE should examine and remodel its organization from what he called a private club structure. The NYSE administration subsequently established the Conway Committee, named for its Chairman, Carle C. Conway. The Secretary of the Conway Committee was future NYSE President, William McChesney Martin, Jr. Among the recommendations, which went into effect, were that: the NYSE appoint a full-time, salaried President; members of the public be representatives on the Board of Governors; committee organization be restructured; and the Constitution and rules be revised and simplified.

The second event that brought about changes was the case of Richard Whitney, President of the NYSE from 1930-1935. In 1938, Whitney, Senior Partner of Richard Whitney & Co. was arrested on two separate indictments which charged him with grand larceny. It was discovered that Whitney had misappropriated a customer's securities as early as 1926 and similar misappropriations were practiced later on a regular basis. The lateness of disciplinary action led to investigation and revision of rules regarding the New York Stock Exchange's supervision and monitoring of its members and their activities.

The years of the Second World War brought about significant innovations at the NYSE. The NYSE assisted the war effort with the sale of major defense loans. With an increase in women employees on the homefront, the NYSE hired women as quotation clerks and carrier pages on the trading floor.

The post-war era was a time of a great increase in investors. NYSE President G. Keith Funston (1951-1967) embarked on an educational program, "Own Your Share of American Business" to attract more investors. Part of the campaign was advertising in newspapers and magazines as well as on the radio. Throughout the fifties, the numbers of individual shareholders increased from about 6.5 million to 12.5 million by the end of the decade. The NYSE published its first shareownership survey in 1952; this survey offered statistics on the numbers of investors and their characteristics. For the most part, the fifties was the time of a bull market, with brief setbacks including the market decline after President Dwight D. Eisenhower suffered a heart attack in September 1955.

A major market break occurred in May 1962; both the NYSE and the SEC published reports examining implications of this market break. A landmark report was the SEC's *Special Study of the Securities Markets* (1963) which examined the securities markets, possible reasons for the break, and made recommendations for the future of the markets, including the NYSE. A result of the SEC's *Study* was passage of the Securities Acts Amendments of 1964.

Another crisis at the NYSE took place during the late 1960s when facilities in brokerage offices could no longer handle the vast amount of paper work. The "back office paperwork crunch" caused losses of stock certificates and major delays in the securities sale process. The NYSE, during 1967-1968, reduced its hours of trading to help alleviate the backlog of work. It did not resume its regular hours until May 1970. This time period was also marked by financial difficulties for many member firms of the NYSE. The number of member firms decreased from 647 in 1967 to 572 in 1970 due to bankruptcies, mergers, and acquisitions. The NYSE provided financial assistance to public customers and created a Special Trust Fund to handle much of this compensation. Congress, however, created the Securities Investor Protection Corporation (SIPC) in 1970 to protect customers' money and securities holdings in the event of liquidations.

The 1960s were also a time of great changes and innovations. The NYSE now hired women for jobs on the trading floor and in December 1967, Muriel Siebert, became the first woman member of the NYSE. A major technological innovation was the addition of a new stock ticker which could print 900 characters per minute.

The 1970s was a decade of historic developments, organizationally, for the NYSE. In 1971, former NYSE President, William McChesney Martin, Jr. was commissioned by the NYSE to prepare a study of its organizational structure and make recommendations for change. The NYSE adopted some of these recommendations, notably: 1.

incorporation of the NYSE as a not-for-profit organization and 2. change in Board structure to include ten directors from the securities industry, ten public directors, and a full-time Chairman and Chief Executive Officer to be elected by the Board.

May 1, 1975 or "May Day" marked the end of the fixed brokerage commission rate structure in existence at the NYSE since its beginnings. During the same year, Congress enacted the Securities Acts Amendments of 1975 which was designed to promote the development of a competitive national market system.

To work toward the national market system, the NYSE developed the Intermarket Trading System (ITS) and Consolidated Tape. During the late 1970s, the NYSE renovated its trading floor to accommodate new electronic systems including the Opening Automated Report Service (OARS). During the 1970s, the NYSE inaugurated its fully automated Designated Order Turnaround (DOT) system to electronically transmit smaller orders and reports between the NYSE and member firms.

Among key events during the first half of the 1980s were: opening of the New York Futures Exchange (NYFE) as a subsidiary of the NYSE (1980); beginning of trading through experimental linkage between ITS and six other exchanges (1982); beginning of trading in options on NYSE Common Stock Index Futures (1983); implementation of NYSE's SuperDOT (Designated Order Turnaround) 250 (1984); and a visit to the Exchange by President Ronald Reagan, the first such visit by a U.S. President (1985). The 1980s was also a time of the insider trading scandal whose key participants were Ivan Boesky, Martin Siegel, Michael Milken, and Dennis Levine.

On October 19, 1987, a day to be forever known as "Black Monday," the Dow Jones Industrial Average fell a record 508 points. "Terrible Tuesday," October 20, 1987 was characterized by a continuation of high volume and volatility as well as uncertainty and nervousness among market participants. However, due largely to a series of announced stock buyback programs by major corporations, the Dow closed with a 102.27 net gain at the end of the trading day. Investigating and making recommendations to prevent another Black Monday were the goals of reports by the President's Task Force or the Brady Commission; the Securities and Exchange Commission; the Commodity Futures Trading Commission (CFTC); the New York Stock Exchange; the Chicago Mercantile Exchange (CME); and the General Accounting Office. The New York Stock Exchange has reviewed and practices and its specialist system.

The late 1980s and early 1990s were a time for the NYSE to continue its examination of the implications of Black Monday, to explore ways for the NYSE to compete effectively with other exchanges; and to implement and improve technological innovations.

An event that tested preventive measures against another Black Monday was the market decline of October 13, 1989. The decline was approximately 190 points as compared to 508 in 1987 but caused concern that another Black Monday could occur. The NYSE prepared a report, *Market Volatility and Investor Confidence* (1990), which offered recommendations to help maintain a strong market and deal with the implications of the 1987 and 1989 market breaks. Also in 1990, the Market Reform Act was enacted; it is designed to strengthen the SEC's regulatory oversight of the securities markets and to authorize the SEC to take appropriate action during market emergencies.

Innovations undertaken by new NYSE Chairman and CEO, William Donaldson include plans for twenty-four hour trading by the end of the decade and completion of MetroTech, a backup center for all NYSE systems.

In its two hundred year history, the NYSE has advanced from a group of twenty-four brokers who signed a formal agreement to an organization with: over 1400 members, managed by a Board of Directors and a Chairman; over 1700 companies that list their companies on the Exchange; over 50 million shareholders in these companies; and a fully automated trading system. The NYSE Chronology in Appendix I provides an overview of these changes from 1792 to the early 1990s.

CHAPTER II
GENERAL GUIDES AND DICTIONARIES

Some of the authors whose works are listed and annotated in *The New York Stock Exchange: A Guide to Information Sources* may assume that readers are familiar with various terms regarding the NYSE. Examples of these terms are "Odd-Lot," "Specialist," "Big Board," and "the Club." For those just learning about the NYSE, associated words and jargon may be totally unfamiliar. For this purpose, listed here are selected general guides and dictionaries. The general guides concisely and clearly explain various facets of NYSE operations among which are how the trading floor of the NYSE is arranged; how securities are bought and sold; and how to read the listings of stock prices. The dictionaries offer succinct and precise definitions of associated terms. It should be noted that six of the seven sources listed cover securities and investments in general, but contain chapters or sections about the New York Stock Exchange.

1. Hildreth, Sandra S. *The A to Z of Wall Street*. Chicago: Longman Financial Services Publishing, 1988. 299 pages.

    Provides concise definitions for over 2500 common investment terms and phrases among which are: "New York Stock Exchange," "NYSE Maintenance Call," "penny stock," etc.

2. New York Stock Exchange. *Investor's Information Kit*. New York:

13

516 - 454 - 1800

New York Stock Exchange, 198- series of pamphlets.

Contents of kit: "The New York Stock Exchange: The Capital Market," (52 pages)--describes history and operations of the NYSE, role of Securities and Exchange Commission, etc; "Understanding Stocks and Bonds," (11 pages)--discusses stocks and bonds and how they are traded; "Understanding Financial Statements," (23 pages)--guide to using financial statements to evaluate a company's financial status; "Margin Trading Guide," (20 pages)--explains margin trading or trading on credit when a customer makes only partial payment for securities and borrows the rest from his/her broker; "Glossary," (31 pages)--defines terms such as "Bull Market," "Callable," "Bear Market," "Blue Chip," "Capital Stock," "Conglomerate," and "Premium;" and "Getting Help When You Invest," (18 pages)--discusses ways in which NYSE member firm brokers can assist you in selecting a broker, opening an account, etc.

3. Odean, Kathleen. *High Steppers, Fallen Angels, and Lollipops: Wall Street Slang.* Foreword by Leonard Silk. New York: Dodd, Mead & Co., 1988. 212 pages.

Describes terms and how they came to be used. Based on interviews with brokers and research in the New York Stock Exchange Archives. Examines terms: "Sleeper," "Glamour Stocks," "Go Public," "Junk Bonds," etc. Studies nicknames of people such as Jay Gould, the "Wizard of Wall Street." Chapter 8 chronicles the history of the NYSE and terminology associated with it such as "Buttonwood Tree Agreement," "Blue Room," "Big Board," "Trading Post," etc. Chapter 9 analyzes nicknames of various events including stock market crashes; among these names are "Blue Monday," "Black Monday," "Black Thursday," "Black Friday," "Great Crash," etc. With a bibliography.

4. Pessin, Allan H. and Joseph A. Ross. *Still More Words of Wall Street.* Homewood, Illinois: Business One Irwin, 1990. 292 pages.

Third volume in series defines terms associated with the securities industry in the United States, Japan, Great Britain, etc. Among terms are "Black Monday," "Black Friday," "NYSE Rule 387," and "Index Arbitrage."

5. Pessin, Allan H. and Joseph A. Ross. *More Words of Wall Street: 2000 More Investment Terms Defined.* Homewood, Illinois: Dow Jones-Irwin, 1986. 269 pages.

Second volume in series offers concise definitions of various terms among which are "Bull Market," "Futures Contract," and "Bear Spread.

6. Pessin, Allan H. and Joseph A. Ross. *Words of Wall Street: 2000 Investment Terms Defined.* Homewood, Illinois: Dow Jones-Irwin, 1983. 297 pages.

First volume in series offers definitions of: "New York Stock Exchange," "Blue Chip," "Margin," "Securities Act of 1933," "Securities Exchange Act of 1934," etc.

7. Wurman, Richard Saul, Alan Siegel, and Kenneth M. Morris. *The Wall Street Guide to Understanding Money and Markets.* New York: Access Press, a division of Simon & Schuster, 1990. 119 pages.

Illustrated guide to the securities markets defines terms, explains how to read the financial pages, etc. Provides brief histories of the Crashes of 1929 and 1987, a history of the NYSE, an illustration of the NYSE trading floor, and definitions of terms associated with the NYSE including "Designated Order Turnaround (DOT)," "Post Display Units," and "Specialist."

CHAPTER III
BIBLIOGRAPHIES

Listings and annotations of materials concerning the New York Stock Exchange are found in the following sources. None of the sources listed below have as their only topic, "the New York Stock Exchange." Rather, the listings of books on the NYSE comprise a chapter or section of the bibliographical citations. Some of the bibliographies are exclusively on securities markets and investments and others appear as parts of guides to business materials. Each bibliography has a different emphasis. Henrietta Larson's focus is on historical sources regarding the NYSE. Other works will cover only statistical sources such as those published by *Value Line, Standard & Poor's*, and *Moody's*.

It should be noted that much of the literature of the New York Stock Exchange will contain bibliographies and/or bibliographic footnotes or endnotes.

8. *The Basic Business Library: Core Resources*. Edited by Bernard S. Schlessinger, Rashelle S. Karp and Virginia S. Vocelli, Associate Editors. Phoenix, Arizona: Oryx Press, 1989. 278 pages.

Guide to business information sources covers investment information publications. Includes essay: "The Best Investment Sources," by Carla Martindell Felsted; this essay provides citations and annotations for investment advisory services, investment periodicals and statistical sources, Moody's and Standard & Poor's services, a reference bookshelf, and an investment bookshelf (lists citations only). Additional investment sources are part of the "Core List," compiled by Virginia S. Vocelli. Includes index.

9. Daniells, Lorna M. *Business Information Sources.* Rev. ed. Berkeley: University of California Press, 1985. 673 pages.

   Annotated guide to business resources provides chapter on investment sources. This chapter covers comprehensive investment services; industry surveys; concise statistical data and stock prices; charting services; dividends; stock price indexes; weekly investment advisory services; corporate reports; brokerage house reports; computerized financial data; Securities and Exchange Commission publications; capital changes services; new security offerings; stock exchange publications; lists of largest U.S. companies; credit rating services; investment companies; government, municipals, and other fixed income securities; guides to financial services and statistics; indexes to financial publications; investment newspapers and periodicals; international investment services; foreign corporate annual reports; European sources; United Kingdom sources; Japanese sources; lists of largest foreign companies; bibliographies and indexes on foreign companies and industries; general books on investments; security analysis and portfolio management; the stock market and investment management guides; bonds and money markets; options market; commodities and financial futures markets; law and securities regulations; bibliographies of investment books; investment dictionaries; investment management journals; directories of the securities industry; and security industry associations. Includes index.

10. Daniells, Lorna M., comp. *Business Reference Sources: An Annotated Guide for Harvard Business School Students* Reference List, No. 33. Boston, Massachusetts: Harvard University. Graduate School of Business Administration. Baker Library, 1987. 131 pages.

Selective bibliography of business sources whose stated purpose is to introduce Harvard University business students to the Baker Library collection. Each entry includes full citation, call number and/or location, and an annotation. Chapter five contains descriptive information on: resources for company and industry information; investment manuals and services; concise financial data; current statistics on stock and bond prices; charting services; dividends; stock price indexes; weekly investment advisory services; new securities offerings; brokerage house reports; financial newspapers and periodicals; periodical indexes, etc. Includes index.

11. *Directory of Business and Financial Services.* Edited by Mary McNierney Grant and Riva Berleant-Schiller. 8th ed. New York: Special Libraries Association, 1984. 189 pages.

Annotated directory of business and financial information services published periodically. Includes an annotated list of services concerning the New York Stock Exchange, stocks and bonds, securities regulation, and investments. Formats included are print sources and online databases. Each entry consists of name and address of publisher, the annotation, frequency of publication, and cost. Indexed by entry number.

12. Hirata, Yoshihoko, comp. *Prosperity, Great Depression, and New Deal: A Bibliography of American Economy During the Interwar Period.* Tokyo: Yushodo Booksellers Ltd., 1972. 262 pages.

Bibliography of books, monographs, and government publications. Includes section on "Securities Markets" listing materials on the New York Stock Exchange during the interwar period.

13. Larson, Henrietta M. *Guide to Business History: Materials for the Study of American Business History and Suggestions for Their Use.* Index by Elsie Hight Bishop. Cambridge, Massachusetts: Harvard University Press, 1948. 1181 pages.

Annotated guide to sources on business history with a section on the New York Stock Exchange. States: "...the books on the history of the Exchange are largely either statistical in nature or deal with striking personalities and episodes." (p. 359). Other relevant annotations are provided in sections on the "Stock Market -- General Works"; "History of Crises, Depressions, and General Business and Economic Conditions"; and the biographies sections of "Business Men," "Financial Capitalists," and "Industrial Capitalists."

14. Mechanic, Sylvia. *Investment Bibliography*. New York: New York Stock Exchange, 1983. 17 pages.

Prepared by Sylvia Mechanic, Business Librarian, Brooklyn Public Library, Business Library for the New York Stock Exchange. Annotated guide to: Newspapers and Periodicals; Books; Reference Works; Investment and Financial Services; and Selected Financial Organizations' names and addresses. Books described include histories of Wall Street and investment guides.

* Nagarajan, K.V. *The Stock Market Crash of October 1987: A Bibliography*. See item 381 below.

15. Strauss, Diane Wheeler. *Handbook of Business Information: A Guide for Librarians, Students, and Researchers*. Englewood, Colorado: Libraries Unlimited, 1988. 537 pages.

Guide to business information sources includes several chapters concerning investments, stocks, bonds, futures, and options. Describes various sources among which are introductory guides, almanacs and encyclopedias, dictionaries, directories, investment advisory services, stock price information sources, New York Stock Exchange information services and sources, stock index information sources, corporate reports, comprehensive investment information services, stock reporting services, online databases and disks, information sources for bonds, and statistical materials for bonds. Explains basic terms such as common and preferred stock, earnings per share, dividend yield, Dow Jones Industrial Average, etc. Provides brief description of history and operations of the NYSE.

16. Zerden, Sheldon. *Best Books on the Stock Market: An Analytical Bibliography.* New York: Bowker, 1972. 168 pages.

Foreword by Robert Sobel. Annotated listing of books concerning: methods of investing, history, biography, books for the beginner, and general works. Also includes list, not annotated, of textbooks, reference works, and supplementary reading list. The History section features books on the history of Wall Street and the New York Stock Exchange. Cites Stedman and Sobel works as most comprehensive sources on the history of the NYSE.

CHAPTER IV
BIOGRAPHIES

The New York Stock Exchange's history has been affected by the actions of brilliant, colorful, and, sometimes, notorious individuals. Many have changed the course of the NYSE's history as well as the history of American business.

This chapter lists and annotates biographies and autobiographies of men and women who, directly or indirectly, influenced the history of the New York Stock Exchange. It should be noted that a multitude of works have been written about some of these individuals, notably Jay Gould, J. Pierpont Morgan, Sr., and Commodore Cornelius Vanderbilt. Some of the works, including *Jubilee Jim* and *The Embezzler,* are in the form of historical fiction, but follow closely the facts of the individual's life and times. Other works are written by people who have worked for the New York Stock Exchange for many years and have recorded their recollections in autobiographies. Also included are biographies of selected NYSE Presidents and Chairmen. Biographies containing sketches of groups of individuals such as *Our Crowd* and *Mystery Men of Wall Street* are also a part of this chapter.

Additional biographical sketches can be located by scanning the *Dictionary of American Biography* and by consulting the *Biography Index*. Encyclopedias also contain entries concerning the more prominent individuals.

Cross-references to these biographies are provided throughout the book. Additionally, individuals profiled in the biographies are included in the Subject Index.

17. Allen, Frederick Lewis. *The Great Pierpont Morgan*. New York: Harper & Row, 1949. 306 pages.

Story of Morgan and his times from early life to the Pujo Committee testimony. Reviews previous biographies, laudatory and critical, including those by Lewis Corey (*The House of Morgan*); Matthew Josephson (*The Robber Barons*); Herbert L. Satterlee (*J. Pierpont Morgan: An Intimate Portrait*); and Carl Hovey (*The Life Story of J. Pierpont Morgan*). With bibliographical references.

18. Andrews, Wayne. *The Vanderbilt Legend: The Story of the Vanderbilt Family, 1794-1940*. New York, 1941. 454 pages.

Biographies of the Vanderbilts: Commodore Cornelius Vanderbilt, his son, William H. Vanderbilt and their descendents including Frederick W. Vanderbilt, Alfred Gwynne Vanderbilt, and Gloria Vanderbilt. With: "The Vanderbilt Family Tree." Describes business and financial enterprises of Commodore Vanderbilt and his son. With illustrations and bibliography.

19. Anonymous. *The Mirrors of Wall Street*, with drawings by Hugo Gellert. New York: Putnam's, 1933. 268 pages.

Studies, some of which are unsympathetic, of: John Pierpont Morgan, Jr., John Davison Rockefeller, Jr., George Fisher Baker, Thomas William Lamont, Winthrop Williams Aldrich, William Chapman Potter, Charles Edwin Mitchell, Otto Herman Kahn, Clarence Dillon, Walter Percy Chrysler, Eugene Meyer, Jr., Charles Gates Dawes, and Bernard Mannes Baruch. With drawings of each person profiled. Also includes an essay examining relationship between Wall Street and Washington from the passage of the Federal Reserve Act through the early 1930s.

20. Auchincloss, Louis. *The Embezzler*. Boston: Houghton Mifflin, 1966. 277 pages.

Novel's main character is Guy Prime. Events in Prime's life are similar to those in Richard Whitney's life. Background of novel is Wall Street during the nineteen-thirties.

21. Babson, Roger W. *Actions and Reactions: An Autobiography of Roger W. Babson.* New York: Harper, 1935. 404 pages.

Autobiography of the investment adviser, founder of the forecasting service, *Babson's Reports*, the predictor of September 1929's "Babson Break" and the October 1929 Panic, and organizer of the Babson Statistical Organization. After witnessing events on the floor of the NYSE during the Panic of 1907, Babson resolved to seek to prevent large losses in the stock market. *Babson's Reports* advised investors when to buy and when to sell as well as what to buy and what to sell. The *Reports* presented the "Babsonchart," a statistical chart for stocks, bonds, and commodities. Forecasting based on Law of Action and Reaction which assumes that period of abnormal depression always follows a period of abnormal prosperity. Also presents Babson's views of education, marriage, health, writing, and politics. Recalls acquaintanceships with Presidents Theodore Roosevelt, Taft, Wilson, Harding, Coolidge, Hoover, and Franklin D. Roosevelt.

*   Barrett, Walter [pseud] *The Old Merchants of New York City* see item 126 below

22. Barron, Clarence W. *More They Told Barron: Conversations and Revelations of An American Pepys in Wall Street.* Edited and arranged by Arthur Pound and Samuel Taylor Moore. New York: Harper & Brothers, 1931. 334 pages.

Sequel to *They Told Barron.* Foreword includes the Barron family genealogy. Barron was the publisher of the *Wall Street Journal*, the *Boston News Bureau*, etc. Records of Barron's meetings with Bernard Baruch, Charles Francis Adams, John D. Rockefeller, Jr., etc. Comments on world, political, economic, and financial events.

23. Barron, Clarence W. *They Told Barron: Conversations and Revelations of an American Pepys in Wall Street.* Edited and arranged by Arthur Pound and Samuel Taylor Moore. New York: Harper & Brothers, 1930. 372 pages.

Based upon notes Barron kept for an autobiography. Includes foreword and beginning of first chapter for the autobiography, "Financial Reminiscences" and record of his meetings with Bernard Baruch, J.P. Morgan, Jesse Livermore, William C. Durant, Henry Ford, Calvin Coolidge, Samuel Insull, etc. Lists publications of Barron.

24. Baruch, Bernard. *Baruch: My Own Story.* New York: Henry Holt and Co., 1957. 337 pages.

The first volume of Baruch's autobiography is an account of his family background, his childhood, college years, and career as a Wall Street speculator and member of the New York Stock Exchange Board of Governors.   Describes experiences during panics of 1893, 1901, 1903, and 1907 and Stock Market Crash of 1929.   Includes a chapter on his investment philosophy.   Volume two of autobiography is *Baruch: The Public Years.*

25. Baruch, Bernard. *Baruch: The Public Years.* New York: Holt, Rinehart, and Winston, 1960. 431 pages.

Covers nearly fifty years of Baruch's experiences in public life from World War I to the Cold War. Includes a chapter concerning events, causes, and effects of the Great Crash of 1929.

26. Birmingham, Stephen. *Our Crowd: The Great Jewish Families of New York.* New York: Harper & Row, 1967. 404 pages.

Chronicles lives and times of New York's Jewish banking families: the Seligmans, Guggenheims, Loebs, Lehmans, Lewisohns, Goldmans, Warburgs, Sachs, Kuhns, Baches, and Belmonts. Covers time period 1837 through mid 1960s. Presents genealogical backgrounds of the families, with a "Family Business Tree." Relates families' business dealings with Jay Gould, J.P. Morgan, Daniel Drew, and E.H. Harriman. Historic events described include: Panics of 1837, 1857, 1873, and 1907; Black Friday, 1869; the Pujo Committee investigation; the 1929 Crash; and the Pecora Hearings. With illustrations.

27. Borkin, Joseph. *Robert R. Young: The Populist of Wall Street.* New York: Harper & Row, 1969. 236 pages

Biography of Robert R. Young, private businessman who was involved in contests for control of various railroads, including the Allegheny Corporation and New York Central. Concentrates on Young's life and career from 1937 through his suicide twenty-one years later. Also relates history of railroads and railroad financing from 1831 through the 1930s. Includes bibliographical references and illustrations.

28. Browder, Clifford. *The Money Game in Old New York: Daniel Drew and His Times.* Lexington: University Press of Kentucky, 1986. 319 pages.

Biography of Daniel Drew describing his work as a cattle drover, his career on Wall Street, and his founding of the Drew Theological Seminary. Provides account of the "Erie Wars" and Drew's business dealings with Fisk, Gould, and Vanderbilt. Refutes some of *The Book of Daniel Drew*.

29. Carosso, Vincent P. *The Morgans: Private International Bankers, 1854-1913.* Harvard Studies in business history; 38. Cambridge, Mass.: Harvard University Press, 1987. 888 pages.

Story of the House of Morgan concentrates primarily on the lives of Junius Spencer Morgan (1913-1890) and John Pierpont Morgan (1837-1913). Includes some biographical information on John Pierpont Morgan, Jr. (1867-1943). Research based on study of personal papers of the Morgan family and the Morgan firms' business records. With a bibliography.

30. Chernow, Ron. *The House of Morgan: An American Dynasty and the Rise of Modern Finance.* New York: Atlantic Monthly Press, 1990. 812 pages.

Story of the House of Morgan (the firms, J.P. Morgan & Co., Morgan Stanley, and Morgan Grenfell) and the most notable Morgans: J.P. Morgan, Sr. and J.P. Morgan, Jr. Profiles the Morgan partners: Thomas W. Lamont, Dwight W. Morrow, and Russell Leffingwell. Chronicles effects of the Stock Market Crashes and Panics, including the Crashes of 1929 and 1987. With a chronology of the Morgan Empire from 1838 to 1988, a bibliography, and illustrations.

31. Churchill, Allen. *The Incredible Ivar Kreuger.* New York: Rinehart & Co., 1957. 301 pages.

The life of Ivar Kreuger, the "Match King,"a financier of great influence on Wall Street in the 1920s. Concentrates on psychological influences in Kreuger's life from his early years through his development of internationally based corporations including 160 match factories through his death. Kreuger found many financial backers during his visits to Wall Street in the 1920s and his stocks were traded on the New York Stock Exchange. Kreuger's realization that he was about to be exposed as a swindler and forger led to his suicide in 1932. His death was kept a secret in the United States until the New York Stock Exchange closed for the day. With illustrations and bibliographical references.

32. Corey, Lewis. *The House of Morgan: A Social Biography of the Masters of Money.* New York: G. Howard Watt, 1930. 479 pages.

History of the House of Morgan from its colonial origins to 1929. Provides biographical information for Miles Morgan, the colonial ancestor; Joseph Morgan; Junius Spencer Morgan; John

Pierpont; J. P. Morgan, Sr.; and J. Pierpont Morgan, Jr. Studies key events among which are: the Erie Wars; the Panic of 1907; the Pujo Committee Hearings; and the 1929 Crash. With bibliography and illustrations including family portraits, organizational charts, and political cartoons.

33. Dimock, Anthony Weston. *Wall Street and the Wilds*. New York: Outing Publishing Co., 1915. 476 pages.

Autobiography of a New York Stock Exchange member as well as a hunter and photographer. Started work on Wall Street as a teenager and during his career witnessed first-hand such events as Black Friday, 1869.

*   Douglas, William O. *Go East Young Man: The Early Years: The Autobiography of William O. Douglas*. see item 263 below.

*   Dunnan, Nancy. *The Stock Market*. see item 97 below

34. Ehrlich, Judith Ramsey and Barry J. Rehfeld. *The New Crowd: The Changing of the Jewish Guard on Wall Street*. Boston: Little, Brown, 1989. 444 pages.

Profiles members of the "New Crowd," influential Jewish financiers who prospered on Wall Street during the decades after World War II. Examines careers of Sidney Weinberg, Felix Rohatyn, Sanford "Sandy" Weill, William R. "Billy" Salomon, John Gutfreund, Lewis Glucksman, Alan C. Greenberg, John Loeb, Michael Milken, Saul Steinberg, Peter Cohen, Carl Icahn, Ivan Boesky, and Dennis Levine. Discusses insider trading scandals involving Boesky, Levine, and Milken. Relates developments during the time period from the late 1940s to 1989 on the NYSE and Wall Street. With a bibliography of books, magazines and newspapers, and other material.

35. Emery, William Morrell. *The Howland Heirs: Being the Story of a Family and a Fortune and the Inheritance of a Trust Established for Mrs. Hetty H. R. Green.* With an introduction by Hon. William W. Crapo, 1919. 484 pages.

   Genealogy of the Howland Family among whose members are Sylvia Ann Howland and her niece Hetty Howland Robinson Green. Provides biographical sketches of family members and the history of the fortune, most of which was inherited by Green and her two children. Studies Green's business investments and provides excerpts from some of her interviews. Among portraits are those of Green; her son, Colonel Edward Green; and Sylvia Ann Howland. See also Sparkes' biography, *Hetty Green.*

36. Flynn, John T. *Men of Wealth: The Story of Twelve Significant Fortunes from the Renaissance to the Present Day.* New York: Simon and Schuster, 1941. 531 pages.

   Biographical essays of people (eleven men and one woman) of great wealth among which are Hetty Green, Cornelius Vanderbilt, and J.P. Morgan, Sr. Each essay is accompanied by a portrait of the individual profiled.

37. Forbes, John Douglas. *J.P. Morgan, Jr., 1867-1943.* Charlottesville: University Press of Virginia, 1981. 262 pages.

   Biography of the younger J.P. Morgan is separated into three time periods: 1867-1913; 1913-1933; and 1933-1943. Covers: his early life, marriage, and start in the family business; his activities as senior partner of J.P. Morgan & Co.; his experiences during the 1929 Crash; and his testimony at the Pecora investigations. Research based on access to Morgan papers, including the letters from J.P. Morgan, Jr. to his mother. Studies role of the younger Morgan as book collector who expanded the Pierpont Morgan Library collection. With bibliography and description of the J.P. Morgan, Jr. papers.

38. Fuller, O.M. *John Muir of Wall Street: A Story of Thrift*. New York: Knickerbocker Press, 1927. 325 pages.

Concerns an odd-lot broker on the New York Stock Exchange and an executive for United States railroads, Kansas Pacific and Union Pacific. Studies his business career and family life. He was also publisher of the *Odd-Lot Review*.

39. Fuller, Robert H. *Jubilee Jim: The Life of Colonel James Fisk, Jr*. New York: Macmillan, 1928. 566 pages.

Biographical novel of the life and career of Jim Fisk from his boyhood to his murder by Edward S. Stokes. The story is told from the viewpoint of Fisk's lifelong friend, Rufus Phelps, who gives first-hand account of major events in Fisk's life including the Erie Wars and Black Friday. Character studies are also provided for Daniel Drew, Commodore Vanderbilt, Jay Gould, Josie Mansfield, and Edward S. Stokes. Illustrated with photographs and illustrations from *Harper's Weekly*.

40. Glynn, Lenny. "Arthur Cashin, Floor Broker, New York Stock Exchange." *Institutional Investor* 21 (June 1987): 491-492.

Cashin reflects on his experiences as a governor of the NYSE and his work as a floor broker for over twenty years. Changes discussed by Cashin include growth in volume; introduction of such innovations as program trading. Studies role of floor broker, including what happens during panics.

41. Grant, James. *Bernard M. Baruch: The Adventures of a Wall Street Legend*. New York: Simon and Schuster, 1983. 376 pages.

The life and times of Baruch, emphasizing his Wall Street career. Discusses Baruch's work as a New York Stock Exchange governor, as an investor, and his experiences during the 1929 Crash. Studies Baruch's contributions as head of the War Industries Board during World War I, delegate to the United Nations Atomic Energy

Commission, and adviser to U.S. presidents.

42. Grodinsky, Julius. *Jay Gould: His Business Career, 1867-1892*. Philadelphia: University of Pennsylvania Press, 1957. 627 pages.

   Examines policies of Gould as a businessman and his involvement with the Erie Railroad, Union Pacific, Western Union, and Manhattan Elevated. Discusses Erie Wars and Gold Corner of 1869. Assesses importance of Gould to business history and his contribution to the United States railroad industry. Includes bibliographical references.

43. Hoisington, Harland W., Jr. *Wall Street, 1920-1970: Five Fabulous Decades*. New York: Vantage Press, 1972. 207 pages.

   Autobiographical account of an investment counselor. Describes Wall Street during the Great Crash, the Depression Years, the role of the Securities and Exchange Commission, the bull and bear markets during the post-World War II years, etc. Profiles Ivar Kreugar, Emil Schram, Keith Funston, etc. Projects future of the stock market.

44. Holbrook, Stewart H. *The Age of the Moguls*. Garden City, N.Y.: Doubleday, 1953. 373 pages.

   Profiles Commodore Cornelius Vanderbilt, Daniel Drew, Jim Fisk, Jay Gould, Jay Cooke, J.P. Morgan, Henry Clay Frick, Andrew Carnegie, John D. Rockefeller Sr., Henry Ford, Sam Insull, William Randolph Hearst, Andrew Mellon, etc. Includes accounts of the Erie Wars; Black Friday, 1869; Panic of 1873; and the Stock Market Crash of 1929.

*   Hoover, Herbert. *Memoirs of Herbert Hoover: The Great Depression, 1929-1941*. see item 215 below.

45. Hovey, Carl. *The Life Story of J. Pierpont Morgan.* New York: Sturgis & Walton, 1911. Reprint: Freeport, N.Y.: Books for Libraries Press, 1971. 352 pages.

Biography of Morgan written during his lifetime and with Morgan's "cognizance" emphasizes his business career. Discusses: his ancestry; childhood and youth; the establishment of Drexel, Morgan & Co. in 1871; the formation of the United States Steel Trust; the Panic of 1907; and his philanthropy. Illustrations include: portraits of Morgan; Junius Spencer Morgan; the Library on Thirty-Sixth Street; Charles M. Schwab; Henry C. Frick; Elbert H. Gary; J.A. Farrell; and Wall Street in the Panic of 1907.

46. Hoyt, Edwin P., Jr. *The House of Morgan.* New York: Dodd, Mead, 1966. 428 pages.

The life and times of the Morgan family from colonial times through the early 1960s. Story of: Miles Morgan, Joseph Morgan, Junius Spencer Morgan, J. Pierpont Morgan, Sr., J. Pierpont Morgan, Jr., Junius Morgan, and John Pierpont Morgan II. Provides descriptions of Panics of 1893 and 1907; the Pujo Committee Investigation; the 1929 Crash; and 1930s legislation including the Glass-Steagall Act. With bibliography of sources.

47. Jackson, Stanley. *J.P. Morgan: A Biography.* New York: Stein and Day, 1983. 332 pages.

Biography of the highly influential financier and adviser of U.S. presidents. Covers: genealogy of the Morgan family; his career on Wall Street; his family; and his establishment of the Morgan Library. Discusses his role in Wall Street history including his halting the panic of 1907 and his business dealings with Bernard Baruch, Jay Gould, William C. Durant, and E.H. Harriman. Includes bibliography.

48. *James Fisk, Jr.: His Life and Death. Also, the Trial of Edward S. Stokes for the Murder. With a Biography of Josie Mansfield.*

New York, 187-. 48 pages.

Mostly illustrations depicting scenes from the lives of Fisk,
Mansfield, and Stokes. Illustrations for Fisk include: "Black
Friday," "The Lunch before the Murder (by Stokes)," and "Death
Bed Scene."

49. Johnston, Joanna. *Mrs. Satan: The Incredible Saga of Victoria C.
    Woodhull.* New York: Putnam's, 1967. 319 pages.

The story of feminist Victoria C. Woodhull (1838-1927), who
with her sister, Tennessee "Tennie" Claflin, was the first woman
broker on Wall Street (1870). Tells of Woodhull's and Claflin's
friendship and business association with Commodore Vanderbilt.
Additionally, Woodhull was the first woman candidate for President
of the United States. With a bibliography of newspapers and
periodicals; pamphlets; and books. Includes illustrations.

50. Jones, Willoughby. *The Life of James Fisk, Jr., The Story of His
    Youth and Manhood, with Full Accounts of all the schemes and
    enterprises in which he was engaged, including the Great Frauds
    of the Tammany Ring, Biographical Sketches of Railroad
    Magnates and Great Financiers, with Brilliant Pen Pictures in
    Light and Shadows of New York Life. Josie Mansfield, "The
    Siren" how a Beautiful Woman Captivated and Ruined her
    victims. The Mansfield Mansion. The Rejected and Accepted
    Suitors. Edward S. Stokes, The Assassin and an Account of the
    Assassination.* Philadelphia, Chicago: Union Publishing Co.,
    1872. 512 pages.

Legacy of Fisk, written the year of his death. Covers: his youth
in Vermont; years on Wall Street and association with Jay Gould;
his involvement in the Gold Ring and Erie Railroad; his marriage;
his liaison with Josie Mansfield, etc. Provides: excerpts of Fisk's
testimony on the Gold Ring before a Committee of Congress; the
Fisk-Mansfield letters; and descriptions of and comments about
Fisk by contemporaries including Henry Ward Beecher.
Illustrations include portraits of Fisk, Daniel Drew, Edward S.

Stokes, Josie Mansfield, William M. Tweed, Jay Gould, etc.

51. Josephson, Matthew. *The Robber Barons: The Great American Capitalists, 1861-1901*. New York: Harcourt, 1934. 474 pages.

The lives and careers of: Commodore Cornelius Vanderbilt; Daniel Drew; Jay Cooke; Jay Gould; Andrew Carnegie; John D. Rockefeller; J. Pierpont Morgan; James Fisk, Jr.; Collis Huntington; William H. Vanderbilt; James J. Hill; Henry Villard; Henry Clay Frick; Edward H. Harriman; William C. Whitney. Studies key business events of the time period 1861-1901 among which are: the Erie Wars; the Gold Ring and Black Friday; the Panics of 1873, 1884, 1893, and 1901; and the growth of the Trust or great monopoly. Includes bibliography.

52. Kempner, S. Marshall. *Inside Wall Street, 1920-1942*. New York: Hastings House, 1973. 140 pages.

Autobiographical account of an investment banker and partner in Stern, Kempner & Co. Describes Great Crash of 1929 and events leading to the Securities Exchange Act of 1934.

53. Kennan, George. *E.H. Harriman: A Biography*. Boston: Houghton Mifflin, 1922. 2 volumes.

Detailed biography of railroad president, stock speculator, and broker. Covers: his ancestry and boyhood; his character; marriage; establishment of his broker's office; work as director of Erie Railroad Company and Union Pacific and as president of Southern Pacific; the Panic of 1901; and his directorship of Equitable Life Assurance Society. Discusses Harriman's business dealings and associations with: J.Pierpont Morgan, Sr., Theodore Roosevelt, Charles Evans Hughes, James R. Keene, and James J. Hill. Includes a chronology of Harriman's life. With bibliographical references, illustrations, and a railroad map of the Harriman lines.

54. Klein, Maury. *The Life and Legend of Jay Gould.* Baltimore: Johns Hopkins University Press, 1986. 595 pages.

Biography of Gould discusses his life and business career. Analyzes legacy of Gould in history. Tells of lives and contributions of Gould's descendents. Describes and analyzes other biographies of Gould. With bibliographical references.

55. Lamont, Thomas W. *Henry P. Davison: The Record of a Useful Life.* New York: Harper, 1933. 373 pages.

Biography of a partner in J.P. Morgan & Co, written by a partner in J.P. Morgan & Co.

56. Lane, Wheaton J. *Commodore Vanderbilt: An Epic of the Steam Age.* New York, 1942. 357 pages.

Primarily a narrative of the business career of Commodore Cornelius Vanderbilt. Much of research based on access to correspondence, family records, and interviews with family members. Studies: genealogy of the Vanderbilt family; childhood; his early business venture as a boatman carrying passengers and freight between Staten Island and Manhattan; the expansion of the business to steamboat lines; his directorship of the Long Island, New Jersey Central, Stonington, the Hartford and New Haven, the Erie, and the New York and Harlem Railroads; the Erie Railroad Wars with Daniel Drew, Jay Gould, and James Fisk, Jr.; the construction of the Grand Central Station in Manhattan; his marriages; the lives and fortunes of his twelve children, including William H. Vanderbilt. With bibliographical notes and maps. Includes portraits of: Phebe Hand Vanderbilt, the Commodore's mother; Commodore Vanderbilt; Daniel Drew; William Henry Vanderbilt, the Commodore's son; and Jacob Hand Vanderbilt, his brother. With copy of engraving of NYSE at the time of the Panic of 1873.

57. Larson, Henrietta M. *Jay Cooke: Private Banker.* Harvard Studies

in Business History. Cambridge, Massachusetts: Harvard University Press, 1936. 512 pages.

Studies rise, success, and ultimate failure of private banker, Jay Cooke. Covers: his family background; childhood; early business experiences; marriage and children; establishment of Jay Cooke & Co.; his financing of the Northern cause in the Civil War; effects of Black Friday, 1869; his financing of the Northern Pacific Railroad; the failure of Jay Cooke & Co. that triggered the Panic of 1873; and his later years from 1873-1905. Appraises Cooke's role in American business history. Much of research based on Jay Cooke's collection of manuscripts, including his memoirs. Includes illustrative portraits of Cooke. With bibliographical references and notes.

58. Lefevre, Edwin. *Reminiscences of a Stock Operator.* New York: George H. Doran Co., 1923. 299 pages.

The reminiscenses of the fictional Larry Livingston are based on events in the life of Jesse Livermore. In-depth account of Livingston's successes as a speculator on Wall Street during the early part of the twentieth century.

59. McAlpine, Robert W. *The Life and Times of Col. James Fisk, Jr. A Full and Impartial Account of the Remarkable Career of a Most Remarkable Man; Together with sketches of all the important personages with whom he was thrown in contact, such as Drew, Vanderbilt, Gould, Tweed, etc. etc., and a Financial History of the Country for the last three years. Embracing, also, the Lives of Helen Josephine Mansfield, The Enchantress, and Edward S. Stokes, The Assassin.* New York: New York Book Company, 1872. 504 pages.

Written the year of Fisk's assassination, studies his business career and life. Relates results of inquest and verdict in the trial of Edward S. Stokes. Provides: illustrations; excerpts from Fisk's correspondence; excerpts from his testimony on the Gold Conspiracy; and excerpts from contemporary newspaper accounts.

60. McDonald, Forrest. *Insull*. Chicago: University of Chicago
    Press, 1962. 350 pages.

Biography of the financier who controlled a United States gas
and electric empire worth over three billion dollars. Insull started
out in the electric business as Thomas Edison's private secretary in
1881 and subsequently was responsible for founding the business
of centralized electric supply. He organized the Edison General
Electric Company, forerunner of today's General Electric
Company. Tells of Insull's major financial losses during the 1931
NYSE market decline. Toward the end of his life, Insull was
charged and later acquitted on charges of embezzlement and using
the mails to defraud investors. Insull's son, Samuel, Jr. was called
to testify before the Pecora Committee in 1933. Research based on
interviews, examination of the Samuel Insull Papers, corporation
records, and on books, government reports, and articles. With
bibliographical references.

61. Mansfield, Helen Josephine. *The Truth at Last!: Life of Col.
    James Fisk, Jr. with Full Particulars of the Unpublished Secrets
    and Intimacies Existing between him and Josie Mansfield, his
    former mistress: Sketches of Edward S. Stokes, his successful
    rival and assassin, together with various incidents in the
    checkered career of the murdered millionaire, never before made
    public.* New York: s.n. 188? 65 pages.

Centers on the Mansfield-Fisk-Stokes rivalry and subsequent
murder of Fisk by Stokes. Details Fisk's business career from early
days in Vermont to his business dealings on Wall Street. Provides:
excerpts from court case, Mansfield vs. Fisk; letters of Mansfield
and Fisk; the inquest and last will of Fisk; and events of Stokes'
murder trial.

62. Marion, Larry. "John Phelan, Jr., Chairman and Chief Executive
    Officer, New York Stock Exchange." *Institutional Investor* 21
    (June 1987): 277-281.

Relates Phelan's career at the NYSE, as specialist, board

member, Vice-Chairman and Chairman. Tells of change in organization during the early 1970s when representatives from industry and public members would serve on the board. Phelan considers public board to be best thing that happened to the NYSE. Issues dealt with by Phelan during his years at the Exchange included: automation of the NYSE; development of a national market system; unfixing commission rates; and reorganization and enhancement of a surveillance system. Phelan predicts: enormous swings in the marketplace; a substantial increase in volume; and a major correction in the market.

63. Marton, Andrew. "James Needham, Former Chairman, New York Stock Exchange." *Institutional Investor* 21 (June 1987): 262-269.

Profiles Needham, selected in 1972 to be the first full-time Chairman of the NYSE. Needham previously was a SEC Commissioner. Relates experiences of Needham during his tenure as Chairman, among which were: facing a major recession; preserving NYSE Rule 390 requiring all trading by member firms of listed stocks be done on the Exchange; and lack of full support by the Board of Directors. Defends public relations activities as necessary to the NYSE and denies that he was not accessible as Chairman. Explains conditions regarding his forced resignation as Chair and states he is not bitter about it. He subsequently became a consultant and corporate director.

64. Marton, Andrew. "William Batten, Former Chairman, New York Stock Exchange. *Institutional Investor* 21 (June 1987): 271-273.

Account of experiences of Batten, Chairman of the NYSE from 1976-1984. Before becoming Chairman, Batten was Chief Executive Officer of J.C. Penney Co. and was on the Board of the NYSE. Batten started his tenure as Chairman right after enactments of the Securities Acts Amendments of 1975. As Chairman he: initiated a strenuous communication porgram with CEOs of listed companies asking for their input; proposed what later became known as ITS (International Trading System); expanded number of shares per day with a goal of handling 100 million shares per day; and worked to open up access to the New York Stock Exchange.

*   Medbury, James K. *Men and Mysteries of Wall Street.* see item 105 below.

65. Minnigerode, Meade. *Certain Rich Men: Stephen Girard, John Jacob Astor, Jay Cooke, Daniel Drew, Cornelius Vanderbilt, Jay Gould, Jim Fisk.* New York: Putnam, 1927.Reprint: Freeport, N.Y.: Books for Libraries Press, 1970. 210 pages.

Series of biographical sketches, including Wall Street brokers and financiers: Jay Cooke, Daniel Drew, Cornelius Vanderbilt, Jay Gould, and Jim Fisk. Studies Cooke's involvement in the Panics of 1857 and 1873. Relates Drew's, Gould's, Fisk,'s and Vanderbilt's roles in the Erie Wars and the Panic of 1873. Analyzes Gould's and Fisk's Gold Corner and events leading up to Black Friday, 1869. With illustrative portraits and bibliography.

*   "Mr. Chocolate." see item 266 below.

66. Morgello, Clem. "Robert Haack, Former President, New York Stock Exchange." *Institutional Investor* 21 (June 1987): 254-258.

Portrait of Haack, President of the NYSE from 1967 to 1972. Problems faced by Haack during his tenure were: the market's slump and volume shrinkage; the beginnings of negotiated rates; a major back-office paperwork crunch; and failure of undercapitalized firms. During these years, the Central Stock Depository was established. In November 1970, Haack caused controversy by stating that the NYSE examine and experiment with negotiated commission rates for large orders.

67. Nicolson, Harold. *Dwight Morrow.* New York: Harcourt, Brace

and Company. 1935. 409 pages.

Biography of partner (1914-1927) at J.P. Morgan & Co. Describes events on Wall Street during this time period including the Crisis of 1914 and the closing of the New York Stock Exchange. Research based on access to letters, diaries, and recollections of members of the Morrow family.

68. Northrop, H.D. *Life and Achievements of Jay Gould, the Wizard of Wall Street, being a complete and graphic account of the greatest financier of modern times...a remarkable story abounding in fascinating incidents, thrilling episodes, and marvelous achievements.* Philadelphia: M. Southard Pub. Co., 1892. 512 pages

Story of Gould, the "Wizard of Wall Street," details his ancestry, boyhood and youth, work in the tannery business, his career as President of Erie Railroad and involvement in the Erie Wars; his business association with James Fisk, Jr.; his involvement in Black Friday and the Gold Corner; and his ownership of the Manhattan Elevated Company, Union Pacific, and Western Union. Also discusses family life, hobbies, contributions to charities, and stories of his interviews with newspaper reporters. The author had interviewed Gould on several occasions and provides some first-hand reports of these meetings. Presents excerpts from Gould's autobiographical testimony before the U.S. Senate Committee on Education and Labor in September 1883. Illustrated with portraits of Jay Gould; his son, George J. Gould; Mrs. George J. Gould; his son, Edwin Gould; William H. Vanderbilt; James Fisk, Jr.; Russell Sage; Cornelius Vanderbilt; and Daniel Drew. Other illustrations include sketches of Brokers Vaults under the Stock Exchange; the New York Stock Exchange building; the New York Stock Exchange Board in session; and Broad Street on Black Friday, 1869. With extracts from newspaper accounts published at the time of Gould's death. Contains an abstract of Gould's last will and testament. Analyzes legacy of Gould to American business. This biography published year of Gould's death.

69. Oberholtzer, Ellis Paxson. *Jay Cooke: Financier of the Civil War.*
    Philadelphia: George W. Jacobs & Co., 1907: Reprint: New
    York: Burt Franklin, 1970. 2 vols.

    Some of research for book was based on access by author to
    Cooke's correspondence and papers. The author also had
    cooperation of Cooke's children and had consulted them regarding
    some facts of biography. Details Cooke's ancestry and early life;
    business career; marriage and family life; personal characteristics;
    founding of Jay Cooke & Co.; financing of the Northern Cause
    during Civil War; and failure of Jay Cooke & Co., an event which
    led to Panic of 1873. Correspondence of Cooke is presented
    throughout the work. Contemporary accounts from newspapers are
    also included. Describes NYSE trading floor at the time of the
    Panic of 1873. With photographs of Cooke, his family, and
    business associates. Includes bibliographical references.

70. O'Connor, Richard. *Gould's Millions.* New York: Doubleday &
    Co., 1962. Reprint: Westport, Connecticut: Greenwood Press,
    1973. 335 pages.

    Biography of Jay Gould describes his childhood, work in the
    tannery business, work on Wall Street, and involvement in the Erie
    Wars and the Gold Corner. Relates business dealings of Gould
    with Commodore Vanderbilt, Daniel Drew, and Jim Fisk.
    Chronicles Gould's acquiring of control over Manhattan Elevated
    Railway Company, Union Pacific, and Western Union. Describes
    family of Gould--his wife Helen and the lives and fortunes of their
    six children. Includes illustrations and bibliography.

71. Porter, Donald. *Jubilee Jim and the Wizard of Wall Street: A
    Novel.* New York: Dutton, 1990. 568 pages.

    Fictionalized narrative of financial intrigues of Jim Fisk or
    "Jubilee Jim" and Jay Gould, "the Wizard of Wall Street." Main
    characters are: Gould, Fisk, William Vanderbilt, Cornelius
    Vanderbilt, Ulysses S. Grant, Josie Mansfield, and the fictional
    Annabelle Stokes, who represents a composite of several historical

figures. Describes Erie Wars and Black Friday.

72. Pyle, Joseph Gilpin. *The Life of James J. Hill. New York:*
     Doubleday, Doran & Co., 1917. 2 volumes.

Biography of American railroad builder Hill based on the author's access to his subject's letters, papers, and other documents. Additionally, the author had interviewed Hill and his family members and associates. Studies Hill's ancestry; childhood; early business career as partner in steamboat line; marriage and family; his establishment of railroad lines and their consolidation into the Great Northern Railway Company; his rivalry with E.H. Harriman; his reorganization of the Northern Pacific; his business dealings with J.P. Morgan; and the effects of Morgan's and Hill's dealings on the stock market--one effect was the Panic of 1901. Also discusses causes and consequences of the Panics of 1893 and 1907. Appendixes contain business documents and letters and statistics concerning Hill's railroad systems. Among illustrations are portraits of: James J. Hill at various ages; Mrs. James J. Hill; and Lord Mount Stephen, a business associate and friend.

73. Rheinstein, Sidney. *Trade Whims: My Fifty Years on the New York*
     Stock Exchange. New York: Ronald Press, 1960. 211 pages.

Anecdotes and reminiscenses of a fifty year member of the NYSE. Joined Exchange in 1909, served as a specialist, became member of the Board of Governors in 1940, and President of the Specialists Association of the New York Stock Exchange. Profiles individuals: G. Clinton Miller, Jesse L. Boskowitz, Harold Weekes, Allen Lehman, and Col. Henry Breckinridge. Includes text of Rheinstein's "Report to the Board of Governors of the New York Stock Exchange," September 1942 which called for improvement of public relations to get more traders on the Exchange. Discusses events of October 1929 Stock Market Crash. Provides reprint of *New York Times* article, October 30, 1959: "A Trader Recalls the Dark Day of Bulls' Slaughter on Wall Street," by Elizabeth M. Fowler; this article concerns Rheinstein's recollections of the day of the 1929 Crash.

74. Rochester, Anna. *Rulers of America: A Study of Finance Capital.*
New York: International Publishers, 1936. 367 pages.

Analyzes industries and economic developments from the 1860s
through the 1930s. Examines influence of the Morgans, Mellons,
and Rockefellers. Of special significance to NYSE history is the
study of the House of Morgan and the contributions of J. Pierpont
Morgan and J. Pierpont Morgan, Jr.

75. Sarnoff, Paul. *Jesse Livermore: Speculator King.* Palisades Park,
N.J.: Investors' Press, 1967. 136 pages.

Life of Jesse Livermore outlines his techniques for success on
Wall Street. Selections of various interviews with Livermore are
included. Describes early life, experiences during 1929 Crash, his
marriages, friendships, and 1940 suicide.

76. Satterlee, Herbert L. *J. Pierpont Morgan: An Intimate Portrait.*
New York, 1939. 595 pages.

Biography of Morgan by his son-in-law Herbert L. Satterlee.
Research based on first-hand experiences and observations as well
as access to diaries and letters of Morgan. Studies ancestry of
Morgan based on family records among which is the diary of
Joseph Morgan, the paternal grandfather. Describes key events in
Morgan's life: his marriages; family life; business activities at J.P.
Morgan & Co.; the U.S. Treasury crisis of 1895; founding of the
Morgan Library; the Panic of 1907; and testimony before the Pujo
Committee. Illustrations include photographs of Morgan from
boyhood to his later years; portraits of his parents and
grandparents; photographs of family homes and business offices;
and portraits of his first and second wives, children, and
grandchildren.

* Scoville, Joseph Alfred. *Old Merchants of New York City.* see
item 126 below.

* Sharp, Robert M. *The Lore and Legends of Wall Street.* see item 125 below.

77. Sinclair, Andrew. *Corsair: The Life of J. Pierpont Morgan.* Boston: Little, Brown, 1981. 269 pages.

Biography of J. Pierpont Morgan, Sr. analyzes his impact on American economic history and development. Relates: his early years; the influence of his father, Junius Spencer Morgan; his marriages and children; his conflicts with Jay Gould and Jim Fisk; his yachts, *Corsair, Corsair II,* and *Corsair III*; the development of the Morgan Library; the Panics of 1901, 1903, and 1907; and the Pujo Committee hearings. Includes a bibliography.

* Sloane, Leonard. *The Anatomy of the Floor: The Trillion Dollar Market at the New York Stock Exchange.* see item 324 below.

78. Smith, Arthur D. Howden. *Commodore Vanderbilt: An Epic of American Achievement.* New York: McBride, 1927. 339 pages.

The story of Vanderbilt, with some parts told in form of imagined conversations among protagonists. Tells of: his early years; his steamboat lines; his control over railroad including the Erie Railroad and Harlem and Hudson lines; his marriages; and his business dealings with Jay Gould, Daniel Drew, and Jim Fisk. Among illustrations: portraits of Vanderbilt; Daniel Drew; Wall Street in the Early Days; the Late Colonel James Fisk, Jr.; the Erie War; Tennie C. Claflin; Victoria C. Woodhull; the Old Terminal of the New York Central; and the Locomotive "Commodore Vanderbilt."

79. Sparkes, Boyden and Samuel Taylor Moore. *Hetty Green: A Woman Who Loved Money.* New York: Doubleday, Doran, 1930. 338 pages.

Biography of Hetty Howland Robinson Green, the "Witch of

Wall Street" from her early days in New Bedford, Massachusetts as the heiress to a whaling company fortune to her years as a multimillionaire with a fortune of approximately $100,000,000. Describes her ancestry, marriage to Edward Henry Green, her family life, business dealings and investments, and various legal disputes. Provides account of her years on Wall Street; she was called the "Witch of Wall Street" primarily because of the black mourning outfit she wore on her visits to Wall Street. Tells of conditions on Wall Street during this time (1870s - 1916) including events of the 1873, 1884, and 1907 Panics. Presents excerpts from newspaper accounts of the time, many dealing with Green's legal disputes and her practices of extreme thrift. Among illustrations are portraits of Green, her husband, children, and parents. See also Emery's *The Howland Heirs*.

80. Sparling, Earl. *Mystery Men of Wall Street: The Powers Behind the Market*. Illustrated with portraits by Seymour Marcus. New York: Greenberg Publisher, 1930. 254 pages.

Presents series of profiles on lives and contributions of: William C. Durant, Jesse L. Livermore, Arthur W. Cutten, Frank E. Bliss, Benjamin Block, Michael J. Meehan, Joseph E. Higgins, The Fisher Brothers, Louis W. Zimmerman, John J. Raskob, George Breen, and Harry Content. These biographical sketches first appeared, in abbreviated form, in *The New York Telegram* during December 1929. The introduction reviews past contributions of individuals including J.P. Morgan, Jay Gould, and Jay Cooke. The conclusion describes conditions at the NYSE during the 1929 Crash.

81. Stafford, Marshall P. *The Life of James Fisk, Jr.: A Full and Accurate Narrative of All the Enterprises in Which he was Engaged. The Railroads*. New York: Polhemus & Pearson, 1871. Reprint: New York: Arno Press, 1981. 300 pages.

Account of Fisk's life published a year before his death. Discusses business relationship with Jay Gould through Erie Wars and Black Friday, 1869. Among other aspects of his life examined:

his election to Colonel of the Ninth Regiment National Guard State
of New York, his family life in Boston with his wife, and his
association with Josie Mansfield. Illustrations include portraits of
Daniel Drew, Jay Gould, James Fisk, Jr., Commodore Vanderbilt,
and Josie Mansfield.

*   Stewart, James B. *Den of Thieves*. see item 419 below.

82. Swanberg, W.A. *Jim Fisk: The Career of an Improbable Rascal.*
     New York: Scribner's, 1969. 310 pages.

     The life and business career of James Fisk, Jr. from his
     childhood in Brattleboro, Vermont to his final days on Wall Street.
     Tells of the Erie Wars, the Gold Ring, and his dealings with Jay
     Gould, Josie Mansfield, William "Boss" Tweed, Daniel Drew,
     Commodore Vanderbilt, and Ulysses S. Grant. Provides excerpts
     of Fisk-Mansfield correspondence.   Postscript relates what
     happened to family, friends, and associates of Fisk after his death.
     Includes bibliography.

83. "Those Powerful Powder Puff Executives." *Nation's Business* 58
     (November 1970): 80-88.

     Profiles of women executives feature a brief biographical sketch
     of Muriel Siebert, the first woman member of the New York Stock
     Exchange. She heads her own company Muriel Siebert, Inc. With
     a photograph.

84. Warshow, Robert Irving. *Bet-a-Million Gates: The Story of a
     Plunger.* New York: Greenberg, 1932. 187 pages.

     Biography of noted Wall Street speculator, John Warne Gates
     (1855 -1911) concentrates on his business career. Concentrates on
     business career of individual known as the "Prince of Gamblers,"
     a speculator and manipulator who started out in the barbed wire
     industry.

85. Warshow, Robert Irving. *Jay Gould: The Story of a Fortune*. New York: Greenberg, 1928. 200 pages.

Biography of Gould discusses his childhood, start in the leather business, his roles in the Erie Wars and the Gold Conspiracy and acquisition of Union Pacific, Western Union, and the Manhattan Elevated Railway Company. Features Gould's school composition from April 9, 1850: "Honesty is the Best Policy." With an imaginary conversation between the Reader and Gould with the latter telling his side of the story.

86. Weiss, Gary. "William Donaldson." *Business Week*. Annual 1000 Issue, 1991, 78.

Profiles the Chairman (1991-   ) of the New York Stock Exchange. His career began thirty-two years ago when he founded, with Dan Lufkin and Richard H. Jenrette, the Wall Street firm, Donaldson, Lufkin & Jenrette, Inc. After leaving the firm in 1973, he went on to become an Undersecretary of State, then Dean of the Yale School of Management, and subsequently, proprietor of the investment firm, Donaldson Enterprises, Inc. His first major action as new chairman was to downsize the NYSE operation by cutting staff through layoffs, early retirements, and attrition. Among challenges faced by Donaldson as Chairman of the NYSE are: competition from NASDAQ's national market system, regional and international exchanges, and automated transaction systems including Instinet and POSIT. With a portrait.

87. Wheeler, George. *Pierpont Morgan & Friends: The Anatomy of a Myth*. Englewood Cliffs, N.J.: Prentice-Hall, 1973. 338 pages.

Life and career of Morgan and his business relationships with Andrew Carnegie, John W. "Bet-a-Million" Gates, James R. Keene, Henry Clay Frick, James J. Hill, James Fisk, Jay Gould, Daniel Drew, Commodore Vanderbilt, etc. Examines myth versus reality in Morgan's life. Explains how Morgan attained heroic image and analyzes how Morgan was depicted by the press and various biographers. Includes selections of Morgan's testimony before the Pujo Committee in 1912. With a bibliography of books; documentary sources at the Library of Congress; state, federal, and other reports, etc.; general references, magazines; and newspapers.

88. White, Bouck. *The Book of Daniel Drew: A Glimpse of the Fisk-Gould Regime from the Inside*. Garden City, N.Y.: Doubleday, Page & Co., 1913, c1910. 423 pages.

Based on "bundle of manuscript" by Drew found thirty years after his death. Discovered diary was left to grandniece. White states that "share in the preparation of this volume has had to be so large, even writing with my own hand parts which were needed in order to supply the connection." Covers events of Drew's life: childhood, work as cattle drover, in circus business, marriage to Roxana Mead, religious beliefs, steamboat business, work on Wall Street, role in the Erie War, founding of Drew Theological Seminary, the Panic of 1873, and bankruptcy. Gives account of Drew's business dealings with Jay Gould, Jim Fisk, and Commodore Vanderbilt.

89. White, Trumbell. *The Wizard of Wall Street and his Wealth, or the Life and Deeds of Jay Gould*. Chicago: Mid-Continent Publishing Co., 1892. 312 pages.

The life, contributions, and legacy of Jay Gould. Discusses: the Erie Wars; the Gold Corner; Gould's controlling interests in the Manhattan Elevated Railway, the Western Union Telegraph Company, and the Missouri Pacific System; his marriage and family life; and his personal characteristics. Among illustrations: "Black Friday" in Wall Street; Gould before the Congressional committee; the Men of Black Friday: Jay Gould, Jim Fisk, Daniel Drew, Commodore Vanderbilt, Peter B. Sweeney, and E.R. Stokes; and Jay Gould's Private Car and his yacht, "Atalanta."

90. Winkler, John K. *Morgan the Magnificent: The Life of J. Pierpont Morgan (1837-1913)*. New York: Vanguard Press, 1930. 313 pages.

Biography of Morgan tells of his personal and family life; his nearly exclusive control over U.S. cash and credit; his conflicts with President Theodore Roosevelt; the Panic of 1907; and the Pujo Committee testimony.

91. Wyckoff, Richard D. *Wall Street Ventures and Adventures through Forty Years.* New York: Harper & Brothers, 1930. 313 pages.

Records experiences on Wall Street from 1888-1928 as stock runner, telephone boy on the floor of NYSE, salesman, partner in a brokerage firm, writer, and editor. Describes work as founder, publisher, writer, and editor for *The Ticker, The Magazine of Wall Street,* and *Trend Letter.* Recalls meetings with Jay Gould, Diamond Jim Brady, Jesse Livermore, and Edward H. Harriman. Discusses Panics of 1893, 1901, and 1914.

CHAPTER V
GENERAL HISTORIES

The majority of sources listed and annotated in this chapter cover the general history of the New York Stock Exchange and do not concentrate on a specific time period. The works by Robert Sobel and Francis Stedman are considered by some historians and bibliographers to be the best and most comprehensive histories of the NYSE.

Other materials listed here have special significance to the history of the NYSE. These are: Charles Mackay's *Extraordinary Popular Delusions and the Madness of Crowds*, a treatise on the nature of panics and Wayne Westbrooks's *Wall Street and the American Novel*, an analysis of fiction about Wall Street, including the New York Stock Exchange.

It should be noted that some books listed in later chapters which cover various time periods contain a brief history of the New York Stock Exchange.

92. Clews, Henry. *Fifty Years in Wall Street: 'Twenty-Eight Years in Wall Street,' Revised and enlarged by a Resume of the Past Twenty-Two Years Making a Record of Fifty Years in Wall Street.* New York: J.S. Irving Publishing Co., 1908. 1062 pages.

Updated edition of financier Clews' history of Wall Street covers years 1857-1907. Includes history of the NYSE, examination of stock market panics, biographical information, etc. Discusses Panics of 1903 and 1907. With illustrations and directories of NYSE Officers.

93. Clews, Henry. *Twenty Eight Years in Wall Street.* New York: J.S. Irving Publishing Co., 1888. 716 pages

First-hand account of men and events of Wall Street, from 1857 through early 1887 also chronicles history of Wall Street and NYSE. Clews states that "...the great aim of the book is to place Wall Street in its true light before the eyes of the world, and help to efface the many wrong impressions the community have received..." Chapter XI is a history of the NYSE from the Buttonwood Tree Agreement though 1886 with a list of the Presidents of the Exchange and the Ten Oldest Living Members of NYSE. Chapter XLVI is a synopsis of key events on Wall Street from 1816 through January 1887. Discusses Panic of 1837, Panic of 1857, the Gold Ring (1869), the Erie Wars, and the Panic of 1873.   Provides biographical information on: Daniel Drew, Commodore Vanderbilt, Jay Gould, James R. Keene, and Jacob Little.   Among illustrations are: photographs of the New York Stock Exchange (exterior and board room) and portraits of W.R. Travers, Jay Gould, E.C. Stedman, Daniel Drew, Commodore Vanderbilt, and Jacob Little.   Author was a noted Wall Street financier.

94. Collins, Frederick. *Money Town: The Story of Manhattan Toe: That Golden Mile Which Lies Between the Battery and the Fields.* New York: Putnam's, 1946. 327 pages.

Wall Street's history from the 1600s to 1946. Reviews key events in history of the New York Stock Exchange, from 1792. With illustrations and photographs of: the Tontine Coffee House and various views of the NYSE.

95. Collman, Charles Albert. *Our Mysterious Panics: 1830-1930.* New York: William Morrow & Co., 1931: Reprint: Westport, Connecticut: Greenwood Press, 1968. 310 pages.

Studies Wall Street's panics of 1837, 1857, 1873, 1884, 1893, 1901, 1907, and 1929. Defines panic and analyzes its causes and effects. Examines roles of individuals in panics described, including

J.J. Hill, J.P. Morgan, and Jay Cooke. Compares earlier panics with market crash of 1929. Includes bibliographical references.

96. *Crashes and Panics: The Lessons from History*. Edited by Eugene N. White. Homewood, Illinois: Dow Jones-Irwin, 1990. 260 pages.

Papers presented at a Conference held at the Salomon Brothers Center for the Study of Financial Institutions at New York University's Stern School of Business in October 1988. Contents: Preface by A.W. Sametz; Introduction by Eugene N. White; Part 1. Before the Modern Age: Flower Bulbs and Life Annuities; Part 2. The Stock Market in the Nineteenth Century; Part 3. The Great Crashes of 1929 and 1987; Part 4. Are There Any Lessons from History? Part 1 is comprised of the papers: "Who Put the Mania in the Tulipmania?" by Peter M. Garber; "How the South Sea Bubble was Blown Up and Burst: A New Look at Old Data," by Larry D. Neal; and "Discussion," by Frederic S. Mishkin and Forrest Capie. Part 2: "The Panic of 1873 and Financial Market Volatility in Panics Before 1914," by Charles P. Kindleberger; "Financial Market Panics and Volatility in the Long Run, 1830-1988," by Jack W. Wilson, Richard E. Sylla, and Charles P. Jones; and "Discussion," by Michael D. Bordo and Gary Gorton. Part 3: "When the Ticker Ran Late: The Stock Market Boom and Crash of 1929," by Eugene N. White; "Bubbles and Fundamentals: New Evidence from Great Bull Markets," by Gary J. Santoni and Gerald P. Dwyer; "Comments on the Stock Market Crash: Six Months After," by Hayne Leland and Mark Rubinstein; and Discussion by Robert J. Schiller, Peter C. Warman, and Merton H. Miller. Part 4 is a Roundtable Discussion, with papers: "Are There Any Lessons from History?" by Eugene N. White; "Historical Perspective and Proposed Changes," by Franklin R. Edwards, "1929 and 1987: Parallels and Contrasts," by Barry J. Eichengreen; and "The Achilles Heel of the Financial Sector: A Comment on the Crash," by William L. Silber. Provides historical background for interpretation of the Crash of 1987. Examines causes, effects, and the nature of panics. With statistical tables and bibliographical references.

97. Dunnan, Nancy. *The Stock Market.* The Inside Track Library. Englewood Cliffs, N.J.: Silver Burdett Press, a division of Simon & Schuster, Inc. 1990. 128 pages.

Describes, for young people, the history and organization of major stock exchanges including the NYSE, provides historical information concerning the Crashes of 1929 and 1987, etc.. Provides some biographical information on notable individuals: Jay Gould, J. Pierpont Morgan, John J. Phelan, Jr., and Muriel F. Siebert. With a bibliography.

98. Eames, Francis L. *The New York Stock Exchange.* s.l.: Thomas G. Hall, 1894: Reprint: Westport, Connecticut: Greenwood Press, 1968, 139 pages.

Reprint of 1894 edition published by Thomas G. Hall. History of the NYSE from 1792-1894. Initial purpose of author was to prepare the book solely for members of the NYSE who have an interest in the history of their organization. Provides organizational history of Exchange with names of members and officers, statistics on sales at the Stock Exchange, By-Laws, Constitution, Standing Committees,etc. With illustrations and photographs of the NYSE. Reprints Constitution of The New York Stock and Exchange Board.

* Fowler, William Worthington. *Ten Years in Wall Street.* Hartford, see item 141 below.

99. Friedman, Maxine. *Wall Street: Changing Fortunes.* New York: Fraunces Tavern Museum, 1990. 58 pages.

Issued in conjunction with an exhibition at the Fraunces Tavern Museum on view from January 31, 1990 through August 12, 1990. Chronicles history of Wall Street from its seventeenth century origins to the start of World War I. Describes exhibits, with illustrations included for some. Among exhibits: "The Buttonwood Agreement"; painting of the Tontine Coffee House; chair from the New York Stock Exchange (c.1865-1871); portraits of Daniel

Drew, Jay Gould, and Cornelius Vanderbilt; a photograph of the New York Stock Exchange (1903); and the first issue of the *Wall Street Journal*. With a selected bibliography.

100. Hemming, H.G. *Hemming's History of the New York Stock Exchange*. New York: Henry Glover & Co., 1905. 1 vol. (various pagings)

Subtitle: "Historical Sketch of the Foundation of Stock Exchanges. The Basis Essential to Permanence. The Relation of the Exchange to the Bank. The Rise of the New York Stock Exchange, Its Career, Leaders and Methods. Its Functions and Relative Part in the Machine of International Finance. The Money Market of the World." Chronicles events in the history of the NYSE from 1792-1903, includes discussion of classical and European predecessors; the founding of the NYSE; the Panics of 1837, 1857, 1873; Black Friday, 1869; the various headquarters of the NYSE, etc. With steel engravings of members of the Exchange (ca. 1905). Text followed by illustrations of four views of old New York. NYSE members in portraits includes those of: Bernard M. Baruch, Henry Clews, Francis L. Eames, George J. Gould, and J.P. Morgan, Jr.

101. Hoisington, Harland W., Jr. *Reforms! Wall Street, 1790-1974*. New York: Vantage Press, 1976. 172 pages.

Reforms by the U.S. Government and by various stock exchanges are reviewed. Provides information concerning: key dates in NYSE's history; presidents of the NYSE who made reforms; establishment of the Securities and Exchange Commission; Reforms and Cases of the SEC, etc.

102. Kindleberger, Charles Poor. *Manias, Panics, and Crashes: A History of Financial Crises*. Rev. ed. New York: Basic Books, 1989. 302 pages.

Concerns international financial crises explained through economic models. Defines and explains nature of financial crises and evaluates measures to manage crises. Appendix A is essay, "Irrationality in Economics," and Appendix B, "A Stylized Outline of Financial Crises, 1720-1987." The "Stylized Outline" is in chart form and, for each financial crisis, lists key facts including year, country, speculative peak, and lender of last resort. With bibliographical references.

*   Lamb, Martha J. *Wall Street in History.* see item 125 below.

103. Levinson, Leonard L. *Wall Street: A Pictorial History.* New York: Ziff-Davis Publishing, 1961. 376 pages

Wall Street from its beginnings to 1960, with illustrations and photographs. Describes: founding of the NYSE; Panics of 1837, 1857, 1884, 1907, 1929; the Wall Street explosion of 1920; the Senate Banking and Currency Committee hearings of the early 1930s; the financial district during World War II, etc. Provides photographs and drawings of: Jay Gould; James Fisk, Jr.; William H. Vanderbilt; J.P. Morgan, Sr.; Bernard M. Baruch; Hetty Green; Charles E. Mitchell; Richard Whitney; J.P. Morgan, Jr., etc. Includes illustrations of the NYSE buildings throughout its history.

104. Mackay, Charles. *Extraordinary Popular Delusions and the Madness of Crowds.* With a foreword by Bernard M. Baruch. Boston: L.C. Page & Co., a subsidiary of Farrar, Straus and Cudahy, 1932. 724 pages.

With facsimile title pages and reproductions of original illustrations from the editions of 1841 and 1852. Reprinting recommended by Baruch who used book as guide that saved him millions of dollars. Baruch, in foreword, mentions crowd madness as factor in 1929 market crash. Mackay asserts; "men, it has been well said, think in herds; it will be seen that they go mad in herds, while they only recover their senses slowly, and one by one." Contains the stories of the following historical incidents which resulted from madness of crowds. These stories are: "The Mississippi Scheme," "The South-Sea Bubble," "The Tulipomania

(Tulips used as means of speculation)," "The Alchymists," "Modern Prophecies," "Fortune-Telling," "The Magnetisers," "Influence of Politics and Religion on the Hair and Beard," "The Crusades," "The Witch Mania," "The Slow Poisoners," "Haunted Houses," "Popular Follies of Great Cities," "Popular Admiration of Great Thieves," "Duels and Ordeals," and "Relics." Mackay is often cited in books and articles about crashes and panics.

105. Medbury, James K. *Men and Mysteries of Wall Street.* s.l.: Fields, Osgood, & Co., 1870: Reprints: Wells, Vermont: Fraser Publishing Co., 1968. New York: Greenwood Press, 1968. 344 pages.

History of the New York Stock Exchange from its origins in 1792 to conditions in 1870. Provides explanations of terms such as "block," "corners," "jobbers," "short," and "washing." Reviews activities of brokers and the procedures to buy and sell stock. Examines historical contributions of Commodore Vanderbilt, Jim Fisk, Daniel Drew, Jay Gould, and Leonard W. Jerome.

106. Meeker, James Edward. *The Work of the Stock Exchange.* Rev. ed. New York: Ronald Press, 1930. 720 pages.

History of the New York Stock Exchange studies its organization, administration, and relation to American business. With illustrations, sample forms used at the NYSE, etc.

107. *Men and Idioms of Wall Street: Explaining the Daily Operations in Stocks, Bonds and Gold.* New York: John Hickling & Co., 1875. Reprint: Burlington, Vermont: Fraser Publishing Co., 1988. 72 pages.

Provides brief history of Wall Street from 1653 to 1875. Explains terms such as "Speculation," "Cliques and Pools," "Commission," "Investments," and "Tight Money Market." With list of defaulted R.R. Bonds, list of stocks dealt in the New York Stock Exchange, highest and lowest prices of stocks, 1860-1874, and railroad statistics. Relates stories of Black Friday, 1869 and the South Sea Bubble. Profiles Commodore Vanderbilt, Henry Keep, John Morrissey, Daniel Drew, A.G. Jerome, L. W. Jerome, A.W. Morse, Thurlow Weed, Moses Taylor, Rufus Hatch, Henry Clews, A.S. Hatch, Alexander Taylor, Jay Gould, Russell Sage, Jay Cooke, and James Fisk.

108. Neill, Humphrey B. *The Inside Story of the Stock Exchange: A Fascinating Saga of the World's Greatest Money Market Place.* New York: B.C. Forbes & Sons, 1950. 345 pages.

Covers history of NYSE from 1792 through 1950. Explains historical and economic role of NYSE. Provides historical information for topics such as: the Buttonwood Tree Agreement; the careers of Jim Fisk, Jay Gould, and Daniel Drew; the Pujo Investigation; the Crash of 1929; and the establishment of the Securities and Exchange Commission. Among statistical tables: Reported Volume of Trading, 1900-1949 and Membership ("Seat") Prices, 1922-1932. With bibliographical references.

109. *The New York Stock Market.* Wall Street and the Security Markets. New York: Arno Press, 1975. 1 v. (various pagings)

Reprint of *History of the New York Stock Exchange, The New York Stock Exchange Directory* published in 1887 by Financier Co., N.Y.; of *Share Ownership in the United States: A Study Prepared at the Request of the New York Stock Exchange,* by Lewis H. Kimmel, published in 1952 by the Brookings Institution, Washington; of *The Consolidated Stock Exchange of New York,* by Samuel A. Nelson, published in 1907 by A.B. Benesch Co., New York; and of *The New York Stock Exchange in the Crisis of 1914,* by Henry G.S. Noble, published in 1915 by Country Life Press, Garden City, New York. *History of the New York Stock Exchange* presents a brief history of NYSE and a list of officers (1824-1886); the oldest members of the NYSE to December 1886; Total Number of Shares of Stock Value of Government, State and Railroad Bonds Sold at the NYSE, 1880-1886; Prices of Active Shares on the NYSE, 1885-1886; members of Exchange; Transfer of Membership, 1886; Alphabetical List of Firms that are members of the Exchange; and Constitution of the NYSE, Amended to June 1, 1886. *Share Ownership in the United States* is a study of facts concerning share ownership and provides statistics on occupations, educational level, etc. of shareholders. *The Consolidated Stock Exchange of New York* is a history of that Exchange. *The New York Stock Exchange in the Crisis of 1914* is an account by the President of NYSE and describes the temporary closing of the Exchange.

110. Perkins, D.W. *Wall Street Panics, 1813-1930 "Upon Record."* Waterville, N.Y.: D.W. Perkins, 1931. 214 pages.

Stories of panics of: 1813-14; 1818-19; 1826; 1837-39; 1841; 1847; 1851; 1857; 1861; 1863; 1864; 1869; 1873; 1884; 1889-90; 1893; 1895; 1899; 1901; 1903; 1907; 1914; 1919; and 1929. The first two chapters relate the history of the New York Stock Exchange from its beginnings in 1792 through 1930. Provides biographical information for the founders of the New York Stock Exchange. Lists Presidents of the NYSE from 1816 to 1930. Among illustrations are: the Market Place, Wall Street, ca. 1792; the Tontine Building, 1794; trading floor of the New York Stock Exchange, 1920s; and the New York Stock Exchange building, ca. 1903. Provides statistical data and an index.

111. Sharp, Robert M. *The Lore and Legends of Wall Street.* Homewood, Illinois: Dow Jones-Irwin, 1989. 246 pages.

The story of Wall Street with accounts of key events and characters. Chapter 17 concerns the origins of the New York Stock Exchange. Provides stories of notable individuals: Daniel Drew, Commodore Vanderbilt, Jay Gould, Jim Fisk, William Travers, James R. Keene, Hetty Robinson Green, Charles Dow, J. Pierpont Morgan, Bernard Baruch, Russell Sage, etc. Discusses crashes of 1929 and 1987. With a bibliography and a glossary of terms.

*   Shultz, Birl E. *The Securities Market--And How it Works.* see item 322 below.

*   Sloane, Leonard. *The Anatomy of the Floor: The Trillion Dollar Market at the New York Stock Exchange.* see item 324 below.

112. Sobel, Robert. *The Big Board.* New York: Free Press, 1965. 395 pages.

Foreword by Broadus Mitchell. History of the New York money market concentrates on the New York Stock Exchange from 1792-1965. Examines social, political, locational, and financial influences on the New York money market. Describes roles in history of Jay Cooke, J.P. Morgan, E.H. Harriman, Charles Merrill, Jim Fisk, Daniel Drew, Jay Gould, Samuel Insull, Jesse Livermore, Richard Whitney, etc. Among subjects covered: Panics of 1837, 1857, 1873; the Gold Ring, 1869; the 1929 Crash; and the Securities and Exchange Act. Statistical tables include: Cost of an Exchange Seat, 1884-1892; Key Market Indicators, 1939-1943; Stock Losses, October 29, 1929; Dow Jones-Averages, 1921-1929, etc. With a bibliography. Sobel's *N.Y.S.E.: A History of the New York Stock Exchange, 1935-1975* (see item 325 below) covers NYSE history during that forty-year time span.

113. Sobel, Robert. *Panic on Wall Street: A History of America's Financial Disasters.* New York: Macmillan, 1968. 469 pages.

Studies nature of panics with specific reference to twelve episodes in the history of Wall Street. Covers: the panics of 1792, 1837, 1857, 1869, 1873, 1884, 1893, 1901, 1907, and 1929; and the aborted panics of 1914 and 1962. Describes roles of individuals in various panics such as: William Duer (1792); Jay Gould and Jim Fisk (1869); and J.P. Morgan (1893, 1901, 1907). Outlines possible causes of a panic of the future. Includes statistical tables and bibliography.

114. Stedman, E.C. *The New York Stock Exchange: Its History, Its Contribution to National Prosperity, and Its Relation to American Finance at the Outset of the Twentieth Century.* New York: Stock Exchange Historical Company, 1903. Reprint: New York:

Greenwood Press, 1969, 518 pages.

Detailed history of NYSE chronicles: early days; first Constitution; Crisis of 1818; the NYSE during the Civil War; Black Friday, 1869; the Erie Ring; the Panic of 1873, the dedication of the new Stock Exchange Building, April 22, 1903, etc. Discusses roles of Commodore Cornelius Vanderbilt, Jay Gould, Jim Fisk, and Daniel Drew. The article: "The New Stock Exchange" by John Rodemeyer examines the architecture of the new building. Provides: "Constitution and Rules for the Government of the New York Stock Exchange as Amended and Adopted in March 1902"; a list of officers of the NYSE, 1817-1904; and statistics on "Transactions on the New York Stock Exchange, 1879-1903." With bibliographical references.

115. Thomas, Dana L. *The Plungers and The Peacocks: An Update of the Classic History of the Stock Market.* Rev. ed. New York: William Morrow and Co., 1989. 384 pages.

Brings 1967 edition up to date through coverage of recent development, most notably the 1987 Stock Market Crash. Story of Wall Street, the New York Stock Exchange, and notable events and individuals. Among events presented are: Jay Gould's Gold Corner; development of the Dow Theory; the Panic of 1907; investment activities of J. Pierpont Morgan, Willam Durant, and Jesse Livermore; the Crash of 1929; establishment of the Securities and Exchange Commission; computerization of the stock market; the Crash of 1987; and projections for the future. With illustrations and bibliography.

116. Waggoner, John M. *Money Madness: Strange Manias and Extraordinary Schemes On and Off Wall Street.* Homewood, Illinois: Business One Irwin, 1991. 177 pages.

Stories of money madnesses in forms of manias, panics, crashes, and scams. Among incidents covered: the Erie War; the Panic of 1837; and the 1929 Crash. Includes selected, annotated bibliography at the end of each chapter.

117. Warshow, Robert Irving. *The Story of Wall Street*. New York: Greenberg, 1929. 362 pages.

Story of people and events of Wall Street from 1792 founding of the NYSE to the 1920s. Provides biographical information on Alexander Hamilton, Daniel Drew, Cornelius Vanderbilt, Jay Gould, Jim Fisk, J. Pierpont Morgan, Andrew Carnegie, etc. Author calls the NYSE: "the mmost powerful single exchange organization in the world." (page 344) Illustrations include portraits of Jay Gould, Jim Fisk, W.R. Travers, Cyrus W. Field, Daniel Drew, and Cornelius Vanderbilt.

118. Wendt, Lloyd. *The Wall Street Journal: The Story of Dow Jones and the Nation's Business Newspaper*. Chicago: Rand McNally & Co., 1982. 448 pages.

Story of the *Wall Street Journal*, its founders, editors, and coverage of major news stories. Covers the newspaper's history from its first appearance in 1889 to 1982. Includes brief history of the New York Stock Exchange.

119. Westbrook, Wayne W. *Wall Street and the American Novel*. New York: New York University Press, 1980. 213 pages.

Study of Wall Street as a subject in American novels. Among novels analyzed are: Josiah Gilbert Holland's *Sevenoaks: A Story of To-Day*; Henry James's *The Ivory Tower*; William Dean Howells' *The Rise of Silas Lapham*; Edwin Lefevre's *Samson Rock of Wall Street*; Lefevre's *Reminiscences of a Stock Operator*; Upton Sinclair's *The Moneychangers*; Jack London's *Burning Daylight*; Edith Wharton's *The House of Mirth*; F. Scott Fitzgerald's *The Beautiful and Damned*; John P. Marquand's *Point of No Return*; Theodore Dreiser's *The Financier*; and Louis Auchincloss's *The Embezzler*. Reviews key events in Wall Street's history and profiles prominent individuals. Fictional characters in some of the novels have been based upon: J. P. Morgan, Sr.; Jesse Livermore; Richard Whitney; and Jay Gould. Bibliographical references.

120. Wyckoff, Peter. *Wall Street and the Stock Markets: A Chronology (1644-1971).* Philadelphia: Chilton Book Company, 1972. 304 pages.

Record of events of the Stock Market from 1644 to 1971. Comprised of four sections: 1: A Chronology (1644-1971) - covers important historical incidents, annual or monthly net gains or losses for Dow Jones Averages, total number of trading days per year, etc.; 2: The Exchanges - includes history of seat prices, listing requirements, short sales, share turnover, etc.; 3: The Averages - provides statistical data on the Dow Jones Averages, Standard & Poor's 500-Stock Price Index, New York Stock Exchange Index (Composite), American Stock Exchange Index; and 4: Market Influences - factors responsible for price movements, market theories, etc. With a glossary of terms and bibliography.

CHAPTER VI
1792-1816

The time period covered in this Chapter starts with the signing of the Buttonwood Agreement on May 17, 1792 and ends with the time period right before the establishment of the New York Stock and Exchange Board in 1817.

Key documents for the early years of the Exchange are: The Buttonwood Agreement and Constitution and Nominations of the Subscribers to the Tontine Coffee House. Original copies of these documents are found in the New York Stock Exchange Archives. Other materials listed and annotated are early histories of the Exchange and the Wall Street area.

* Barrett, Walter see Scoville, Joseph Alfred, item 127.

121. Bayles, Harrison. *Old Taverns of New York.* New York: Frank Allen Genealogical Company, 1915. 489 pages.

Describes the history of old taverns and their place in the history of New York City from 1609 through 1820s. One chapter concerns the Tontine Coffee House which was completed in 1793 and became the location of the Stock Exchange of New York.

122. *The Birth of America.* Compiled, edited and with an Introduction by Raymond Friday Locke. The Mankind Series of Great

Adventures of History. New York: Hawthorn Books, 1971. 256 pages.

Among series of essays on United States history during the eighteenth and nineteenth centuries, is "William Duer and the Origins of the New York Stock Exchange," by Robert Sobel. Profiles William Duer and his speculative activities which helped make a formal securities market necessary and led to the Buttonwood Agreement or Corre's Hotel Pact of May 17, 1792. Describes founding of Tontine Coffee House at corner of Wall and Water Streets. Duer, although he did not sign the agreement and was not a member of the Tontine, made New York the central city for buying and selling of securities. He also greatly influenced the bull market of 1792. Discusses panic of 1792 and its effects. Illustrations include a diorama of the first investors meeting under the Buttonwood tree at 69 Wall Street and Wall Street soon after the Stock Exchange was founded in 1792.

123. *The Buttonwood Agreement* (document), signed by Leonard Bleecker, et al. New York, May 17, 1792. original copy at the New York Stock Exchange Archives.

Agreement signed by twenty-four brokers and merchants. Named after Buttonwood Tree on Wall Street under which brokers met to conduct business. Foundation document for first organized stock market in New York; this market later became known as the New York Stock Exchange. States that brokers would avoid public auctions, charge a minimum commission on sales of public stock, and give preference to one another trading securities. The twenty-four men who signed the document are considered to be the first members of the NYSE. Document is reprinted in various histories of the New York Stock Exchange.

124. *Constitution and Nominations of the Subscribers to the Tontine Coffee House.* Comfort Sands, Cornelius Ray, Anthony L. Bleecker, James Tillary, and William Henderson. New York, 1796. 47 pages.

After meeting under the Buttonwood Tree, the first brokers of the NYSE moved to the Tontine Coffee House in 1793. This pamphlet lists names of stockholders of the Tontine Coffee House and the stockholders' nominees. Brief biographical data is provided for each shareholder and nominee. 203 shares of the Tontine Coffee House were sold at $200 each.

*   Friedman, Maxine. *Wall Street: Changing Fortunes.* see item 99 above.

125. Lamb, Martha. *Wall Street in History.* New York: Funk and Wagnalls, 1883. 95 pages

Comprised of series of essays originally written for the May, June, and July 1883 numbers of the *Magazine of American History.* The first chapter covers the years, 1642-1774, the time of Wall Street's early development; the second concentrates on historical and political developments during the years 1774-1830; and the third treats the history of the financial institutions on Wall Street, including the New York Stock Exchange. Studies the NYSE's history from 1792-1883. With illustrations, among which are: Wall Street in 1883-Sub-Treasury and Stock Exchange; A.S. Hatch, President of the Stock Exchange; Edmund Clarence Stedman; and Wall Street in 1832.

126. Scoville, Joseph Alfred. *Old Merchants of New York City,* by Walter Barrett [pseud] New York: Carleton, 1863-70. Reprint: New York: Greenwood Press, 1968. 5 volumes.

Biographical sketches of early New York City merchants, 1700s-mid 1800s, concentrating on financial district in downtown Manhattan. Presents genealogies of families among which are those of John Jacob Astor and Nathaniel Prime. Describes founding of the Tontine Coffee House in 1793 and lists original subscribers. Contains excerpts from correspondence, obituaries, and articles from contemporary newspapers. With indexes of names and businesses at end of each volume.

127. Severini, Lois. *The Architecture of Finance: Early Wall Street.* Studies in fine arts. Art patronage; no. 1. Ann Arbor, Michigan: UMI Research Press, 1983. 237 pages.

Concentrates on architectural styles of buildings on Wall Street from 1609 to 1862. Among illustrations: View of Broad Street, Wall Street, and the City Hall. 1797; Tontine Building, Wall Street, 1792-94; Wall Street, 1798; Wall Street, c. 1829; and Contemporary Wall Street.

* Sobel, Robert. "William Duer and the Stock Exchange." see item 122 above.

128. Werner, Walter and Steven T. Smith. *Wall Street.* New York: Columbia University Press, 1991. 306 pages.

Story of the early American securities markets from the 1790s to 1840, with a briefer analysis of the years, 1840-1890 ("The Railroad Age"). Covers: securities markets in England during the early 1700s; the 1792 stock market crash of 1792; the story of the Buttonwood Agreement of 1792; establishment of the New York Stock and Exchange Board in 1817; biographies of early American securities professionals including Nathan Prime and Jacob Little; contributions of early American investors including John Jacob Astor; the first American speculators, among which is John Michael O'Connor; the first publicly owned businesses; early governance of the securities markets; the renaming of the New York Stock and Exchange Board to the New York Stock Exchange in 1863; the Erie War; Black Friday, 1869; and the Panic of 1873. Studies events of the early securities market in light of developments in the 1980s. With Appendixes: A. "New York Securities Market Statistics: 1790-1840"; B. "Comparison of Securities Markets in New York and Other U.S. Cities: 1790-1840"; C. "Broadside of Securities Trading Rules, September 1791"; D. "New York Stock and Exchange Board 1817 Constitution and Selected Early Resolutions"; E. "John Michael O'Connor -- Stock Trading, January to August 1824"; and F. "Early Securities Regulation in New York."

Includes selected bibliography of manuscripts, legal authorities, books and articles, and newspapers and periodicals.

CHAPTER VII
1817-1860

The sources provided in Chapter VII cover the time period from the establishment of the New York Stock and Exchange Board (NYS & EB) on March 8, 1817, through the early panics of 1819, 1837, and 1957. This chapter lists and describes the 1817 Constitution and includes material describing conditions at the NYS & EB as well as sources of information on the Panics of 1819, 1837, and 1857.

129. Armstrong, William. *Stocks and Stock-Jobbing in Wall Street, with Sketches of the Brokers, and Fancy Stocks Containing a Full Account of the Nature of All Kinds of Stocks and Securities, by a Reformed Stock Gambler.* New York: New York Publishing Co., 1848. 39 pages.

Presents nature of stocks and stock transactions, defines and describes "bulls and bears," "corners," "wash sales," "insiders and outsiders," etc. Lists and studies fancy stocks that include the Bank of Vicksburgh, the Harlem Rail Road, Commercial Rail Road, etc. Provides sketches of brokers and brokerage houses.

130. Boston Board of Trade. *Report of the Committee of the Boston Board of Trade, appointed at the annual meeting, January 20, 1858, "to make a deliberate and thorough investigation into the causes of the recent monetary difficulties and mercantile embarrassments, with a view to the adoption of such remedies as*

71

the nature of the case will allow. " Boston: T.R. Marvin & Son, 1858. 20 pages.

Concerns, among other topics, the causes of the panic of 1857.

* Birmingham, Stephen. *Our Crowd.* see item 26 above.

131. Evans, D. Morier. *The History of the Commercial Crisis, 1857-1858 and the Stock Exchange Panic of 1859.* London: Groombridge & Sons, 1859. Reprint: New York: Augustus M. Kelley, 1969. 1 v. (various pagings)

Concentrates on the financial crisis in England. Includes section on the crisis in America in 1857. Section presents statistical charts with reprints of newspaper articles from the *New York Herald*.

132. Jackson, Frederick. *A Week in Wall Street, by One Who Knows.* s.l.: F. Jackson, 1841. Reprint:New York: Greenwood Press, 1969. 152 pages.

Describes six days on Wall Street. Features definition of panics their causes, beginnings, and advantages with reference to the Panic of 1837.

* Lamb, Martha J. *Wall Street in History.* see item 125 above.

133. McGrane, Reginald Charles. *The Panic of 1837: Some Financial Problems of the Jacksonian Era.* Chicago: University of Chicago Press, 1924 Reprint: New York: Russell & Russell, 1965. 260 pages.

Examines causes and consequences of the Panic of 1837. Studies political and economic considerations involved and roles of Andrew Jackson, Nicholas Biddle, and Martin Van Buren. With a bibliography of manuscripts; newspapers; memoirs, correspondence, speeches, and works; diaries and travels; public documents: Federal; state statutes; special articles, works, and monographs; collections of documents and magazines; and general works.

134. Michie, R.C. *The London and New York Stock Exchanges, 1850-1914.* London: Allen & Unwin, 1987. 312 pages.

Explains history, roles, and functions of the London and New York Exchanges, comparing and contrasting them. Studies the NYSE in relationship to other United States exchanges.

135. New York Stock and Exchange Board. *Constitution.* New York: New York Stock and Exchange Board, 1817. 12 pages.

Constitution which established the New York Stock and Exchange Board (NYS & EB), an organization of brokers who agreed to meet on a regular basis at set hours. Constitution, adopted on March 8, 1817, set rules regarding membership, commission rates, and conduct of sales. Fictitious sales or contracts were forbidden.

136. Rothbard, Murray Newton. *The Panic of 1819: Reactions and Policies.* New York: Columbia University Press, 1962. Reprint: New York: AMS Press, 1973. 261 pages.

Account of the Panic of 1819, America's first major economic crisis and depression. Concentrates on time period 1819-21 and describes remedial proposals. Appendixes consist of: A. Minor Remedies Proposed and B. Chronology of Relief Legislation. With a bibliography of government publications, primary sources, and secondary sources.

137. *'37 and '57. A Brief Popular Account of All Financial Panics and Commercial Revulsions in the United States, from 1600 to 1857: With a more particular history of the two great revulsions of*

1837 and 1857. By members of the New York Press. New York: J.C. Haney, 1857. 59 pages.

Discussion of panics and their natures, with emphasis on causes and consequences of panics of 1837 and 1857. Offers a brief history of panics in the United States.

138. Van Vleck, George Washington. *The Panic of 1857: An Analytical Study.* New York: Columbia University, 1943. Reprint: AMS Press, 1967. 126 pages.

Originally presented as author's thesis, Columbia University, 1943. Analyzes events of the Panic of 1857 and factors envolved. Studies: Long-term factors (foreign and domestic commerce, banking and credit structure, central position of Great Britain in the world economy) and Short-term factors (recent economic developments, political and social conditions reacting unfavorably on business conditions). With a bibliography of newspapers; public documents; collections of documents and magazines; and general bibliography.

*   Winkelman, Barnie F. *Ten Years of Wall Street.* see item 198 below.

CHAPTER VIII
1861-1870

This time period encompasses the Civil War Years, the decade of the struggle for control of the Erie Railroad, and the attempt to corner the gold market by Jay Gould and Jim Fisk, Jr. Fisk, Gould as well as Daniel Drew, Cornelius Vanderbilt and Jay Cooke were financiers of great influence during this time period. Fisk, Gould, Drew, and Vanderbilt are the subjects of innumerable biographies and works of fiction.

Material listed and annotated in this chapter include the "Gold Corner" Hearings and sources describing Wall Street during the 1860s. A large percentage of biographical materials concern Gould, Fisk, Vanderbilt, and Drew. These materials have been listed and cross-referenced to Chapter IV.

139. Ackerman, Kenneth D. *The Gold Ring: Jim Fisk, Jay Gould, and Black Friday, 1869.* New York: Harper Business, A Division of Harper & Row, 1988. 340 pages.

Mostly a narrative of events leading up to, including, and following Friday, September 24, 1869. Provides vivid presentation of events of Black Friday. Early chapters cover "Erie Wars" of the late 1860s. Tells what later happened to protagonists of Black Friday: William Belden, George Boutwell, James Brown, George Butterfield, Albert Cardozo, George G. Barnard, Abel and Jennie

75

Corbin, Ulysses S. Grant, William Marcy Tweed, James Fisk, Jr., Jay Gould, etc. Appendix contains the poem, "Israel Freyer's Bid for Gold," by Edmund C. Stedman, *New York Tribune*, September 28, 1869. Includes bibliography.

140. Adams, Charles Francis and Henry Adams. *Chapters of Erie*. New York: Henry Holt, 1886. Reprint: Ithaca, N.Y.: Great Seal Books, a division of Cornell University Press, 1956. 193 pages.

Contents: "A Chapter of Erie," by Charles Francis Adams; "The New York Gold Conspiracy," by Henry Adams; and "An Erie Raid," by Charles Francis Adams. Examination of the legal and moral ramifications of the Erie Railway Wars and the Gold Conspiracy of 1869. Studies natures of the protagonists: Jay Gould, Jim Fisk, Daniel Drew, and Cornelius Vanderbilt.

* Andrews, Wayne. *The Vanderbilt Legend: The Story of the Vanderbilt Family, 1794-1940*. see item 18 above.

* Birmingham, Stephen. *Our Crowd: The Great Jewish Families of New York*. see item 26 above.

* Browder, Clifford. *The Money Game in Old New York: Daniel Drew and His Times*. see item 28 above.

* Chernow, Ron. *The House of Morgan: An American Dynasty and the Rise of Modern Finance*. see item 30 above.

* Corey, Lewis. *The House of Morgan: A Social Biography of the Masters of Money*. see item 32 above.

* Dimock, Anthony Weston. *Wall Street and the Wilds*. see item 33 above.

*   Forbes, John Douglas. *J.P. Morgan, Jr., 1867-1943.* see item
      37 above.

141. Fowler, William Worthington. *Ten Years in Wall Street; or
     Revelations of Inside Life and Experience on the 'Change.*
     Hartford, Connecticut: Worthington, Dustin & Co., 1870. 536
     pages.

     Based on first-hand observations of Wall Street in the 1860s.
     Explains terms such as "put," "call," "bear," "bull," "speculators,"
     etc. Provides biographical information about key individuals
     including: Cornelius Vanderbilt, Daniel Drew, Jacob Little, Jay
     Gould, James Fisk, Jr., etc. Details events of the 1860s on Wall
     Street among which are the Gold Corner of 1869, the Erie Railroad
     Wars; development of cliques and pools; panics, etc. Contains a
     chapter about women who speculate in stock. Updated in 1880
     under title, *Twenty Years of Inside Life in Wall Street.*

*   Fowler, William Worthington. *Ten Years of Inside Life in Wall
      Street, or Revelations of the Personal Experience of a
      Speculator...* See item 154 below

*   Fuller, Robert H. *Jubilee Jim: The Life of Colonel James Fisk, Jr.*
      see item 39 above.

142. Gordon, John Steele. *The Scarlet Woman of Wall Street: Jay
     Gould, Jim Fisk, Cornelius Vanderbilt, the Erie Railway Wars,
     and the Birth of Wall Street.* New York: Weidenfeld & Nicolson,
     1988. 421 pages.

     Story of the Erie Wars involving Gould, Fisk, Drew, and
     Vanderbilt. Provides biographical details concerning participants.
     Also describes the Gold Corner of 1869 involving Gould and Fisk.
     With a brief description of the NYSE in its early days. Illustrations
     are from *Harper's Weekly, Frank Leslie's Illustrated Newspaper*,
     and William Worthington Fowler's *Ten Years in Wall Street.* With

a bibliography.

*   Grodinsky, Julius. *Jay Gould: His Business Career, 1867-1892.*
      see item 42 above.

143. Hamon, Henry. *The New York Stock Exchange Manual,
     Containing Its Principles, Rules, and Its Different Modes of
     Speculation: Also, a Review of the Stocks Dealt in on 'Change,
     Government and State Securities, Railway, Mining, Petroleum,
     etc.* New York: John F. Trow, 1865. Reprint: Westport,
     Connecticut: Greenwood Press, 1970. 405 pages.

     Comprised of Constitution and Bylaws of the New York Stock
     Exchange, the Open Board of Stock Brokers, the Gold Exchange,
     Evening Exchange, Mining Exchange, Public Petroleum Exchange,
     and Petroleum Stock Board. Reviews trading operations, defines
     key terms, describes stocks and bonds traded, and lists members of
     the stock exchanges in 1865.

*   Holbrook, Stewart. *The Age of the Moguls.* see item 44 above.

*   Hovey, Carl. *The Life Story of J. Pierpont Morgan.* see item
      45 above.

*   Hoyt, Edwin P., Jr. *The House of Morgan.* see item 46 above.

*   *James Fisk, Jr: His Life and Death...*see item 48 above.

*   Johnston, Johanna. *Mrs. Satan: The Incredible Saga of Victoria
      C. Woodhull.* see item 49 above.

*   Jones, Willoughby. *The Life of James Fisk, Jr...*see item 50 above.

* Josephson, Matthew. *The Robber Barons: The Great American Capitalists, 1861-1901*. see item 51 above.

* Klein, Maury. *The Life and Legend of Jay Gould*. see item 54 above.

* Lamb, Martha J. *Wall Street in History*. see item 125 above.

* Lane, Wheaton J. *Commodore Vanderbilt: An Epic of the Steam Age*. see item 56 above.

* Larson, Henrietta M. *Jay Cooke: Private Banker*. see item 57 above.

* McAlpine, Robert W. *The Life and Times of Col. James Fisk, Jr...* see item 59 above.

* Mansfield, Helen Josephine. *The Truth at Last!* see item 61 above.

* Medbery, James K. *Men and Mysteries of Wall Street*. see item above.

* Michie, R.C. *The London and New York Stock Exchanges, 1850-1914*. see item 134 above.

* Minnigerode, Meade. *Certain Rich Men...* see item 65 above.

144. Mott, Edward Harold. *The Story of Erie: Between the Ocean and*

the Lakes. New York: Ticker Publishing Co., 1908. 524 pages.

Story of the Erie Railroad from 1779 to 1898. Chronicles the Erie Wars of the late 1860s and the administration of Jay Gould, 1868-1872. Provides biographical sketches of Presidents of the Erie and famous characters in Erie history such as James Fisk, Jr. and Daniel Drew. With illustrative portraits of Presidents of Erie, Drew, Fisk, Gould, etc.

*   Northrop, H.D. *Life and Achievements of Jay Gould...* see item 68 above.

*   Noyes, Alexander Dana. *The Market Place.* see item 166 below.

*   O'Connor, Richard. *Gould's Millions.* see item 70 above.

*   Porter, Donald. *Jubilee Jim and the Wizard of Wall Street: A Novel.* see item 71 above.

*   Satterlee, Herbert L. *J. Pierpont Morgan: An Intimate Portrait.* see item 76 above.

*   Sinclair, Andrew. *Corsair: The Life of J. Pierpont Morgan.* see item 77 above.

*   Smith, Arthur D. Howden. *Commodore Vanderbilt: An Epic of American Achievement.* see item 78 above.

145. Smith, Matthew Hale. *Twenty Years Among the Bulls and Bears of Wall Street.* Hartford: J.B. Burr & Co., 1871. 557 pages.

Studies Wall Street with emphasis on the 1860s. Covers diverse topics among which are: Black Friday, 1869; Wall Street language; daily operations on the New York Stock Exchange in the 1860s; the stories of Commodore Vanderbilt, Daniel Drew, James Fisk, Jacob Little, Victoria Woodhull, Tennessee Claflin, and Jay Cooke; and a description of early Wall Street. With illustrations.

*   Stafford, Marshall P. *The Life of James Fisk...* see item 81 above.

*   Swanberg, W.A. *Jim Fisk: The Career of an Improbable Rascal.* see item 82 above.

146. Twain, Mark. *Mark Twain's (Burlesque) Autobiography and First Romance.* New York: Sheldon & Co.; New York: Electrotyped by Smith & McDougal, 1871. 47 pages.

Satirical study Twain's life and genealogy plus a medieval tale. Stories are accompanied by a series of cartoons by H.L. Stephens, with captions from nursery rhyme, "The House that Jack Built." These cartoons contain caricatures of Daniel Drew, Jay Gould, James Fisk, Jr., etc. in the midst of their involvement with the Erie Railroad.

*   United States. Congress. House. *Gold Panic Investigation.* see item 147 below.

147. United States. Congress. House. *Investigation into the Causes of the Gold Panic: Report of the Majority of the Committee on Banking and Currency, March 1, 1870 [and the views of the Minority]* 41st Congress, 2d. sess., House Rep. No. 31. Washington, D.C.: U.S. Government Printing Office, 1870. Reprint: New York: Arno Press, 1974., issued in series: Gold: historical and economic aspects. 483 pages.

Investigation of causes of gold panic of September 21 - 27, 1869. With a brief history of events and testimony of bankers, brokers, and merchants, January 15 - February 15, 1870. Committee on Banking of Currency was directed by a resolution of the House of Representatives, passed December 13, 1869, "to investigate the causes that led to the unusual and extraordinary fluctuations of gold in the city of New York from the 21st to the 27th of September, 1869." Report studies: 1. The Gold Exchange and the Gold Exchange Bank, concerning their history, character of their ordinary operations, and their relation to the Gold Panic; 2. The alleged conspiracy to raise the price of gold, the persons engaged in it, and the instrumentalities made use of; and 3. Whether any National government officers were directly or indirectly engaged in the alleged conspiracy. Among testimonies are those of: Jay Gould; James Fisk, Jr.; Abel Rathbone Corbin; George S. Boutwell, Secretary of the Treasury; Albert Speyers, gold broker; and Caleb C. Norvell, financial editor of the *New York Times*. Exhibits include: reprints of articles from the *New York Times* at the time of the Gold Panic and letters of Gould, Corbin, Boutwell, and Ulysses S. Grant. Committee concludes: attempts of conspirators to compromise the President or members of his family failed and that the Gold Exchange and Gold Exchange Bank had become instruments of reckless speculation, with disastrous consequences. The Committee recommends possible legislation to: define and punish conspiracy against the credit of the United States and the business of its people; to levy a tax on transactions such as those of the Gold Exchange and Gold Exchange Clearing House; and to prevent improper use of certified checks by national banks. Also provides views of the Minority. Includes index.

*   Warshow, Robert Irving. *Jay Gould: The Story of a Fortune.* see item 85 above.

*   Wheeler, George. *Pierpont Morgan & Friends: The Anatomy of a Myth.* see item 87 above.

*   White, Bouck. *The Book of Daniel Drew: A Glimpse of the Fisk-Gould Regime from the Inside.* see item 88 above.

148. White, Horace. "Black Friday." *Yale Review* 3 (May 1894): 8-
    23.

   Relates events leading up to Black Friday, September 24, 1869
following progress of its participants Jay Gould and James Fisk, Jr.
Examines the operations of the Gold Room during the 1860s.
Presents text of newspaper account describing the scene in the Gold
Room on Black Friday. On Black Friday, the price of gold fell
from 162 to 135. Studies possible causes of the price decline; these
causes include: the order by the President for the Treasury to sell
gold and actions in the Gold Room by James Brown, a broker
acting for various clients. Relates what happened to participants
after events of Black Friday. With statistics providing the highest
and lowest prices of gold each day in September 1869.

*   White, Trumbell. *The Wizard of Wall Street and his Wealth...* see
     item 89 above.

*   Winkelman, Barnie F. *Ten Years of Wall Street.* see item 198
     below.

*   Winkler, John K. *Morgan the Magnificant: The Life of J. Pierpont
     Morgan (1837-1913)* see item 90 above.

CHAPTER IX
1871-1914

The years 1871-1914 were a time of many changes and events affecting the New York Stock Exchange. Occurring during this time period were: the Panics of 1873, 1884, 1893, 1901, and 1907; the building of new headquarters for the NYSE which opened in 1903; investigations of the NYSE by the Hughes and Pujo Committees; and the 1914 Crisis which brought about the temporary closing of the NYSE.

Sources of Chapter IX include books and articles about the Panics; the report of the Hughes Committee; and the Pujo Committee report or Money Trust Investigation, with testimonies of J. Pierpont Morgan, Sr. and James B. Mabon, President of the NYSE.

* Allen, Frederick Lewis. *The Great Pierpont Morgan.* see item 17 above.

149. American Academy of Political and Social Science. *Lessons of the Financial Crisis.* Annals of the Academy of Political and Social Science. Philadelphia: The Academy, 1908. 169 pages.

Series of essays concerning the Panic of 1907 and its consequences. Contents: "The Panic as a World Phenomenon," by Frank A. Vanderlip; "The Panic of 1907 and Some of Its Lessons," by Myron T. Herrick; "An Elastic Credit Currency as a Preventative of Panics," by William Barret Ridgely; "The

Readjustment of Our Banking System and the Unification of the
Currency," by Charles H. Treat; "The Need of a Central Bank," by
George E. Roberts; "A Central Bank as a Menace to Liberty," by
George H. Earle, Jr.; "Clearing-house Certificates and the Need for
a Central Bank," by William A. Nash; "Foreign Experience a
Guide to Currency Reform," by Isaac N. Seligman; "Relation of a
Central Bank to Elasticity of the Currency," by Jacob H. Schiff;
"Diagnosis of the World's Elastic Currency Problems," by Andrew
J. Frame; "Panic Prevention and Cures," by Henry W. Yates; "The
Northwest in the Recent Financial Crisis," by A.L. Mills;
"Neglected Aspects of Currency and Banking," by F.A. Cleveland;
"The Lessons of the Panic of 1907," by S. Wexler; "The Obstacles
to Currency Reform," by Lyman J. Gage; "A National Clearing
House as a Safeguard against Panics," by J.M. Elliott; and "Trust
Companies and Reserves," by A.S. Frissell.

150. American Academy of Political and Social Science. *Stocks and the
Stock Market*. Annals of the Academy of Political and Social
Science. Philadelphia: The Academy, May 1910. 232 pages.

Series of essays concerning stocks and stock exchanges, including
the New York Stock Exchange. Contents: "The Scope and
Functions of the Stock Market," by S.S. Huebner; "The Purchase
or Sale of Securities through a Stock Broker," by Eliot Norton;
"Stocks and Their Features--Division and Classification," by John
Adams, Jr.; "Preferred Stocks as Investments," by John Moody;
"The Declaration and Yield of Stockholders' Rights," by B.B.
Burgunder; "Convertible Bonds and Stocks," by Montgomery
Rollins; "Barometric Indices of the Condition of Trade," by Roger
W. Babson; "The Sources of Market News," by Roger W. Babson;
"Influences Affecting Security Prices and Values," by Thomas
Gibson; "Economic Crises and Stock Security Values," by Arthur
Selwyn-Brown; "Railroad Stocks as Investments," by Carl Snyder;
"Electric Railway Stocks," by Wallace McCook Cunningham;
"Industrial Stocks as Investments," by Edgar J. Meyer; "Stocks of
Financial Institutions," by L.A. Norton; "The Wrongs and
Opportunities in Mining Investments," by Francis C. Nicholas; and
"Bibliography on Securities and Stock Exchanges," by S.S.
Huebner. Huebner's bibliography lists general works; leading legal

treatises; leading court cases; leading magazine articles; leading manuals, handbooks, dictionaries, directories, constitutions of exchanges, and tables of values, American and Foreign; and leading journals and news services.

* Barron, Clarence W. *More They Told Barron.* see item 22 above.

* Barron, Clarence W. *They Told Barron.* see item 23 above.

* Birmingham, Stephen. *Our Crowd: The Great Jewish Families of New York.* see item 26 above.

* Carosso, Vincent P. *The Morgans: Private International Bankers, 1854-1913.* see item 29 above.

151. Clews, Henry. *The Wall Street Point of View.* New York: Silver Burdett & Company, 1900; Reprint: New York: Greenwood Press. 290 pages.

Studies Wall Street in terms of U.S. government, social problems, and international affairs. Examines events of Panic of 1893. Studies contributions to events on Wall Street by Russell Sage, Commodore Vanderbilt, Jay Gould, Grover Cleveland, and William McKinley.

* Corey, Lewis. *The House of Morgan: A Social Biography of the Masters of Money.* see item 32 above.

* Dimock, Anthony Weston. *Wall Street and the Wilds.* see item 33 above.

152. Dos Passos, John R. *A Treatise on the Law of Stock-Brokers and*

Stock Exchanges. New York: Harper, 1882. Reprint: New York: Greenwood, 1968. 1042 pages.

Studies role of stock exchanges in the economy and their legal nature. Covers stock exchanges throughout the world including the New York Stock Exchange, the London Exchange, and the Paris Bourse. Examines origins of the NYSE, its rules and organization, and major cases. Covers rules and cases for: suspension and expulsion; seats on the Exchange; dividends; short sales; and nature of transactions. With table of cases and the text of the NYSE's Constitution and by-laws, as revised September 15, 1978, with amendments to February 1882. Analyzes legal aspects of transactions between stock-brokers and their clients.

153. Dow, Charles H. *Charles H. Dow: Economist: A Selection of His Writings on Business Cycles.* Edited, with comments by George W. Bishop, Jr. Princeton, N.J.: Dow Jones Books, 1967. 307 pages.

Provides brief biographical sketch of Dow and commentary concerning his writings. Selected writings of Dow included are from time period April 21, 1899 through October 24, 1902. Mostly writings are editorials written by Dow for the *Wall Street Journal.* Dow's writings comment on current activity including NYSE market conditions. With bibliographical references and epilogue: "Dow's Place in the History of Economic Thought."

*   Emery, William Morrell. *The Howland Heirs: Being the Story of a Family and Fortune and the Inheritance of a Trust Established for Mrs. Hetty H. R. Green.* see item 35 above.

*   Fowler, William W. *Ten Years in Wall Street.* see item 141 above.

154. Fowler, William Worthington. *Twenty Years of Inside Life in Wall Street, or Revelations of the Personal Experience of a Speculator...*New York: Orange Judd, 1880. 576 pages.

Updated edition of *Ten Years in Wall Street* by Fowler focuses on Wall Street events between 1860 and 1880. Discusses events of the Gold Corner; the Erie Wars; the Panic of 1873; and various speculations of the late 1870s. Studies business activities of Jay Gould and William H. Vanderbilt. Explains key terms and their origins.

* Fuller, O.M. *John Muir of Wall Street: A Story of Thrift.* see item 38 above.

* Fuller, Robert H. *Jubilee Jim: The Life of Colonel James Fisk, Jr.* see item 39 above.

155. Goldman, Samuel P. *Handbook of Stock Exchange Law Affecting Members, Their Customers, Brokers, and Investors.* Garden City, N.Y.: Doubleday, Page & Co., 1914. 290 pages.

Written for lawyers and stockbrokers, presents and explains the New York Stock Exchange's constitution, by-laws, and rules of the Governing Committee. Also presents and analyzes the laws of the State of New York relating to Stockbrokers. Defines key terms such as "Margin," "Short Sale," "Bull," "Option," "Put," and "Call." With table of cases cited and an index.

* Grodinsky, Julius. *Jay Gould: His Business Career, 1867-1892.* see item 42 above.

156. Historical Publishing Company (N.Y.) *Finance and Industry: The New York Stock Exchange: Banks, Bankers, Business Houses, and Moneyed Institutions of the Great Metropolis of the United States:* Embracing also a List of Prominent Banks in Other Cities of Importance and a Brief History of the New York Mercantile Exchange. New York and London: Historical Publishing Co., 1887. 208 pages.

Contains: sketches of NYSE's leading members, banks, bankers, and other moneyed institutions of New York City; a brief history of Wall Street; illustrative portraits of NYSE's officers, 1886-87; and a history of the New York Mercantile Exchange. With sketches of banks in Boston, Massachusetts; Providence, Rhode Island; Worcester, Massachusetts; Springfield, Massachusetts; and Hartford, Connecticut. With advertisements and index of banks, brokers, etc.

157. Historical Publishing Company (N.Y.). *Finance and Industry: The New York Stock Exchange: Banks, Bankers, Business Houses, and Moneyed Institutions: The Great Metropolis of the United States.* New York and Philadelphia: Historical Publishing Co., 1886. 224 pages.

Contains: sketches of the NYSE's leading members, banks, bankers, and other moneyed institutions of New York City; a brief history of Wall Street and the NYSE; illustrative portraits of NYSE officers, 1886-86; study of Wall Street personalities Jay Gould, James Fisk, Jr., etc.; transcript of a speech by NYSE President J. Edward Simmons; and a history of Manhattan with a list of theatres, churches, etc. The second section of the work concerns the Philadelphia Stock Exchange, its history and organization. With advertisements and an index of brokers, banks, etc.

*   Hovey, Carl. *The Life Story of J. Pierpont Morgan.* see item 45 above.

*   Hoyt, Edwin P., Jr. *The House of Morgan.* see item 46 above.

*   *James Fisk, Jr.: His Life and Death. Also, the Trial of Edward S. Stokes for the Murder. With a Biography of Josie Mansfield.* see item 48 above.

*   Jones, Willoughby. *The Life of James Fisk, Jr...* see item 50
     above.

*   Josephson, Matthew. *The Robber Barons: The Great American
     Capitalists.* see item 51 above.

*   Kennan, George. *E.H. Harriman: A Biography.* see item 53
     above.

158. *King's Views of the New York Stock Exchange: A History and
     Description with Articles on Financial Topics Illustrated with
     More Than Four Hundred Prints and Ninety-Two Views of the
     Exchange and Vicinity.* New York: Moses King, Pub., 1898,
     c1897. 96 pages.

     Chiefly illustrations of notables directly or indirectly identified
     with the NYSE, among which are its ex-presidents and "famous
     men of Wall Street" including Jay Gould, Jay Cooke, Commodore
     Vanderbilt, Jacob Little, William H. Vanderbilt, Daniel Drew, and
     James R. Keene. With exterior and interior views of the various
     homes of the New York Stock Exchange from 1792-1897. Textual
     matter describes the history of the NYSE and offers a comparison
     of the London and New York exchanges. Spans time period, 1851-
     1898, emphasizing the later years.

*   Klein, Maury. *The Life and Legend of Jay Gould.* see item 54
     above.

*   Lamb, Martha J. *Wall Street in History.* see item 125 above.

*   Larson, Henrietta. *Jay Cooke: Private Banker.* see item 57 above.

159. Lauck, W. Jett. *The Causes of the Panic of 1893.* Hart, Schaffner

and Marx Prize Essays. Boston: Houghton, 1907., 122 pages.

Causes of panics of 1890 and 1893 and analysis of their consequences.

*   Lefevre, Edwin. *Reminiscences of a Stock Operator.* see item 58 above.

*   McAlpine, Robert W. *The Life and Times of Col. James Fisk, Jr.*...see item 59 above.

*   McDonald, Forrest. *Insull.* see item 60 above.

*   Mansfield, Helen Josephine. *The Truth at Last!* see item 61 above.

160. Meyer, Eugene, Jr. "The New York Stock Exchange and the Panic of 1907." *Yale Review* 18 (May 1909): 34-46.

Article is transcript of an address delivered before the American Association for the Advancement of Science, Baltimore, Maryland, December 1908. Influences which brought about the Panic of 1907 were most clearly seen by the public in effects on the Stock Market and call money market in New York. Enumerates crisis-producing conditions, all present during the period preceding the 1907 Panic, which were described in the book *Crises and Depressions* as: increase in prices of commodities and later of real estate; increased activity of established enterprises and formation of many new ones; an active demand for loans at higher rates of interest; general employment of labor at increasing or well-sustained wages; increasing extravagance in public and private expenditure; development of a mania for speculation, with dishonest business methods; and a great expansion of discounts and loans and resulting rise in rate of interest. Describes the New York Stock Exchange as, in many respects, the best market for securities in the world. Author's purpose is to demonstrate that Stock Exchange speculation was not responsible for the overextension clearly indicated in 1906-1907 time period, but that the immobilization of capital occurred in enterprises different in character from those dealt in on the NYSE. Stresses importance of maintaining a free market for liquid securities. With statistical tables.

*   Michie, R.C. *The London and New York Stock Exchanges, 1850-1914.* see item 134 above.

*   Minnigerode, Meade. *Certain Rich Men...* see item 65 above.

161. Moody, John. *The Masters of Capital: A Chronicle of Wall Street.* The Chronicles of America. New Haven: Yale University Press, 1921. 234 pages.

Concentrates on time period, 1860s to 1914. Profiles industrialists and financiers: Andrew Carnegie, Edward H. Harriman, James J. Hill, etc.

162. New York State. *Report of Committee on Speculation in Securities and Commodities, June 7, 1909, submitted to the legislature by the governor with his annual message of January 5, 1910.* Albany, N.Y.: J.B. Lyon Co., 1910. 44 pages.

Hughes Committee report on operation of New York's security and commodity exchanges. The *Report of Governor Hughes' Committee on Speculation in Securities and Commodities* is the result of an investigation by a Committee appointed by Governor Charles E. Hughes on December 14, 1908. Horace White was appointed Chairman of the Committee. The objective of the Committee was to make an inquiry into facts regarding speculation in securities and commodities. Included in the report is an examination of the NYSE and describes its history, organization, and identifies patrons of the NYSE (i.e., investors, manipulators, floor traders, outside operators, and inexperienced persons). Report severely criticizes practices of manipulation of prices; pyramiding;

and "wash sales"; "matched orders." A further goal is to reduce the volume of speculation of the gambling type. Additionally, examines structures and histories of: the Consolidated Stock Exchange; the Curb Market; the Produce Exchange; the Cotton Exchange; the Coffee Exchange, and other exchanges. Studies results of Germany's 1896 investigation of the Berlin Exchange.

163. New York Stock Exchange. *Answers of the New York Stock Exchange to the Questions of Governor Hughes' Committee.* New York: New York Stock Exchange, 1909. 1 vol. (various pagings)

First part of report is comprised of series of questions and answers; the second is the text of the *Report of Governor Hughes' Committee on Speculation in Securities and Commodities.* The questions and answers cover topics of: possible incorporation of the Stock Exchange; possibility of the NYSE to be subject to state control; regulation of short-selling; "wash sales"; "matched sales"; corners; role of specialists; margins; the possible rule that no securities be admitted to quotation unless the issuing corporations furnish full statements of their standing and periodical reports of their businesses, etc. See item 162 above for description of the *Report of Governor Hughes' Committee on Speculation in Securities and Commodities.*

164. *The New York Stock Exchange.* Wall Street and the Security Markets. New York: Historical Publishing Co., 1886. Reprint: New York: Arno Press, 1975. 224 pages.

Contains: the "Origin, Growth and Usefulness of the New York Stock Exchange: Sketches of Its Leading Members, Banks, Bankers, and Other Moneyed Institutions of the City"; "A Bird's Eye View of the Great Metropolis"; "The Bankers and Brokers of New York City," a directory with addresses and biographical information; "The Banks of New York"; "The Philadelphia Stock Exchange--Its History, Progress, and Importance"; "The Banks and Brokers of Philadelphia"; "The Banks of Philadelphia"; and "Leading Merchants, Manufacturing and Business Firms of New

York City." With reprints of advertisements from 1886.

*   Nicolson, Harold. *Dwight Morrow.* see item 67 above.

165. Noble, H.G.S. *The New York Stock Exchange in the Crisis of*
     1914. Garden City, N.Y.: Country Life Press, 1915. 89 pages.

     Written by NYSE President during Crisis of 1914 who
     authorized closing of the Exchange.   Analyzes events and
     implications of the 1914 Crisis. Discusses the NYSE C l e a r i n g
     House Committee; contracts settlement; and unemployment relief.

*   Northrop, H.D. *Life and Achievements of Jay Gould...* see item
     68 above.

166. Noyes, Alexander Dana. *The Market Place: Reminiscences of a*
     Financial Editor, with illustrations. Boston: Little, Brown, 1938;
     Reprint: New York: Greenwood Press, 1969. 383 pages.

     In his recollections, financial editor and author Noyes describes
     conditions on Wall Street from the 1860s through 1937. Details
     events of: Black Friday, 1869; the Panics of 1873, 1893, 1901, and
     1907; the closing of the NYSE from July - December 1914; and the
     1929 Stock Market Crash. Among illustrations are: "A Frantic Day
     on the Exchange, 1863"; "the Gold Room on September 24, 1869";
     "The Panics of 1873 and 1869 as Portrayed by *Harper's Weekly*";
     "Bank Run During Panic of 1907"; and "Wall Street During the
     Crash of 1929."

*   Noyes, Alexander Dana. *The War Period of American Finance,*
     1908-1925. see item 192 below.

*   O'Connor, Richard. *Gould's Millions.* see item 70 above.

167. *One Hundredth Anniversary of the New York Stock Exchange: Brief Sketches of Wall Street of To-day.* New York: J.B. Gibson, 1892. unpaged.

Includes: reproduction of the Buttonwood Tree Agreement (1792); NYSE members in 1892; and list of officers for 1824-1892.

168. Osborne, Algernon Ashburner. *Speculation on the New York Stock Exchange, September 1904-March 1907.* Studies in History, Economics, and Public Law. New York: Columbia University, 1913. Reprint: New York, AMS Press, 1968. 172 pages.

Reports results of stock speculation investigation on the New York Stock Exchange, 1904-1907. Chooses time period because of the sustained activity of stock trading. Written in light of recent criticism of the NYSE and call for reforms. Refers to recommendations of the Hughes Committee and the House Committee on Banking and Currency (the "Money Trust" committee). Aims to prove the effectiveness of the NYSE organization for fulfillment of certain economic and social purposes. Appendixes consist of two statistical charts: I. Number of Shares Sold on the New York Stock Exchange, Each Month, 1900 to 1912, Inclusive and II. Prices of Leading Speculative Stocks on the New York Stock Exchange, on the First of Each Month, September 1904, to March, 1907, and on March 29, 1907.

169. "The Panic of 1873." *Nation* 57 (August 3, 1893): 76-77.

Describes causes of Panic of 1873. The Panic had been preceded by a time of great speculation soon after the end of the Civil War in 1865. Premature and excessive railway building took place after the War. Great speculation took place in iron, in lands, and in town lots. The time of prosperity and speculation, 1869-1873, ended on September 17, 1873 with the failure of the New York and Oswego Midland Railway. Subsequently, the banking house of Jay Cooke & Co. failed, nineteen other banking and brokerage houses in New York failed, and the Stock Market declined. Due to the

Panic, the NYSE closed for ten days. A general bank suspension took place throughout the country, marked by failures of banks. In New York, Philadelphia, Baltimore, Cincinnati, and St. Louis the clearing houses adopted a pooling plan of loan certificates, thus reducing public panic and runs on banks. The pooling plan was adopted by all cities which had clearing houses. The Panic ended on November 1 when banks were able to resume their full activities. Effects of the Panic lasted until 1879.

170. *Papers and Proceedings of the Twenty-Seventh Annual Meeting of the American Economic Association, Princeton, N.J., December 1914.* The American Economic Review, Vol. 5, No. 1, Supplement, March 1915. Ithaca, N.Y.: American Economic Association, 1915. 323 pages.

Papers and Proceedings include two papers with title: "Speculation on the Stock Exchanges and Public Regulation of the Exchanges," one by Samuel Untermyer, the other by Henry C. Emery. With discussion of papers by: Albert W. Atwood, Walter E. Lagerquist, A.R. Marsh, Joseph H. Underwood, William C. Van Antwerp, and William Z. Ripley. Samuel Untermyer's paper studies the possible regulation of the NYSE and other securities exchanges in light of the "Money Trust Investigation" by the Pujo Committee. Henry C. Emery states that misunderstandings exist regarding duties of stock exchanges and stresses the importance of an open speculative market for securities.

* Pujo Committee, Report of the U.S. House of Representatives, February 1913 (on "The Concentration of Control of Money and Credit"), see item 178 below.

* Pyle, Joseph Gilpin. *The Life of James J. Hill.* see item 72 above.

171. "Reopening the Stock Exchange." *Nation* 99 (December 3, 1914): 672.

Describes the recent reopening of the NYSE as ending the longest period of suspended trading in the Exchange's history. The NYSE was closed since July 31, 1914. The reopening does not indicate normal resumption of trading. Trading began in bonds only at a minimum price. The market had been closed because the anticipated outbreak of war was believed to have potential to cause panic in the money markets. The restrictions in trading are in place because conditions to cause a panic may still be present.

* Rheinstein, Sidney. *Trade Whims: My Fifty Years on the New York Stock Exchange.* see item 73 above.

172. Riggs, Edward G. "The New York Stock Exchange." *Harper's Weekly* 38 (June 16, 1894): 562+

Reviews history of the NYSE, defines key terms, and describes the organization and membership structure of the NYSE. With accompanying illustration from the trading floor of 1894.

* Sarnoff, Paul. *Jesse Livermore: Speculator King.* see item 75 above.

* Satterlee, Herbert L. *J. Pierpont Morgan: An Intimate Portrait.* see item 76 above.

173. *The Sayings of Uncle Rufus: He Dreams He is William H. Vanderbilt; His Virtuous Advice to a Lady Contemplating Speculation in Wall Street.* New York: Jesse Haney & Co., 1881. 120 pages.

Satirical study of Wall Street in the 1870s and 1880s. Based on interviews with and correspondence of "Uncle Rufus Hatch" of Rufus Hatch & Co. Offers social commentaries on the times and on Wall Street personalities: Jay Gould, Daniel Drew, William H. Vanderbilt, Russell Sage, etc. "Uncle Rufus" also explains why he

sold his seat on the New York Stock Exchange and presents a
prospectus for a railroad that runs downhill both ways.

*   Sinclair, Andrew. *Corsair: The Life of J. Pierpont Morgan.* see
    item 77 above.

174. Smith, Matthew Hale. *Bulls and Bears of New York, with the
    Crisis of 1873, and the Cause.* New York: J.B. Burr & Co.,
    1875. 576 pages.

    Encompasses subjects of: the language of Wall Street; celebrated
    brokers and stock operators; ethics; and the Panic of 1873.

*   Sparkes, Boyden and Samuel Taylor Moore. *Hetty Green: A
    Woman Who Loved Money.* see item 79 above.

175. Sprague, O.M.W. "The Crisis of 1914 in the United States."
    American Economic Review 5 (September 1915): 499-533.

    Analyzes the 1914 Crisis, its impact on the United States
    economy and its international ramifications. Examines conditions
    on the New York Stock Exchange during the Crisis and reasons
    why it became necessary to close the NYSE. Contends that if the
    NYSE had not closed when it did (July 31, 1914), the decline in
    price of securities on that day would be so extreme that it would
    have caused numerous failings among brokers and their customers
    and large losses to banks. Compares and contrasts the Crisis of
    1914 with earlier crises.

*   Stafford, Marshall P. *The Life of James Fisk, Jr...*see item 81
    above.

176. *The Stock Exchange in Caricature: A Private Collection of
    Caricatures, Cartoons, and Character Sketches of Members of*

the New York Stock Exchange, humorously portraying their Fads and Foibles, and Conveying the Jovial Spirit and Good Fellowship underlying the Serious Side of Everyday Life "On 'Change." Issued under the Direction of a Committee of Members. New York: Abram Stone, 1904. 2 vols.

Issued as a limited edition, presents caricatures of NYSE members, covering time period 1860 through 1904. Each caricature is accompanied by brief poem. Among many caricatures are those of: Russell Sage, Frank Russak, John Muir, William D. Hutton, Charles W. Maury, and Percival Kuhne.

*   Swanberg, W.A. *Jim Fisk: The Career of an Improbable Rascal.* see item 82 above.

177. "To Investigate the Exchanges." *Nation* 87 (December 17, 1908): 612-613.

Relates plans of Committee appointed by Governor Hughes to investigate alleged abuses in NYSE operations and similar organizations. Calls investigation timely and wise. Committee was called to investigate charges that: large capitalists have repeatedly used facilities of the NYSE to create a semblance of abnormal activity by giving out, simultaneously, buying and selling orders and that they have used the same machinery of "matched orders" to produce appearance of a violent rise or violent decline in prices. Committee must question the fact of whether or not NYSE authorities have used their powers to prevent these alleged abuses, or if the State will need to be called upon to protect investors.

178. United States. Congress. House. Committee on Banking and Currency. *Money Trust Investigation. Report of the Committee Appointed Pursuant to House Resolutions 429 and 504 to Investigate the Concentration of Money and Credit.* Washington, D.C.: Government Printing Office, 1913. 3 vols.

Report of the Money Trust Investigation or Pujo (named after

Arsene P. Pujo, Chairman of Subcommittee on the Committee of Banking and Currency) Committee Hearings. Investigates possible concentration of money and credit management in the hands of a few groups of financiers in New York City and their associates in New York and other cities. It had been charged that the groups of financiers have power and influence to: create, avert, and compose panics; control the New York Stock Exchange and other securities markets; regulate interest rates for money; and control railroads, industrial corporations, and moneyed institutions. Refers to Hughes Committee Report and studies NYSE and its organization, listing procedures, margin requirements, short selling, and manipulation. Investigation includes testimonies of: George W. Ely, Secretary of the New York Stock Exchange; James B. Mabon, President of the NYSE; Henry K. Pomroy, member of the NYSE; Charles W. Turner, member of the NYSE; Rudolph Keppler, member of NYSE Board of Governors; and J. Pierpont Morgan, Sr. With statistical tables and charts. Other sections of Investigation review evidence and provide conclusions and recommendations regarding clearing-house associations; the New York Stock Exchange; and concentration of control of money and credit. Recommends: incorporation and regulation of clearing-house associations; examination of clearing-house members; issuance of clearing-house certificates; regulation of rates for collecting out-of-town checks; regulation of rates of discount and of interest on deposits, etc.; that the NYSE and other exchanges be a body corporate of the State or Territory in which it is located; require complete disclosure of corporations listed on securities exchanges; require a margin of not less than 20 percent on all stock purchases; that exchanges keep a full book of account; state in exchange charter the condition on which issues of securities shall be admitted or removed from trading list; prohibiting manipulation regarding execution of simultaneous or substantially simultaneous orders from same person or persons to buy and sell the same security for the purpose of inflating or depressing the price of a security; consolidation of two or more banks should not be permitted unless such action be approved by Comptroller of Currency as in public interest; reorganization of railroad organization under supervision of Interstate Commerce Commission; national banks should be prohibited from engaging in underwritings; prohibition of interlocking bank directorates in same community or locality; and prohibition of interlocking stockholdings among banks.

179. Van Antwerp, W.C. *The Stock Exchange from Within*. Garden City, N.Y.: Doubleday, Page & Co., 1913. 459 pages.

Examines role of stock exchanges in the United States and international economies. Explains basic concepts of "value," "price," etc. Analyzes nature of panics in view of events of the Panic of 1907. Studies day to day events on the New York Stock Exchange, its history and organizational structure, and what happens on the trading floor. Compares the NYSE with the London Stock Exchange. Appendix consists of the text of "The Report of the Hughes Commission of 1909."

* Warshow, Robert Irving. *Bet-a-Million Gates: The Story of a Plunger*. see item 84 above.

* Warshow, Robert Irving. *Jay Gould: The Story of a Fortune*. see item 85 above.

* Wheeler, George. *Pierpont Morgan & Friends: The Anatomy of a Myth*. see item 87 above.

* White, Trumbell. *The Wizard of Wall Street*. see item 89 above.

180. Windmuller, Louis. "A Brief History of the Panic and Some Lessons Which it May Teach Us." *Harper's Weekly* 38 (August 25, 1894): 799+.

Provides details of events of the Panic of 1893, reasons for its occurrence, and offers advice for prevention of similar panics.

* Winkelman, Barnie F. *Ten Years of Wall Street*. see item 198 below.

*   Winkler, John K. *Morgan the Magnificent: The Life of J. Pierpont Morgan (1837-1913)* see item 90 above.

*   Wyckoff, Richard D. *Wall Street Ventures and Adventures through Forty Years.* see item 91 above.

CHAPTER X
1915-1929

Literature in this chapter depicts conditions on Wall Street and at the NYSE during World War I and the post-war years and describes major events among which are the 1920 bomb explosion and the great bull market. Among sources which describe in detail the bull market of the 1920s are John Brooks's *Once in Golconda: A True Drama of Wall Street* and Robert Sobel's *The Great Bull Market: Wall Street in the 1920s*. Also described are several early films of the New York Stock Exchange which are available in the NYSE Archives.

*   Babson, Roger W. *Actions and Reactions: An Autobiography of Roger W. Babson.* see item 21 above.

*   Birmingham, Stephen. *Our Crowd: The Great Jewish Families of New York.* see item 26 above.

181. Brooks, John. *Once in Golconda: A True Drama of Wall Street: 1920-1938.* New York: Norton, 1969. 307 pages.

Chronicles Wall Street events from the 1920 bomb explosion through the years of the Depression. Provides accounts of: the 1920s bull market, the 1929 Crash, and the establishment of the Securities and Exchange Commission. Examines careers of Richard Whitney, J.P. Morgan, Jr., and Jesse Livermore. With bibliographic references.

*   Churchill, Allen. *The Incredible Ivar Kreuger*. see item 31 above.

182. Dice, Charles Amos. *New Levels in the Stock Market*. New York:
     McGraw-Hill Book Co., 1929. 264 pages.

     Describes and examines significance of 1920s bull market. Offers
     advice to investors and studies prices of stocks and of seats on the
     NYSE during this time period. Compares 1920s Coolidge-Hoover
     market with that of McKinley-Roosevelt. Author's preface is dated
     August 1929, two months before Crash. With statistical tables.

183. Huebner, Solomon S. *The Stock Market*. New York: D. Appleton,
     1922. 496 pages.

     Presents the many services of the organized stock market to the
     individual investor, student, and layman. Introduces and defines
     general concepts involved in the organized stock market. Discusses
     specific exchanges throughout the world among which are the
     London Exchange, the New York Curb Market, and the New York
     Stock Exchange. For the NYSE, covers topics of: operation,
     organization, legal status, listing requirements, quotation service,
     etc.   Analyzes specific panics and general nature of panics.
     Appendixes contain: I. Classification and Description of Stock
     Certificates; II. Sample Form of Common Stock Certificate; III.
     Sample Form of Preferred Stock Certificate; IV. Sample Form of
     Bond Certificate; V. Sample Form of a Stock Allotment Warrant;
     VI. Copy of Announcement of Declaration of Rights; VII. Listing
     Requirements of the New York Stock Exchange; VIII. Sample of
     a Corporation's Report as Issued by the Committee on Stock List
     of the New York Stock Exchange; IX. Tabular Outline of "Tape"
     Abbreviations and Their Meaning (Used in Connection with the
     Ticker Service of the New York Stock Exchange); X. Commissions
     Charged on the New York Stock Exchange; XI. Price Fluctuations
     of 20 Railroad Stocks and 20 Industrial Stocks During 1905-1918;
     XII. Composite Price Record of 20 Railroad Stocks; XIII.

Composite Price Record of 40 Stocks; XIV. Bond Prices in (1) Terms of Dollars and (2) Terms of Commodities; and XV. Bibliography.

184. Kahn, Otto H. *The New York Stock Exchange and Public Opinion: Remarks at Annual Dinner, Association of Stock Exchange Brokers Held at the Astor Hotel, New York, January 24, 1917.* New York: New York Stock Exchange, 1917. 31 pages.

Offers answers to several questions regarding the NYSE; these questions are: "Should the Exchange be regulated?" "Is the Exchange merely a private institution?" "Short selling--is it justifiable?" "Does the public get 'fleeced?'" and "Do 'big men' put the market up or down?"

*   McDonald, Forrest. *Insull.* see item 60 above.

185. Martin, H.S. *The New York Stock Exchange: A Discussion of the Business Done; Its Relation to Other Business, to Investment, Speculation and Gambling; the Safeguards Provided by the Exchange, and the Means Taken to Improve the Character of Speculation.* New York: H.S. Martin, 1919. 277 pages.

A study of the NYSE and its history, organization, and role. Focuses on: speculation, investment, short selling, structure of the NYSE, margin trading, stocks and bonds, the NYSE Constitution, odd lot trading, short selling, etc. Defines key terms of Wall Street among which are "floor," "post," "rails," "trader," "whipsawed," "bull," and "bear." Provides definitions of the New York Stock Exchange. Illustrations include: Broad Street in 1797, Floor of the Exchange, map of Wall Street, telegraphers on the Exchange Floor, and the Floor of Exchange decorated for Liberty Loan Rally. Provides facsimile of the Buttonwood Agreement. Appendix contains NYSE Listing Requirements.

186. *Mechanics of the Nation's Market Place* [film] s.l.: Visugraphic

Pictures, Inc., 1928. 35mm, b & w, silent. 25 min.

Examines training and education of NYSE floor employees and the work of the NYSE Institute.

*   Morris, Joe Alex. *What a Year!* see item 221 below.

187. *The Nation's Market Place* [film] New York: New York Stock Exchange, 1928. 35mm b & w, silent, 20 min.

Revised edition of *A Trip to Wall Street*, see item 196. Deals with trading floor procedure and traces a typical investment transaction through machinery of the NYSE. Revised, with sound track added in 1932, see item 241.

188. *A New Service* [film] s.l.: Visugraphic Pictures, 1929. 16mm, b & w, silent.

Produced for the Stock Clearing Corporation, describes functions and procedures of the new Central Delivery Department. With graphic comparing the old to the new way of delivery.

189. New York Stock Exchange. *Constitution of the New York Stock Exchange: Adopted by the Governing Committee, June 10, 1925, Effective June 25, 1925.* New York: New York Stock Exchange, 1925. 124 pages.

Rules of the NYSE describe duties of the President, Vice-President, Treasurer, etc.; roles of the Standing Committees; membership application; transfer of membership; dues and fines; commissions; role of specialists, etc. Defines terms and includes index.

190. New York Stock Exchange. *Report of the President.* New York: NYSE, 1921/23-1936/37.

Trends and developments reported by the NYSE President. Also lists officers and committees of the NYSE. With statistical charts.

191. New York Stock Exchange. Committee on Publicity. *The New York Stock Exchange: History, Organization, Operation, Service.* New York: Committee on Publicity, New York Stock Exchange, 1926. 22 pages.

Presents history of the NYSE and explains how it is organized. Reviews how securities orders are handled, defining terms such as odd lots, specialist, margin, etc. Studies the NYSE's role in the U.S. economy. With illustrations.

* Noyes, Alexander Dana. *The Market Place: Reminiscences of a Financial Editor.* see item 166 above.

192. Noyes, Alexander Dana. *The War Period of American Finance, 1908-1925.* New York: Putnam's, 1926. 459 pages.

United States financial history concentrates on World War I and the early 1920s. Studies events at the NYSE during this time period; the time period in 1914 when the NYSE was closed; and Stock Market declines in 1917 and 1920. With a bibliography of government publications, periodical literature, and other publications.

193. Patterson, Robert T. *The Great Boom and Panic, 1921-1929.* Chicago: Henry Regnery Co., 1965. 282 pages.

Offers answers to two questions: What happened during boom and panic of the 1920s? and What were their causes? Profiles people involved: Jesse Livermore, Arthur W. Cutten, William C. Durant, Van Sweringen Brothers, Samuel Insull, Ivar Kreuger, etc. Statistical tables include Dow Jones stock averages, 1914-1942 and Daily Average Stock Trading.

194. "Remick Nips Panic on Stock Exchange." *New York Times* 69 (September 17, 1920): 1, 5.

Records effects of Wall Street bomb explosion of September 16, 1920 on the operations of the NYSE. Less than one minute after the explosion, William H. Remick, President of the NYSE, rang the gong suspending trading for the day. Suspension of trading nipped in the bud the possibility of a panic among brokers. This emergency suspension was first of its kind in NYSE history. Suspensions, however, have taken place for other reasons: the blizzard of 1888 and the period following outbreak of the first World War.

195. Sobel, Robert. *The Great Bull Market: Wall Street in the 1920s.* Norton Essays in American History. New York: Norton, 1968. 175 pages.

Study of the stock market in the 1920s and events leading up to the 1929 Crash. Examines the bull market, its development, weaknesses in the system, and the key people involved, including Jesse Livermore, Samuel Insull, Ivar Kreuger, the Van Sweringen Brothers, and Richard Whitney. Describes events of the Great Crash and subsequent legislation such as the Glass-Steagall Act and the Securities Act of 1933. Includes bibliographical essay and, as an appendix, a statistical chart of "Growth in Twenty-Five Largest Firms, 1917-1929."

*   Sparling, Earl. *Mystery Men of Wall Street.* see item 80 above.

196. *A Trip to Wall Street* [film] New York: New York Stock Exchange, 1923. 35 mm b & w, silent.

The first motion picture taken on the trading floor of the NYSE. Later revised as *The Nation's Market Place*, see item 241.

197. "Wall Street Explosion Kills 30, Injures 300; Morgan Office hit,

Bomb Pieces Found; Toronto Fugitive Sent Warnings Here."
New York Times 69 (September 17, 1920): 1-2.

Headline story describes bomb explosion on Wall Street. The
explosion at Broad and Wall Streets occurred at noon, shattering
windows for blocks. Damage was estimated at $2,500,000. Lists
identified dead and injured and includes photographs of Wall Street
after the disaster.

198. Winkelman, Barnie F. *Ten Years of Wall Street*. Philadelphia:
John C. Winston, Co., 1932. 381 pages.

Concentrates on stock market conditions from 1919-1929, with
the final three chapters covering the years 1929-1932. Provides
historical background of events from the time of the American
Revolution through the panics of 1837, 1857, 1873, 1893, 1901,
and 1907. Includes excerpts from newspaper articles as well as
copies of cartoons covering the situation on Wall Street. With
bibliographical references.

CHAPTER XI
THE CRASH OF 1929

The Crash of 1929 is the subject of various historical studies, novels, motion pictures, and television programs where fictional and historical protagonists are depicted losing their fortunes. People who experienced great losses in the Crash included the wealthy, the average citizen, and the famous, including Groucho Marx and Eddie Cantor.

The literature listed and annotated below details events, causes, and consequences of the 1929 Crash. Among authors represented are John Kenneth Galbraith, Frederick Lewis Allen, Paul Samuelson, and Irving Fisher. Also included is Eddie Cantor's unique study, *Caught Short*. Materials include newspaper articles written at the time of the Crash, periodical articles, books, and a videocassette. Although many fictional accounts exist, only one representative work of fiction is included.

199. Allen, Frederick Lewis. *The Lords of Creation*. New York: Harper & Brothers, 1935. 483 pages.

Story of the great financial and corporate expansion in the United States between the Depression of the 1890s to the crisis of the 1930s. Events are described in an economic as well as in a human interest and social significance. Among events studied are: the Panics of 1901 and 1907; the Pujo Committee Hearings; World War I and its effect on Wall Street; the years of prosperity in the 1920s; the Crash of 1929, its causes and effects; and reforms on

Pierpont Morgan, E.H. Harriman, Samuel Insull, the Van Sweringen Brothers, and Charles E. Mitchell. The Appendix contains bibliographical references. With illustrations.

200. Allen, Frederick Lewis. *Only Yesterday: An Informal History of the Nineteen-Twenties*. New York: Harper & Brothers, 1931. 370 pages.

Covers the years between the end of World War I through the Crash of 1929. Reviews events in historical, political, economic, social, and cultural contexts. Studies the bull market of the 1920s, the Panic of October 24, 1929 and its aftermath. Offers an hour by hour narrative of events of the Crash, including activities on the NYSE trading floor. The Appendix, "Sources and Obligations" includes bibliographical references.

201. *The American Experience: The Crash of 1929* [videorecording] Host: David McCullough; Writer: Ronald H. Blumer. Producers: Ellen Hovde, Muffie Meyer. Narrator: Philip Bosco. Alexandria, Virginia: PBS Video, 1990. 59 min. color, with black-&-white sequences.

Story of the Crash of 1929 with newsreel footage and interviews. Discusses bull market of the 1920s and causes and consequences of the Crash. Chronicles political, economic, and cultural events of the year 1929 and events leading up to Crash, and an hour by hour account of what happened during the Crash. Features interviews with: John Kenneth Galbraith; Michael Nesbitt, grandson of Michael Meehan; Patricia Livermore, daughter-in-law of Jesse Livermore; Craig Mitchell and Rita Mitchell Cushman, the children of Charles E. Mitchell; Robert Sobel; Tom McCormick, stock sales clerk in 1929; Aristo S. Scrobogna, Secretary to William C. Durant; Arthur Marx, whose father Groucho Marx lost money in the 1929 Crash; Edward Lamont, grandson of Thomas W. Lamont, etc. Studies roles of those who were influential on Wall Street at the time of the Crash, including: Richard Whitney, Jesse Livermore, William C. Durant, Charles E. Mitchell, and Thomas W. Lamont.

202. Angly, Edward. *Oh Yeah!* Compiled from Newspapers and Public
     Records. New York: Viking Press, 1931. 64 pages.

     Series of quotations and political cartoons covering, among other
     topics, Herbert Hoover's presidential campaign of 1928, the Crash
     of 1929 and the early years of the Great Depression. Quotations
     are by: E.H.H. Simmons, President, New York Stock Exchange;
     Jesse Livermore; William Randolph Hearst; Herbert Hoover;
     Andrew W. Mellon, Henry Ford; Irving Fisher; Calvin Coolidge;
     John D. Rockefeller, Sr., etc. Also includes selection of statistics
     about Crash of 1929. Quotes by many concerning prosperity in
     the near future clash with statistics on economic conditions.
     Epilogue is quotation by Calvin Coolidge: "The country is not in
     good condition." Index.

203. Axon, Gordon V. *The Stock Market Crash of 1929.* New York:
     Mason/Charter, 1974. 150 pages.

     Studies causes and consequences of the 1929 Crash. Covers:
     effects on the market by World War I; the bull market during the
     1920s; events of October 1929; the securities reforms of the early
     1930s; the Depression; and the New Deal. Presents biographical
     information on: Calvin Coolidge, Herbert Hoover, Franklin D.
     Roosevelt, Charles E. Mitchell, Richard Whitney, Ivar Kreuger,
     and Jesse Livermore. Speculates on what would have happened if
     no crash had occurred and if Franklin D. Roosevelt had been
     President in 1929. Compares events of 1929 to events on Wall
     Street in 1970 and 1973. With copies of headlines at the time of the
     Crash from the *New York Times* and the *London Times.* The
     appendix consists of text of Franklin D. Roosevelt's first inaugural
     address. Includes glossary and bibliography.

204. "Bankers Halt Stock Debacle: 2-Hour Selling Deluge Stopped
     After Conference at Morgan Offices." *Wall Street Journal.* 44
     (October 25, 1929): 1, 18.

     Account of events of October 24, 1929 when strong support by
     bankers thrown behind the stock market shortly after noon stopped

the great wave of liquidiation, termed "probably the most demoralized condition in stock market history." (p. 1) No official admission was made of the amount of support by bankers, though estimates brought the amount to approximately one billion dollars. The four large banks represented at the conference at in office of J.P. Morgan & Co. were: Chase National, National City, Bankers Trust, and Guaranty Trust. The view expressed by spokesman for meeting of bankers was that the market break was a technical one and "was not based on anything fundamentally wrong." (p. 18) Trading volume of 12,894,600 shares broke all previous Exchange records.

205. Bierman, Harold, Jr. *The Great Myths of 1929 and the Lessons to be Learned*. Contributions in economics and economic history, number 118. New York: Greenwood Press, 1991. 202 pages.

Studies events leading up to the Crash and why the Crash happened. Considers two basic questions: was stock market unreasonably high in October 1929? and was a crash inevitable? Analyzes and refutes many misconceptions of the 1929 Crash. Compares and contrasts the 1929 and 1987 Stock Market Crashes. Discusses lessons to be learned from the 1929 Crash. Includes excerpts from the Stock Exchange Practices Hearings of 1933. With statistical tables and a bibliography.

*   Birmingham, Stephen. *Our Crowd: The Great Jewish Families of New York*. see item 26 above.

206. Bow, James. "The *Times's* Financial Markets Column in the Period Around the 1929 Crash." *Journalism Quarterly* 57 (Autumn 1980): 447-450, 497.

A study of the *New York Times's* "Financial Market" column at the time of the 1929 Crash, concentrating on time period October 13 to November 13, 1929. A crash was not predicted although the column sometimes offered hints and comparisons to earlier panics. Columns are rated optimistic (27.3%); pessimistic (18.2%); and neutral (54.5%). With bibliographical references.

207. "Breaks of the Past Recalled in Street: Comparisons Made to Market Crises of 1920, 1907, 1903, and 1901." *New York Times* 79 (October 25, 1929): 3.

Compares October 24, 1929 decline with conditions during Panics of 1920, 1907, 1903, and 1901. It was generally agreed that the October market break was most severe in scope and violence. Reviews causes of the earlier Panics.

208. "Brokers in Uproar as Market Boils." *New York Times* 79 (October 25, 1929): 3.

First-hand account of events on the NYSE trading floor on October 24, 1929. Describes trading floor and visitors' gallery; among visitors viewing the trading floor was Winston Churchill. Outside the Exchange, large crowds were gathered and rumors of failures, suicides, and other disasters spread throughout Wall Street. After trading ended, over 50,000 Wall Street employees tabulated the day's transactions, with some having to work throughout the night.

*   Brooks, John. *Once in Golconda.* Cited above as item 181 above.

209. *Brother, Can You Spare a Dime? America from the Wall Street Crash to Pearl Harbor: An Illustrated Documentary*, by Susan Winslow, assisted by Wendy Holmes. New York: Facts on File, 1976. 160 pages.

First section concerns the Stock Market Crash of 1929. Mostly, excerpts from newspaper articles about the Crash from the *New York Herald Tribune* and *New York Sunday News*. With a photograph taken at the time of the Crash in front of the New York Stock Exchange building.

210. Cantor, Eddie. *Caught Short! A Saga of Wailing Wall Street.*
     Illustrations by Sid L. Hydeman. New York: Simon and
     Schuster, 1929. 45 pages.

   Written by the "comedian, author, statistician, and victim."
   Humorous account of one person's experiences during the Great
   Crash with descriptions of conversations with other victims. Offers
   definitions of Wall Street terms: "Preferred Stock" - "a security
   with a high hat and spats"; "Call Money" - "Lawful larceny"; and
   "Dividend" - "Salvage from original investment." The publishers
   describe this as a "consoling and hilarious extravaganza."

*   Churchill, Allen. *The Incredible Ivar Kreuger.* see item 31 above.

211. Fisher, Irving. *The Stock Market Crash and After.* New York:
     Macmillan, 1930. 286 pages.

   Appraises Stock Market Crash, causes, prices in years preceding
   Crash.   Outlines proposed measures to alleviate stress of 1929
   Crash including: "Proposal of an 'artificial floor' of Minimum
   Prices," "proposed Basis of Value on Margins," "A New Method
   of Financing Security Purchases," "Proposed Committee on Listing
   of New Issues," "Proposed Repeal of Capital Gains Tax," etc.
   Among charts are: "Stock Prices, Last Half of 1929," "Stock Price
   Index Numbers, 1870-1929," and "Mergers Recorded, 1918-
   1929."

212. Galbraith, John Kenneth. "The Great Crash." *Journal of Portfolio
     Management* 6 (Fall 1979): 60-62.

   Article adapted by Galbraith from Introduction to Fiftieth
   Anniversary Edition of his book, *The Great Crash.* Discusses the
   impact and legacy of October 24, 1929, the day of the Great Stock
   Market Crash. Reviews measures taken to prevent another crash
   including the Securities Exchange Act of 1934. Compares and
   contrasts conditions of the 1920s with those of the 1960s.

213. Galbraith, John Kenneth. *The Great Crash, with a new introduction by the author.* Boston: Houghton Mifflin, 1988. 206 pages.

Analyzes the Crash, its causes and its implications for future generations. Compares 1929 Crash with Panics of 1873, 1907, and 1920. Studies events from December 1928 to November 1929, including events on the New York Stock Exchange trading floor at the time of the Crash. Studies roles of key individuals: Ivar Kreuger, Charles E. Mitchell, Richard Whitney, Herbert Hoover, Irving Fisher, and Roger Babson. With bibliographical references. First published in 1955. New introduction compares and contrasts Crashes of 1929 and 1987. Work is frequently cited in studies of the Crash.

*   Gimlin, Hoyt. "Wall Street: 40 Years After the Crash." see item 295 below.

214. Hirst, Francis W. *Wall Street and Lombard Street: The Stock Exchange Slump of 1929 and the Trade Depression of 1930.* New York: Macmillan, 1931. 180 pages.

Covers time period, 1927-1930. Causes of the Crash and its effects from Wall Street to London. Describes the bull market of 1927 through October 1929. Analyzes findings of Professor Irving Fisher and Roger W. Babson. Reports the newspaper accounts of events of the Crash and events on the trading floor. Studies consequences and ramifications of Crash internationally through 1930.

215. Hoover, Herbert. *Memoirs of Herbert Hoover: The Great Depression, 1929-1941.* New York: Macmillan, 1052. 503 pages.

Covers year of Great Crash, the presidential election of 1932, and the time of the Great Depression. Analyzes causes of Crash of 1929. Urged NYSE to curb manipulation of stocks.

216. Kindleberger, Charles P. "The International Causes and Consequences of the Great Crash." *Journal of Portfolio Management* 6 (Fall 1979):11-14.

Examines international causes and ramifications of the 1929 Crash. Analyzes ideas and observations of Herbert Hoover, Milton Friedman, Peter Temin, W.W. Rostow, and others. Compares and contrasts international economic conditions of 1929 and 1979. With bibliographical references.

217. Klingaman, William K. *1929: The Year of the Great Crash.* New York: Harper & Row, 1989. 393 pages.

The story of the Stock Market Crash and the social, political, and cultural events of that year. Profiles prominent individuals of the time, including: Calvin Coolidge; Herbert Hoover; Franklin D. Roosevelt; Edward, Prince of Wales; Al Capone; Ernest Hemingway; Charles and Anne Lindbergh; F. Scott Fitzgerald; and the Marx Brothers. Discusses causes of the Crash and how it was responsible for the Great Depression. Actual time period chronicled: November 1928 - June 1930. Inspiration for this book was Stock Market Crash of 1987.

218. Knapp, Paul. *The Berengaria Exchange.* New York: Dial Press, 1972. 239 pages.

Concerns events during voyage of the luxury liner, *Berengaria* at the time of the Stock Market Crash. The *Berengaria* had on board a floating brokerage office, a branch of M.J. Meehan & Co. Among passengers on board were: Helena Rubinstein, Edgar Wallace, and Jay Cooke III.

219. Levien, J.R., comp. *Anatomy of a Crash--1929.* New York: Traders Press, 1966. 121 pages.

Compilation of material which reviews causes and consequences of the 1929 Crash. Contains: "General Motors--Decades'

Achievement," a chapter from Barnie F. Winkelman's *Ten Years of Wall Street; "Incidents which led up to and Followed the October Crash told in Chronological Order," from the* New York Times; a group of monthly charts of Dow Jones averages; a transcript of Richard Whitney's address, "The Work of the Stock Exchange in the Panic of 1929"; "Pool Operations," from Barnie F. Winkelman's *Ten Years of Wall Street*; "Crisis-Producing Conditions," from *Crises and Depressions*, by Senator Theodore Burton; and a section of Victor de Villers' Point and Figure course reviewing price movements of the Crash.

* McDonald, Forrest. *Insull.* see item 60 above.

220. Migneco, Ronald and Timothy Levi Biel. *The Crash of 1929.* Illustrations by Maurie Manning and Michael Spackman, Robert Caldwell, and Randol Eagles. World disasters. San Diego, California: Lucent Books, 1989. 64 pages.

The story of the Stock Market Crash for young people. Discusses causes and effects of Crash. Explains basics of investing, the procedures for buying and selling stocks, and the differences between bull and bear markets. Profiles notable businessmen and investors of the time including Henry Ford, William C. Durant, Charles Mitchell, and Thomas Lamont. Compares the Crash of 1929 with that of 1987. Provides glossary of terms including "broker," "margin," "stock," "ticker tape," "Wall Street," etc. With a bibliography and an index.

221. Morris, Joe Alex. *What a Year!* New York: Harper & Brothers, 1956. 338 pages.

Concerns political, economic, and cultural events of 1929. Includes chapter on the 1929 Crash that studies causes and effects. Provides description of events of the Crash on the trading floor of the NYSE. With illustrations among which are: the New York Stock Exchange during the 1929 Crash and a portrait of Mr.and Mrs. Richard Whitney.

*   New York Stock Exchange. *Report of the President.* see item 190
     above.

*   Noyes, Alexander Dana. *The Market Place: Reminiscences of a
     Financial Editor* see item 166 above.

222. Noyes, Alexander Dana. "The Stock Market Panic." *Current
     History* 31 (December 1929): 618-623.

     Written by the Financial Editor, *New York Times.* Contends that
     Stock Market Crash was inevitable since credit facilities were
     seriously overstrained. Credit facilities were from domestic and
     international sources. Credit acquired was used to facilitate further
     stock purchases at wildly increasing prices. Among contributing
     factors to violence and timing of Panic were: protective measures
     taken by European markets after use as a credit resource by Wall
     Street; warnings regarding the American credit situation by
     responsible bankers; and many of the ringleaders of the Wall Street
     speculation, finding themselves in an overextended position, were
     attempting to extricate themselves. Discusses the extremely violent
     decline and great losses of personal savings experienced by
     speculators. States that a reasurring consideration is that the
     reckless speculation had not extended into field of general trade.

*   Patterson, Robert T. *The Great Boom and Panic, 1921-1929. see*
     item 193 above.

223. Rogers, Donald I. *The Day the Market Crashed.* New Rochelle,
     N.Y.: Arlington House, 1971.

     Tells the story of October 24, 1929 or Black Thursday and of
     October 29, 1929 or Black Tuesday.

224. Samuelson, Paul A. "Myths and Realities about the Crash and
     Depression." *Journal of Portfolio Management* 6 (Fall 1979):

7-10.

Offers perspectives concerning the historical and economic significance, the myths, and realities of the 1929 Crash. Refutes some of the misconceptions regarding the Crash. Recommends, for further reading, Frederick Lewis Allen's *Only Yesterday*, John Kenneth Galbraith's *The Great Crash,* and Charles Kindleberger's *Manias, Crashes, and Panics.* With bibliographical references.

*   Schabacker, R.W. *Stock Market Theory and Practice.* see item 246 below

225. Schachtman, Tom. *The Day America Crashed.* New York: Putnam's, 1979. 336 pages.

Story, hour by hour, of October 24, 1929 or "Black Thursday." Provides social, political, economic, and cultural background to events of the Crash. Describes events on trading floor of the New York Stock Exchange. Some information based on correspondence and accounts of people involved in the market Crash. Final chapter "Children of the Crash" tells what happened to people involved in crash including : Herbert Hoover, Franklin D. Roosevelt, Jesse Livermore, Richard Whitney, Arthur W. Cutten, Andrew W. Mellon, and the Van Sweringen Brothers. With bibliographical references.

226. Schlesinger, Arthur M. *The Crisis of the Old Order: 1919-1933.* The Age of Roosevelt. Boston: Houghton Mifflin, 1956. 557 pages.

Volume in series covering presidency of Franklin D. Roosevelt discusses historical background from 1919 to outset of Roosevelt's first term of office. Provides analysis of 1920s bull market through Stock Market Crash of 1929. Examines causes of the Stock Market Crash, developments during this crisis, and their consequences. With bibliographical references.

*   Schwed, Fred, Jr. *Where are the Customers' Yachts? or A Good Hard Look at Wall Street.* see item 270 below.

227. Simmons, Edward Henry Harriman. *Principal Causes of the Stock Market Crisis of 1929: Address delivered...at the twenty-first annual dinner of the Transportation Club, the Pennsylvania Railroad, at Philadelphia, Pennsylvania, January 25, 1930.* Philadelphia: Transportation Club, the Pennsylvania Railroad, 1930. 29 pages.

Transcript of an address delivered by the author. Analyzes causes to reduce chances of a recurrence. States that primary cause of the 1929 Crash was the high level of prices attained by a large number of leading American share issues. Among other factors described are: lack of equilibrium in speculation due to greater willingness to buy than sell securities; large proportion of securities purchased on margin; and the large output of new stock issues placed on the market during September and October 1929. Pinpoints three ways stock market affects business as: by psychological influences of stock market activity on the public; by facilitating flow of capital into corporate enterprise; and by increased consumption made possible by realized stock market profits. Statistical charts provided with text are: "Standard Statistics Weekly Stock Price Index, 1929"; "Indices of Industrial Production (1923-1929)"; "New York Stock Exchange Share Market Activity: Actual and Relative to Share Listings (1925-1929)"; "Current Values of Securities Listed as Result of Right Financing and Cash Received by the Companies (1926-1929)"; "Monthly Public Security Offerings of Corporate Securities (Net Capital) By Type of Security (1926-1929)"; "Monthly Public Security Offerings of Corporate Securites (Net Capital) By Type of Enterprise (1926-1929)"; "Relationship Between Brokers' Loans and Commodity Prices (1917-1923)"; "Relationship Between Brokers' Loans and Commodity Prices (1924-1930)"; and "Annual Public Security Flotations--Net Capital (1919-1929)."

228. Sirkin, Gerald. "The Stock Market of 1929 Revisited: A Note." *Business History Review* 49 (Summer 1975): 223-231.

Studies and questions findings of economists regarding 1929 Crash. Evaluates behavior of 1929 stock market using theory of stock values as affected by growth of earnings and applying a formulation on stock prices, devised by Burton Malkiel. Using evaluation, refutes the time period as one of "speculative orgy" in "a time of madness." With bibliographical references.

*   Sobel, Robert. *Panic on Wall Street: A History of America's Financial Disasters.* Cited above as item 113 above.

229. Sparkes, Boyden. *Customers' Man.* New York: Frederick A. Stokes Company, 1931. 182 pages.

Novel concerns a singer gaining employment in a brokers office and how he became a customers' man. Covers effects of 1929 Crash on the protagonist.

*   Sparling, Earl. *Mystery Men of Wall Street: The Powers Behind the Market.* see item 80 above.

230. "Stocks Collapse in 16,410,030-Share Day, But Rally at Close Cheers Brokers; Bankers Optimistic, to Continue Aid." *New York Times* 79 (October 30, 1929):1-2.

Reports collapse of stock prices in what was referred to as "the most disastrous trading day in the stock market's history." (p. 1) A market rally did occur, however, during the closing minutes of trading. The market decline had started on Thursday, October 24, followed by a moderate rally on Friday, and normal conditions on Saturday. The market declined on Monday, October 28 followed by the severe collapse on October 29. Includes statistics concerning the day's volume and the largest declines in the leading issues on the NYSE.

231. "Stocks Steady After Decline: Bankers State Support Continues-

-Spokesman Expresses View Hysteria is Passing: Record Trading
Volume." *Wall Street Journal* 44 (October 30, 1929): 1, 15.

Reports stock market prices reached new lows with a record
trading volume of 16,410,000 shares. Large banking group which
had met on October 24, met on October 29 and a spokesman for the
group announced it would continue to support the market. The
group's spokesman indicated that hysteria of the past few days
seemed to be passing. Richard Whitney, Vice-President of the
NYSE, issued the statement: "The meeting of the board of
governors of the New York Stock Exchange considered carefully
the present situation, but felt no action was necessary and adjourned
to its regular meeting Wednesday afternoon." (p. 1)

*   United States. Congress. Senate. Committee on Banking and
      Currency. *Stock Market Study.* see item 335 below.

232. Whitney, Richard. *The Work of the New York Stock Exchange in
     the Panic of 1929.* Address delivered by Richard Whitney,
     President, New York Stock Exchange. Boston, Massachusetts,
     June 10, 1930. 9 pages.

     Transcript of an address delivered before the Boston Association
     of Stock Exchange Firms, at the Algonquin Club, Boston
     Massachusetts, June 10, 1930. Chronicles events of October 1929
     Crash, discusses the economic effects of panics, the roles of the
     New York Stock Exchange and the New York banks during the
     1929 panic. Describes events of the Crash from the viewpoint of
     the administration of the New York Stock Exchange. Stresses
     importance of the NYSE as "a free and open security market" and
     does not advocate temporarily closing down the market or adopting
     artificial means of restraint as methods of dealing with panics.

233. Wigmore, Barrie A. *The Crash and Its Aftermath: A History of
     Securities Markets in the United States, 1929-1933. Contributions
     in economics and economic history; no. 58.* Westport,
     Connecticut: Greenwood Press, 1985. 731 pages.

Relates events leading up to the 1929 Crash, developments after 1929, and the effect the Crash had on specific industries and individual stocks. Stocks studied represent various industries including: banks, oil industry, steel industry, food industry, retailers, etc. For the years 1929-1933, analyzes: political and economic influences; bond markets; and status of the stock market. The statistical appendix includes: Ratios for leading stocks, 1929-1933; NYSE Listed Issues, 1914-1938 (annually); Dow-Jones Stock Indices, Month ends, 1929-1933; and NYSE Short Interest, 1931-1936 (weekly). Coverage is from Crash of 1929 to end of President Franklin D. Roosevelt's "First Hundred Days" in June 1933.

*   Winkelman, Barnie F. *Ten Years of Wall Street.* see item 198 above.

*   Winslow, Susan. *Brother, Can You Spare a Dime? America from the Wall Street Crash to Pearl Harbor.*, see item 209 above.

234. "Worst Stock Crash Stemmed by Banks; 12,894,650 - Share Day Swamps Market; Leaders Confer, Find Conditions Sound." *New York Times* 79 (October 25, 1929): 1-2.

Reports events of the stock crash on October 24, 1929. Credit was given to Wall Street banking leaders for arresting decline on the New York Stock Exchange. The five bankers who met at the offices of J.P. Morgan & Co. were Charles E. Mitchell, Albert H. Wiggin, William Potter, Seward Prosser, and Thomas W. Lamont.

CHAPTER XII
1930-1934

The first four years of the 1930s were a period of Congressional investigations and legislation that would bring about great changes in the securities industry.

Among sources which are represented in Chapter XII are the Committee on Banking and Currency Hearings; Ferdinand Pecora's recollections of the Hearings in his study, *Wall Street Under Oath*; the texts of the Securities Act of 1933 and the Securities Exchange Act of 1934; studies of the legislation resulting from the hearings: the Glass-Steagall Act, the Securities Act of 1933, and the Securities Exchange Act of 1934; and the history of the Securities and Exchange Commission.

235. Allen, Frederick Lewis. *Since Yesterday: The Nineteen-Thirties in America, September 2, 1929 - September 2, 1939.* New York: Harper & Brothers, 1940. 362 pages.

Examines economic, social, political, and cultural events. There is some overlap with Allen's *Only Yesterday* (see item 200) which discusses events from November 11, 1918 - November 1929, with an additional chapter covering events between 1929 - 1931. The 1929 Crash's story is told in abbreviated format as opposed to its more lengthy treatment in *Only Yesterday*. This work covers developments after the Crash, including the hearings of the Senate Committee on Banking and Currency and enactment of the Securities Act of 1933 and the Securities and Exchange Act of 1934.

236. Benston, George J. "Required Disclosure and the Stock Market:
An Evaluation of the Securities Exchange Act of 1934."
American Economic Review 63 (March 1973): 132-155.

Reviews disclosure requirements of the Securities Exchange Act
of 1934. According to the Act, a corporation whose stock is traded
on a registered stock exchange or who registered a stock issue
must: file detailed balance sheets, income statements, and
supporting substatements (form 10K) within 120 days after close of
fiscal year; file a less detailed semiannual report (form 9K) within
45 days after the first half of the fiscal year; and file a current
report (form 8K) 10 days after end of any month in which
significant events occurred (i.e. legal proceedings, change in
control of corporation, etc.). Compares and contrasts financial data
before and after passage of the Securities Exchange Act. Examines
statistically change in riskiness and returns in stock prices on the
New York Stock Exchange before and after '34 Act. Concludes that
disclosure requirements of the '34 Act had no measurable positive
effect on securities traded on the NYSE. Includes bibliographical
references.

*   Black, Hillel. *The Watchdogs of Wall Street.* see item 283 below.

*   Churchill, Allen. *The Incredible Ivar Kreuger.* see item 31 above.

*   Dolley, James C. "The Effect of Government Regulation on the
Stock-Trading Volume of the New York Stock Exchange." see
item 261 below.

237. Ellenberger, J.S. and Ellen P. Mahor, comp. *Legislative History
of the Securities Act of 1933 and Securities Exchange Act of 1934
(Act of May 27, 1933, 48 Stat. 74, 15 U.S.C. 77a-77bbb (1970),
and Act of June 6, 1934, 48 Stat. 88, 15 USC 78a-78hhh-1*

(1970). South Hackensack, N.J. Law Librarians' Society of Washington, D.C., 1973. 11 volumes.

Provides text of both the Securities Act of 1933 and the Securities Exchange Act of 1934, with transcripts of hearings, related documents, House and Senate Bills, etc. Contents: V. 1: Securities Act of 1933--the law as enacted and codified, debate (73rd Congress, 1st session) including transcript of remarks by President Franklin D. Roosevelt; V. 2: Securities Act of 1933 - including House Documents and Senate Reports, including "Federal Securities Act," Hearings before the House Interstate and Foreign Commerce Committee, 73rd Congress, 1st Session on H.R. 4314, March 31, April 1, 4, and 5, 1933 and "Securities Act," Hearings before the Senate Banking and Currency Committee, 73rd Congress, 1st Session on S. 875, March 31 - April 8, 1933. V. 3: Securities Act of 1933 Bills and Amendments; V. 4: Securities Exchange Act of 1934 - the law as enacted and codified, debate (73rd Congress, 2nd session), includes message from President Franklin D. Roosevelt and letters from Richard Whitney, President of the NYSE; V. 5: Securities Exchange Act of 1934 - Senate and House Reports; V. 6 and V. 7: Securities Exchange Act of 1934 - Hearings, including "Stock Exchange Practices," Hearings before the Senate Banking and Currency Committee, 73rd Congress; V. 8 and V. 9: Securities Exchange Act of 1934 - Hearings including, "Stock Exchange Regulation," Hearings before the House Interstate and Foreign Commerce Committee, 73rd Congress; V. 10: House Bills; and V. 11: Senate Bills.

238. Hodgson, James Goodwin, comp. *Wall Street: Asset or Liability?* The Reference Shelf, vol. 9, no. 4. New York: H.W. Wilson Co., 1934. 253 pages.

Compilation of articles based on a proposal that a heavy federal tax be levied on every stock transaction where seller has not had possession of stock for at least one year. Topics covered include speculation, short selling, margins and brokers' loans, manipulation, and reforms adopted in 1933. Most articles are reprinted from periodicals such as *Business Week, Nation, New Republic, Collier's,* and *Atlantic Monthly.* Among these articles are:

"Building a Stock Market Boom," "Causes for Complaint," by Marguerite Peyton Sloan; "The Function of a Stock Exchange," by Richard Whitney; "What is Speculation," by Theodore H. Price; "Abolish Stock Gambling," by John T. Flynn; "Where the Money Came From in 1929"; "Who Gets the Money?" by Lewis H. Haney; "Who Speculates," by Lewis Corey; "Speculation and the Stability of Stock Prices," by M.J. Fields; "The Uses of Speculation," by Charles A. Conant; "Short Selling Approved," by Richard Whitney; "The Danger in Margins," by Thomas N. Carver; and "Short Selling Loses Caste," by J. George Frederick. Presents selections from the 1933 Senate Committee on Banking and Currency Hearings. Statistical tables include: "NYSE Money Desk Call Loan Rates," "NYSE Member Borrowings on Security Collateral," and "Listed Stocks--Total Shares and Total Market Values." "What to Read Next" is a bibliographic essay on stock market sources, most of which were published in the early 1930s. With a bibliography of books, pamphlets, and periodicals.

*   Macaulay, Frederick Robertson. *Short Selling on the New York Stock Exchange.* see item 299 below.

*   McDonald, Forrest. *Insull.* see item 60 above.

239. Meyer, Charles H. *The Law of Stock Brokers and Stock Exchanges.* New York: Baker, Voorhis, 1931. 1493 pages.

Concerns law relating to stock brokers and stock exchanges-- judicial decisions, statutes, and exchange rules. Analyzes fundamental concepts of stockbrokerage law; nature of exchanges and exchange membership; organization of the exchanges; relations of members and their firms to the exchange; rights and obligations arising out of security and commodity dealings; contracts for purchase and sale of securities and commodities; contracts between the customer and his/her own broker; and remedies for breaches of contracts. Studies rules of the New York Stock Exchange, the Stock Clearing Corporation, the New York Curb Exchange, the New York Cotton Exchange, and the Chicago Stock Exchange. For the

NYSE, describes: its history; organization; how orders are handled; and court decisions, rules, and statutes. Appendix II contains the text of the NYSE Constitution and Rules, with an official index to Constitution and Rules. Includes references to rules, statutes, and court decisions.

240. Meyer, Charles H. *The Securities Exchange Act of 1934 Analyzed and Explained.* New York: Francis Emory Fitch, 1934. 251 pages.

Comprised of two parts: Part I, the Securities Exchange Act of 1934 (Fletcher-Rayburn Act) and Part II, the Securities Act of 1933, as amended in 1934. Each part consists of a summary and detailed analysis, section by section, of each Act. Discusses key areas among which are the establishment of the Securities and Exchange Commission, registration of securities, and margin requirements. Defines key terms throughout the book. Includes a General Index.

241. *The Nation's Market Place* [film] New York: New York Stock Exchange, 1932. 35mm, color, sound.

Examines trading floor procedure.

*   New York Stock Exchange. *Report of the President.* see item 190 above.

242. New York Stock Exchange. Committee on Public Relations. *New York Stock Exchange: Its Functions and Operations.* New York: New York Stock Exchange, April 1936. 40 pages.

Explains functions, operations, and history of the NYSE. Discusses: membership, transactions, tickers, odd-lots, margin, commissions, specialists, bond brokers, etc. With a glossary of key terms and illustrations, mostly photographs of the NYSE trading floor.

243. Parrish, Michael E. *Securities Regulation and the New Deal.* New Haven: Yale University Press, 1970. 270 pages.

Treatise on New Deal financial regulation examines the Securities Act of 1933; the Securities Exchange Act of 1934; the Public Utility Holding Company Act, and the early history of the Securities and Exchange Commission. Reviews earlier attempts to regulate corporate securities in the United States from 1911-1933. Presents implications of regulation on operations and policies of the New York Stock Exchange. With a bibliography that lists: manuscripts and unpublished records; public documents; newspapers; business, professional, and popular journals; court cases; articles; and books.

244. Pecora, Ferdinand. *Wall Street Under Oath: The Story of Our Modern Money Changers.* Reprints of Economic Classics. New York: Simon & Schuster. Reprint: New York: Augustus M. Kelley Publishers, 1968. 311 pages.

Written by Counsel to the United States Senate Committee on Banking and Currency, January 1933 - June 1934 which conducted an investigation into banking and stock market practices. Investigation resulted in enactment of various regulatory measures by Congress, the most important was the one creating the Securities and Exchange Commission on July 1, 1934. Provides testimonies and descriptions of individuals involved: J.P. Morgan, Jr., Thomas W. Lamont, Otto H. Kahn, Richard E. Whitney, O.P. Sweringen, Samuel Insull, Jr. etc. Analyzes the role of the New York Stock Exchange in these investigations and the relationship between the SEC and the NYSE. As a result, (p. 301): "...even the mighty Stock Exchange must now recognize the existence and authority of the United States Government."

*   Pecora Hearings, see item 250 below.

*   Robbins, Sidney. *The Securities Markets: Operations and Issues.*
       see item 318 below.

245. Salmon, David L. as told to Dr. Edwin F. Bowers. *Confessions
     of a Former Customers' Man.* New York: Vanguard Press, 1932.
     251 pages.

     Report of his fifteen years as a customers' man on Wall Street.
     Documents events on Wall Street during 1920s and early 1930s.
     Calls for industrial and financial reform.

246. Schabacker, R.W. *Stock Market Theory and Practice.* New York:
     B.C. Forbes, 1930. 875 pages.

     Written by Financial Editor of *Forbes*, this guide to the stock
     market is divided into two parts: the first dealing with mechanics
     or tools, the second with practical trading theories. Covers: history
     of the NYSE; odd-lot dealing; information sources for the stock
     market; the stock clearing corporation, stock brokers, etc. Provides
     chapter covering causes, effects, and lessons of the Panic of 1929.
     Appendixes consist of: a Chronology of the New York Stock
     Exchange, 1792 - 1929; New York Stock Exchange Firms in New
     York City; Member Firms of Outside Exchanges; New York Stock
     Exchange Securities and Their Symbols; List of 10-Share Unit
     Stocks on the New York Stock Exchange; Table for Quick
     Calculations of Approximate Annual Yields; Stocks included in
     Representative Market Averages; Market News Factors--When and
     Where to Look for Them; Examples of Arbitrage Operation; Sloan
     Test with Five Different Trading Theories; Data on Charts and
     Statistical Series; and Description of a "New Era" in Great Britain
     of the Early 18th Century. With bibliography and index. Plates
     include illustrations of the New York Stock Exchange building; a
     NYSE trading post; and a sample common stock certificate. With
     a "Financial District Map of New York City."

*   Schwed, Fred, Jr. *Where are the Customers' Yachts? or A Good
       Hard Look at Wall Street.* see item 270 below.

247. Seligman, Joel. *The Transformation of Wall Street: A History of the Securities and Exchange Commission and Modern Corporate Finance.* Boston: Houghton Mifflin, 1982. 701 pages.

History of the Securities and Exchange Commission, from events leading to its founding in 1934 to early 1977. Examines Securities Act of 1933 and Securities Exchange Act of 1934. Profiles and studies contributions of key participants in the history of the SEC including: Franklin D. Roosevelt, Ferdinand Pecora, Felix Frankfurter, Joseph P. Kennedy, James Landis, William O. Douglas, Jerome Frank, and William Cary. Studies effects of SEC regulation on the New York Stock Exchange and analyzes contributions and reactions to SEC legislation and proposed legislation by NYSE Presidents: Richard Whitney, Charles Gay, William McChesney Martin, Emil Schram, Keith Funston, and Robert Haack. Analyzes implications of major reports and legislation of the SEC among which are: *In the Matter of Richard Whitney* (1938); *the Special Study* (1963); Securities Acts Amendments of 1964; and Securities Acts Amendments of 1975. With bibliographical references for each chapter. Follows up history of the SEC from 1977-1985 in *The SEC and the Future of Finance,* see item 321 below.

248. Twentieth Century Fund. *Stock Market Control: A Summary of the Research Findings and Recommendations of the Security Markets Survey Staff of the Twentieth Century Fund, Inc.* Editors: Evans Clark, J. Frederic Dewhurst, Alfred L. Bernheim, Margaret Grant Schneider. New York: Appleton-Century Co., 1934. 209 pages.

Reports and summarizes research findings of the Twentieth Century Fund. Full text findings are found in the Twentieth Century Fund's *The Security Markets*, see item 275 below. Studies and attempts to pass critical judgment on market practices. Provides study of organization and operation of the securities markets, including the New York Stock Exchange. Suggests program for regulation and control of the markets. Studies and makes recommendations for: margin buying, specialists, pool activities, short selling, customers' men, etc. Recommends Federal regulation of securities markets. With statistical charts and tables.

249. United States. Congress. House. Committee on Interstate and
     Foreign Commerce. *Stock Exchange Regulation: Hearing before
     the Committee on Interstate and Foreign Commerce, House of
     Representatives, 73d Congress, 2d session, on H.R. 7852 to
     provide for the registration of national securities exchanges
     operating in interstate and foreign commerce and through the
     mails and to prevent unfair practices on such exchanges, and for
     other purposes [and] H.R. 8720 to provide for the regulation of
     national securities exchanges and of over-counter markets
     operating in interstate and foreign commerce or through the
     mails, and to prevent inequitable and unfair practices thereon,
     and for other purpose,* February 14 to March 24, 1934.
     Washington, D.C.: Government Printing Office, 1934. 941
     pages.

     Series of hearings concerning regulation of securities markets.
     Defines key terms regarding securities markets and regulation. With
     statements and communications from: Richard Whitney, President
     of the NYSE; Frank C. Shaughnessy, President, San Francisco
     Stock Exchange; Frank R. Hope, President of the Association of
     Stock Exchange Firms; Charles A. Collins, President, Boston Stock
     Exchange; Michael J. O'Brien, President, Chicago Stock Exchange;
     Thomas B. Gay, attorney, appearing for the New York Stock
     Exchange; Arthur E. Hetherington, Member of New York Stock
     Exchange Firm of De Coppet & Doremus; Eugene E. Thompson,
     President, Associated Stock Exchanges; New York Stock Exchange
     Floor Traders; New York Stock Exchange Specialists; and Hon.
     John Fitzgerald of Boston, Massachusetts. Features detailed
     testimony of Whitney who discusses: the role of specialists; margin
     requirements; rules and regulations of the NYSE; odd-lot trading,
     etc.

250. United States. Congress. Senate. Committee on Banking and
     Currency. *Stock Exchange Practices: Hearings Before the
     Committee on Banking and Currency, 72nd Congress on S. Res.
     84, a resolution to thoroughly invesigate practices of stock*

*exchanges with respect to the buying and selling and the
borrowing and lending of listed securities, the value of such
securities and the effects of such practices; and S. res. 56 (73d
Congress), a resolution to investigate the matter of banking
operations and practices, the issuance and sale of securities, and
the trade therein.* Washington, D.C.: U.S. Government Printing
Office, 1932-34. 9 volumes.

Series of hearings investigating stock exchange practices provides
testimonies of: Richard Whitney, President of the New York Stock
Exchange; Fiorello H. LaGuardia, a Representative from the
Twentieth District of New York; Charles E. Mitchell, Chairman of
the National City Bank of New York and Chairman of the National
City Co.; Samuel Insull, Jr. of Insull Utility Investments; and
Michael Joseph Meehan of M.J. Meehan & Co. Ferdinand Pecora,
special counsel to the Committee (May 1933 - May 1934)
questioned key witnesses. Witnesses discuss events of the 1920s
including the Crash of 1929. Also described are: short selling on
the NYSE, marginal purchasing, bear raiding, specialists, pools,
etc. With Exhibit No. 24, consisting of text of *Constitution of the
New York Stock Exchange* as of October 28, 1931. With statistical
tables.

251. Vernon, Raymond. *The Regulation of Stock Market Members.*
New York: Columbia University Press, 1941. 152 pages.

Concerns government and New York Stock Exchange regulation
of the stock market since 1929. Written by a member of the
Securities and Exchange Commission. Reviews earlier
investigations leading to regulation of the stock market: the
"Hughes Investigation" of 1909 and the Pujo Committee
investigations of 1912. Discusses self-regulatory efforts of the New
York Stock Exchange including regulations concerning margin
requirements and the specialist system. Analyzes: components of
the Securities Act of 1934; the effects of the Richard E. Whitney
case of 1938; and the Securities and Exchange Commission's
"Segregation Report" of 1936. With a bibliography, statistical
tables, and index. Among statistical tables: "Margin Accounts
Carried by Nineteen Member Firms of the New York Stock

Exchange, May 1937, to June 1938"; "Stock Price Changes Related to Transactions of Specialists on the New York Stock Exchange on the Same Day"; "Price Changes Related to Transactions of Members (Except as Specialists) Initiated on the Floor of the New York Stock Exchange on the Same Day"; and "Sources of Funds for Loans Made to Customers by New York Stock Exchange Firms Carrying Margin Accounts." With a bibliography.

252. *Wall Street and Regulation.* Edited by Samuel L. Hayes, III. Boston, Massachusetts: Harvard Business School Press, 1987. 206 pages.

Series of essays examine regulation of the financial services sector from the 1930s through the 1980s, with brief discussion of regulation from 1837-1933. Contents: Introduction, by Samuel L. Hayes, III; "Regulation-Defined Financial Markets: Fragmentation and Integration in Financing Services," by Richard H.K. Vietor; "Breaking Relationships: the Advent of Price Banking in the United States," by David W. Meerschwam; "The Institutionalization of Wealth: Changing Patterns of Investment Decision Making," by Jay O. Light and Andre F. Perold; "Underwriting Regulation and the Shelf Registration Phenomenon," by Joseph Auerbach and Samuel L. Hayes, III; "Wall Street and the Public Interest," by Warren A. Law; and "Conclusions," by Samuel L. Hayes III. Analyzes: Glass-Steagall Act; the Securities Act of 1933; the Securities Exchange Act of 1934; and insider trading. With bibliographical references.

253. "Wall Street Housecleaning." *Business Week* (August 12, 1933): 11-12.

Concerns reforms in trading adopted by the New York Stock Exchange. Among reforms: an increase in margin requirements; detailed reports are required for pool and syndicate operators; and curbing activities of customers' men. Relates plans of President Franklin D. Roosevelt to bring the NYSE under federal regulation. Written during the investigations by the Senate Currency and Banking Committee.

254. Warshow, Robert Irving. *Understanding the New Stock Market.*
New Rev. ed. New York: Blue Ribbon Books, 1937. 248 pages.

Guide to the stock market in light of the Securities Exchange Act
of 1934. Defines terms such as "asked price," "bears," "bulls,"
"clearing," "margin," "pool," "S.E.C.," "unlisted stocks," etc.
Describes history and organization of the New York Stock
Exchange and the Senate Committee Hearings of 1933-34. With the
text of The Securities Exchange Act of 1934,a bibliography, a
glossary of terms, trading rules issued by the Securities and
Exchange Commission, ticker symbols of the New York Stock
Exchange.

*   Weissman, Rudolph Leo. *The New Wall Street.* See item 277
below

255. Wendt, Paul Francis. *The Classification and Financial Experience
of the Customers of a Typical New York Stock Exchange Firm
from 1933 to 1938.*   Submitted in partial fulfillment of the
requirements for the Degree of Doctor of Philosophy in the
Faculty of Political Science, Columbia University. Maryville,
Texas, 1941. 269 pages.

Presents statistical and factual information regarding types of
accounts found in the clientele of a typical New York Stock
Exchange firm and the actual financial experiences of these
customers from 1933 to 1938.   Includes statistical tables and
bibliography. Among appendixes: the Securities Exchange Act of
1934 and a reprint of an article from the *New York Times*, June 22,
1937: "New Wall Street Code Aims to Win Public," concerning the
first code by a group of employees of NYSE firms.

256. Whitney, Richard. *The Functions of Stock Exchanges: A Collection
of Addresses.* New York: New York Stock Exchange, 1936. 289
pages.

Series of addresses by the New York Stock Exchange President from 1930-1935. Addresses discuss the organization and role of the NYSE. Contents: "The Work of the Stock Exchange in the Panic of 1929," address before the Boston Association of Stock Exchange Firms, at Boston, Massachusetts, June 10, 1930; "Trade Depressions and Stock Panics," Address before the Merchants' Association of New York, at New York, N.Y., September 9, 1930; "Speculation," Address before the Illinois Chamber of Commerce, at Chicago, Illinois, October 10, 1930; "The Place of the Stock Exchange in American Business," Address before the New York State Bankers Association at New York City, January 22, 1931; "Public Opinion and the Stock Market," Address before the Boston Chamber of Commerce, Boston, Massachusetts, January 29, 1931; "Business Honesty," Address before the Philadelphia Chamber of Commerce, at Philadelphia, Pennsylvania, April 24, 1931; "Economic Law in Business," Address before the Merchants' Association of New York, at New York, N.Y., September 17, 1931; "Short Selling," Address before the Hartford Chamber of Commerce, Hartford, Connecticut, and over the National Network of the Columbia Broadcasting System, October 16, 1931; "Short Selling and Liquidation," Address before the Syracuse Chamber of Commerce, Syracuse, New York, and over the Nationwide Network of the Columbia Broadcasting System, Inc., December 15, 1931; "The New York Stock Exchange," Address before the Industrial Club of St. Louis, at St. Louis, Missouri, and over the Nationwide Network of the National Broadcasting Company, Inc., September 27, 1932; "Security Investors and the Future," Address before the Cleveland Chamber of Commerce, Cleveland, Ohio, February 28, 1933; "Economic Freedom," Address at a Dinner of the Chicago Association of Stock Exchange Firms, at Chicago, Illinois, December 10, 1934; "The Investor and Security Markets," An Address over the NBC-WEAF Network of the National Broadcasting Company, January 30, 1935; "Industry and Security Markets," An Address over the NBC-WEAF Network of the National Broadcasting Company, February 6, 1935; "Security Markets and the People," An Address over the NBC-WEAF Network of the National Broadcasting Company, February 13, 1935; and "Elements of Recovery, Address at the 53rd Annual Dinner of the Engineers' Society of Western Pennsylvania, Pittsburgh, Pennsylvania, February 26, 1935. Includes index.

257. Whitney, Richard. "In Defense of the Stock Exchange." *Christian Century* 50 (August 9, 1933): 1009-1011.

Reviews the role of the stock exchanges and refutes many misconceptions concerning them. Stresses the importance of the stock exchanges in the economic system. Defines stock exchanges as organizations by means of which money can be exchanged for securities or securities for money. Provides brief history of the New York Stock Exchange as well as the London Exchange and the New York Curb Exchange. Discusses organization and self-regulation of exchanges including the New York Stock Exchange.

258. "Whitney Confers with Roosevelt: Stock Exchange Head and Its Counsel Tell of Reforms under Consideration." *New York Times* 82 (April 6, 1933): 3.

Results of White House conference between President Franklin D. Roosevelt and Richard Whitney indicated that Roosevelt would not be diverted from his efforts to bring stock exchanges under Federal supervision. Whitney had reported to Roosevelt plans for corrective changes in NYSE practices. According to some sources, Whitney's plans contained measures designed to lessen brokers' loans, curb pool operations, and add further restrictions on short selling.

259. Wickwire, Arthur M. *The Weeds of Wall Street*. New York: Newcastle Press, 1933. 234 pages.

Stated purpose is "to take the layman behind the scenes in Wall Street and show him its abuses." Alerts readers to operation of speculative pools and urges support of readers to write their Congressmen urging prohibition of pools. Author draws upon twenty-five year experience as a member of the New York Stock Exchange. Provides: transcript of hearings by Senate Committee on Banking and Currency, 1932-33; case studies of Kolster Radio Corporation, Anaconda Copper Company, and Radio Corporation of America; and viewpoints offered on the market by Henry Clews, Edmund Clarence Stedman, Forrest Davis, Earl Sparling, etc.

*   Wigmore, Barrie A. *The Crash and Its Aftermath: A History of Securities Markets in the United States, 1929-1933.* see item 233 below.

*   Winkelman, Barnie F. *Ten Years of Wall Street.* see item 198 above.

CHAPTER XIII
1935-1949

The time period covered from 1935-1949 encompasses the NYSE's establishment of the Conway Committee, which recommended organizational changes; the Richard Whitney embezzlement case; and the years of the Second World War.

Chapter XIII contains documents of great significance to the NYSE, among which are the *Conway Committee Report*; a collection of speeches by SEC Chairman, William O. Douglas; and the Securities and Exchange Commission's *In the Matter of Richard Whitney.* Contemporary accounts from periodicals of the time period 1935 to 1940 are also described. Other materials examine the effects of the Securities and Exchange Commission and market regulation. Additionally, the NYSE published its own periodical, *The Exchange*, which reported news of the Exchange as well as contemporary financial and economic developments. *The Exchange* began publication in 1939 and would cease publication in 1975.

*   Auchincloss, Louis. *The Embezzler.* see item 20 above.

*   Borkin, Joseph. *Robert R. Young: The Populist of Wall Street.* see item 27 above.

*   *Conway Committee Report*, see item 268 below.

260. "Crash! Crash! Crash!" *Time* 30 (September 30, 1937): 55.

Discusses the two crashes during the Fall of 1937 during which 463 stocks set new lows. In August 1937, NYSE President Charles R. Gay had warned the Securities and Exchange Commission that the thinness of trading, resulting directly from market regulation, would produce "abnormal market conditions." Restriction that affects the market most during periods of pronounced market weakness is regulation of insider operations. Other possible causes cited were a war scare and the Federal Reserve's announcement that it should ease its 55% margin requirements.

261. Dolley, James C. "The Effect of Government Regulation on the Stock-Trading Volume of the New York Stock Exchange." *American Economic Review* 28 (March 1938): 8-26.

Analyzes effects of Federal regulation on the organized securities markets, including the New York Stock Exchange. Focuses on the effects of the Securities Exchange Act of 1934 which granted control to two Federal agencies extensive control over stock exchange trading and required registration of all national security exchanges and each stock and bond listed on such markets. Conclusions of author are: 1. during time period 1934 to 1937, the NYSE has become a markedly more discontinuous market for stocks; trading both by stock-exchange members and outside public has diminished noticeably in volume; there has been a marked decline in floor trading; regulations relating to initial margin requirements have had the greatest effect on trading volume; and volume of odd-lot trading has increased both in absolute and relative amount. Among statistical tables are: "Average Daily Reported Volume of Stock Transactions on the New York Stock Exchange by Months--January, 1934, to November, 1937"; "Average Number of Shares Traded per Point of Change in the Dow-Jones Average of 70 Stock Prices, December, 1934 to October, 1937"; and "Average Spreads in Bid-Ask Quotations on a Sample of Common Stock Listed on the New York Stock Exchange for May, 1935, and May, 1937." Includes bibliographical references.

262. Douglas, William O. *Democracy and Finance: The Addresses and Public Statements of William O. Douglas as Member and Chairman of the Securities and Exchange Commission.* Edited, with an introduction and notes, by James Allen. New Haven: Yale University Press, 1940. 301 pages.

Collection of Douglas' addresses and public statements during the late 1930s relating to the work of the Securities and Exchange Commission. Introduction, by James Allen tells of events leading up to establishment of SEC and includes a biographical sketch of Douglas. Allen also provides a brief review of events leading up to each address. Consists of Parts: I. Democracy in Finance; II. Stock Exchanges; III. Public Utilities; IV. Reform of Corporate Reorganizations; V. Administrative Government; and VI. Education in Government and Law. Part II concerns reorganization of the exchanges. Part II includes: Douglas' public statement, released November 23, 1937 calling for reorganization of exchanges, especially the NYSE; "Reorganization of the New York Stock Exchange," a speech presented on May 20, 1938 at the Association of Stock Exchange Firms' dinner to honor NYSE's Conway Committee; "Margins and Markets," an address given in 1936 at the University of Virginia, Institute of Public Affairs; "Customers' Men," a speech presented in 1936 at the NYSE's Stock Exchange Institute; and "On Amending the Law," a statement issued in response to proposals for changes, by representatives from the nation's securities markets, in Securities Act of 1933 and the Securities Exchange Act of 1934. Douglas' statements and addresses called for cooperative efforts between the SEC and the exchanges and praised reforms made by the NYSE in 1938. Douglas also expressed opposition to weakening laws against market manipulation. With bibliographical references and a portrait of Douglas.

263. Douglas, William O. *Go East Young Man: The Early Years: The Autobiography of William O. Douglas.* New York: Random House, 1974, 493 pages.

In a section of his autobiography, Douglas describes his experiences as Chairman of the Securities and Exchange

Commission during the late 1930s. Relates events of the NYSE market decline of Fall 1937; NYSE's 1938 reforms; and the Richard Whitney embezzlement scandal.

264. Hardy, Charles Oscar. *Odd-Lot Trading on the New York Stock Exchange.* Washington, D.C.: Brookings Institution, 1939. 192 pages.

Results of an investigation on the structure and functioning of the odd-lot market of the New York Stock Exchange. "Odd-Lots" are defined as orders for smaller quantitites of shares and less than round lot remainders of larger orders. Explains Odd-Lot trading system and its organization.

265. Hutchinson, Keith. "Wall Street in Two Wars." *Nation* 154 (April 4, 1942): 396-397.

Compares and contrasts stock prices during World War I and World War II. With a chart, "Wall Street in Two Wars," concerning Dow Jones Averages of industrial stocks for 1914-1918 and 1939-1941.

*   Macaulay, Frederick Robertson. *Short Selling on the New York Stock Exchange.* see item 299 below.

266. "Mr. Chocolate." *Time* 32 (August 15, 1938): 42-47.

Chronicle of 1937-38 at the New York Stock Exchange, culminating with the appointment of William McChesney Martin, Jr. as its President. Martin was known as "Mr. Chocolate" because of habit of ordering hot chocolates at Sardi's. Tells of 1937 market break for which then President, Charles Gay blamed too strict regulation by the Securities and Exchange Commission. SEC Chairman William O. Douglas indicated that reform of the NYSE was in order and offered a choice between self-reform or being placed under control of SEC. Gay subsequently appointed a committee headed by Carle Cotter Conway, chairman of Continental Can. William McChesney Martin, Jr. was a member of the Conway Committee. The NYSE endorsed Conway Committee recommendations. Resistance to NYSE reorganization was weakened by the Richard Whitney embezzlement scandal; Whitney, represented the "Old Guard," resistant to NYSE reorganization. Martin, at age 31, in 1938 became the first paid NYSE President. Relates biographical background of Martin, his education, personal appearance, business career, and goals as NYSE President.

267. New York Stock Exchange. *The Exchange*. New York: NYSE, V. 1, 1939 - V. 36, 1975.

Features articles on the NYSE and current trends in the economy. Some articles are written by NYSE Presidents. Among regular departments: a statistics section; new companies on the NYSE; book reviews; and a ticker symbol directory. Ceased publication in 1975.

268. New York Stock Exchange. *Final Report of the Committee for the Study of the Organization and Administration of the New York Stock Exchange*. New York: NYSE, 1938. 5 pages.

Report by Conway Committee, appointed by NYSE President, Charles R. Gay for study of the exchange's organization and administration. The Chairman of the Committee was Carle C. Conway. Among recommendations: the office of Chairman of the Board be created and a full-time paid President be elected; reduction of standing committees; reduction of number of members of Board of Governors; revision and simplification of the Constitution and Rules; after serving two consecutive terms as a governor, members should be ineligible for election for at least one year; and the board should include representatives of the public, office partners of New York-based member firms and of firms based outside of New York. The Conway Committee report was submitted for approval in January 1938 and approved in May 1938.

269. New York Stock Exchange. *Program to Afford Additional Protection to the Public in Its Brokerage Dealings with Member Firms of the New York Stock Exchange.* New York: NYSE, 1938.

Program was adopted by the New York Stock Exchange Board of Governors on October 26, 1938. Calls for reforms involving: reporting of member borrowings, an increase in audits of members' financial statements; a prohibition of loans subject to various conditions; capital requirements; margin accounts; partners' accounts; more intensive control and supervision of NYSE members; and stricter enforcement of member firms' business practices.

*   New York Stock Exchange. *Report of the President.* see item 190 above.

270. Schwed, Fred, Jr. *Where are the Customers' Yachts? or A Good Hard Look at Wall Street.* Illustrated by Peter Arno. New York: Simon and Schuster, 1940. 215 pages.

A first-hand look at Wall Street from 1927-1940. Concerns: the New York Stock Exchange, the Securities and Exchange Commission, the consequences of the 1929 Crash, investing and speculating, etc. Defines and explains terms, among which are: margins, bear raiding, options, and specialists. Title is from question of an out-of-town visitor to New York after a tour guide tells him to look at the bankers' and brokers' yachts. With cartoons by Peter Arno.

*   Seligman, Joel. *The Transformation of Wall Street: A History of the Securities and Exchange Commission and Modern Corporate Finance.* see item 247 above.

271. Shultz, Birl E. *Stock Exchange Procedure.* New York: New York Stock Exchange Institute, March 1936. 102 pages.

Manual of NYSE procedures designed for prospective and new employees and for students of the New York Stock Exchange Institute's course, "the Work of the Stock Exchange." Covers: the NYSE in history; the need for and function of stock exchanges; and procedure and operation of the NYSE. Among illustrations: trading posts; the floor of the Exchange; and the Bond Floor. With bibliographical references and a series of questions at the end of each chapter.

*   Sloane, Leonard. *The Anatomy of the Floor: The Trillion Dollar Market at the New York Stock Exchange.* see item 324 below.

272. Sobel, Robert. *N.Y.S.E.: A History of the New York Stock Exchange, 1935-1975.* New York: Weybright and Talley, 1975. 398 pages.

History of the NYSE in three phases: 1935-1941, covering the time of the New Deal and Depression under leadership of Charles Gay and William McChesney Martin, Jr.; 1941-1966, considered by many to be the greatest age in Exchange history, under leadership of Emil Schram and G. Keith Funston; and 1967-1975, a period of stress and slow change. Describes organizational changes at the NYSE during this time period. With essay on research methodology and a bibliography.

273. "Stock Crash Blame: SEC and New York Exchange Pass Buck to Each Other. More "Heat" Expected." *Business Week* (December 4, 1937): 20, 22.

Concerns responsibility for market break of Autumn 1937. As a result, SEC Chairman William O. Douglas demanded a NYSE housecleaning, suggesting reduction in number of brokers and advocating paid officers at the NYSE. NYSE President Charles R. Gay countered that the NYSE always had worked with the SEC and would continue to do so. He is planning a committee study of the possibility of paid executives who would not be members. Furthermore, the idea of paid executives was discussed on Wall

Street before the SEC was organized. Statistics indicate that there are not enough statistics to prove either side's case.

274. Stone, I.F. "Questions on the Whitney Case." *Nation* 148 (January 14, 1939): 55-58.

Considers various questions involving the Richard Whitney case. Among these questions were: what excuse had Richard Whitney given his brother for need of such a large amount of money?; had Richard Whitney told his brother he had hypothecated Stock Exchange securities?; and did his brother know he was insolvent. These answers had not been supplied by District Attorney Dewey or Attorney General Bennett during the indictments. Reviews findings of the Securities and Exchange Commission which increased public knowledge concerning the facts of the case. Studies NYSE's role, especially possible evidence that members of the Exchange or their partners knew of Whitney's criminal conduct and/or condition of his firm. Provides excerpts from the SEC hearings concerning the Whitney case.

275. Twentieth Century Fund. *The Security Markets: Findings and Recommendations of a Special Staff of the Twentieth Century Fund.* Director of Survey: Alfred L. Bernheim. Staff Contributors: N.R. Danielian, et al. Editors: Alfred L. Bernheim and Margaret Grant Schneider. New York: Twentieth Century Fund, 1935. Reprint: New York: Arno Press, 1975. 865 pages.

Full text of research findings of the Twentieth Century Fund's Survey of the Security Markets. Summary of recommendations is found in Twentieth Century Fund's *Stock Market Control*, see item above. Published after passage of the Securities Act of 1933 and the Securities Exchange Act of 1934. Editors note that many weaknesses emphasized in the Twentieth Century Fund's surveys have been largely corrected because of the Federal legislation. Studies: the stock exchange in economic theory; the history, organization, Constitution; reforms; and operations of the NYSE and other major exchanges; margin buying; short selling; the work of the specialist; manipulation; foreign stock exchanges; financial

information sources; recommendations for reform; and analyses of
the Securities Act of 1933 and the Securities Exchange Act of 1934.
Appendixes include: statistical data on numbers of stockholders;
prices of exchange memberships; numbers of stocks listed on major
exchanges; principal committees of the New York Stock Exchange;
rules of stock exchanges regulating broker-customer relationships;
and New York Stock Exchange reforms, 1898-1934. With statistical
charts and tables and a bibliography.

276. United States. Securities and Exchange Commission. *In the Matter
of Richard Whitney, Edwin D. Morgan, Jr., F. Kingsley
Rodewald, Henry D. Mygatt, Daniel G. Condon, John J.
McManus, and Estate of John A. Hayes, individually and as
partners doing business as Richard Whitney & Co.* Washington,
D.C.: Government Printing Office, 1939. 3 vol. in one.

Contents: V. 1. Report on Investigation; V. 2. Transcript of
Hearings; and V. 3. Exhibits. Hearing by SEC concerning former
New York Stock Exchange President Richard Whitney's
embezzlement of customers' funds. Whitney was expelled from the
New York Stock Exchange on March 17, 1938. He was arrested on
two separate indictments that charged him with grand larceny in the
first degree, he pleaded guilty, and was sentenced to an
indeterminate term of five to ten years in Sing Sing Prison. Hearing
reports recommendations of the NYSE for its reorganization and
reform to prevent a recurrence of such a case. Includes testimonies
of witnesses: Richard Whitney; Charles R. Gay, President of the
NYSE; John Pierpont Morgan; Edward H.H. Simmons; and
George Whitney. Recommends: 1. An increase of financial
statement requirements and questionnaires among members and a
required annual independent audit of firms doing a public business;
2. A prohibition of margin transactions and maintenance of margin
accounts by member firms and by partners of member firms doing
business with the public; 3. Establishing a 15 to 1 ratio between
broker's indebtedness and his working capital; 4. A separation of
brokerage and dealer capital; 5. All members and member firms
and partners report to NYSE all substantial loans made to or by
such persons or firms except those fully secured by readily
marketable collateral; 6. Current underwriting information be filed

with NYSE on weekly basis; and 7. The establishment for NYSE
members of a central security depository.

*   Vernon, Raymond. *The Regulation of Stock Exchange Members*.
     see item 251 above.

*   *Wall Street and Regulation*. Edited by Samuel L. Hayes, III. see
     item 252 above.

277. Weissman, Rudolph L. *The New Wall Street*. New York and
     London: Harper & Brothers, 1939. 308 pages.

     Analyzes changes on Wall Street from 1933 through 1938.
     Concentrates on the following groups within the financial district:
     members of the New York Stock Exchange; partners or officers;
     salesmen and customers' men; research; traders; and office
     workers. Discusses financial journalism and leading newspapers
     *Commercial and Financial Chronicle, Barron's, Wall Street
     Journal, Financial World, The Magazine of Wall Street,* and
     Economist. Reviews the organization, history, and work of the
     Securities and Exchange Commission. Analyzes recent reforms of
     the NYSE and studies implications of the Richard Whitney case.
     Appendixes consist of: I. New Securities Regulation; II. Summary
     of Part II of the Report of the Securities and Exchange Commission
     in the Whitney Investigation--Recommendations of the New York
     Stock Exchange and the Commission; III. Program to Afford
     Additional Protection to the Public in Its Brokerage Dealings with
     Member Firms of the New York Stock Exchange. With a
     bibliography of Government Publications and secondary sources.

*   Wendt, Paul Francis. *The Classification and Financial Experience
     of the Customers of a Typical New York Stock Exchange Firm
     from 1933 to 1938.* see item 255 above.

*   *Whitney Report*, see item 276 above.

CHAPTER XIV
1950-1987

The years covered in Chapter XIV began with years of a bull market in the 1950s; continued through a market break in May 1962, significant legislation by the SEC in the 1960s; the time of financial difficulties for NYSE member firms in the late 1960s; important legislation in the 1970s which brought about the end of the NYSE fixed brokerage commission rate structure; development of technological innovations at the NYSE during the 1970s and 1980s; and opening of the New York Futures Exchange in 1980, as a subsidiary of the NYSE. The time period covered ends just prior to the 1987 Crash on October 19.

This chapter contains listings for significant reports of the time among which are the Securities and Exchange Commission's *Special Study* (1963); William McChesney Martin's report (1971); the NYSE's *Stock Market Under Stress* (1963); and texts of the Securities Acts Amendments of 1964 and 1975. Frequently cited as sources in histories of this time period and described here are works by Donald T. Regan, Chris Welles, Richard Ney, John Brooks, and Robert Sobel.

278. Babcock, Charles and Mitch Betts. "Stock-Watch Tools Lag Behind Crooked Traders." *Computerworld* 20 (December 15, 1986): 1, 12.

Describes stock-watch software which monitors fluctuations in price or volume of individual issues. The NYSE and American Stock Exchange use software programs to match stock data against a forty-day history that indicates deviations within that time frame. Contends that, even with software, detecting insider trading is difficult.

279. Baruch, Hurd. *Wall Street: Security Risk.* Washington, D.C.: Acropolis Books, 1971. 356 pages.

Written by Special Counsel, Division of Trading and Markets, U.S. Securities and Exchange Commission. Recommends free and honest competition on Wall Street. Among problems discussed are: continuing use and misuse of customers' funds and securities by their brokers; securities industry's inability to process customers' orders promptly and accurately during record trading volume of 1967-68 and financial crisis of 1969-70; and non-functioning of the self-regulation system during the late 1960s. Concentrates on activities at the NYSE during the late 1960s. Presents case studies and includes bibliographical references.

280. Baumol, William J. *The Stock Market and Economic Efficiency.* The Millar lectures; no. 6, 1965. New York: Fordham University Press, 1965. 95 pages.

Analysis of the stock market by an economic theorist. Studies the stock exchange as a close approximation to a perfect market; the role of the specialist; and security prices and long-run competitive equilibrium. Examines the Random-Walk hypothesis. Includes bibliographical references.

281. *The Big Board* [film] s.l.: On Film, Inc., 1958. 16mm, b & w., 13 minutes. sound.

Explains operations of the market, role of specialist, institutional investing, and large block transactions.

282. "Big Board Subsidiary For Futures Trading Opens Doors Today."
     Wall Street Journal 196 (August 7, 1980): 23.

Reports that first day of trading on the New York Futures
Exchange (NYFE), the NYSE's futures exchange begins on August
7, 1980. On its first day, the NYFE will offer futures contracts in
five foreign currencies and in 20-year Treasury bonds. In June
1979, the NYSE had applied to the Commodity Futures Trading
Commission for permission to open a futures market.

283. Black, Hillel. *The Watchdogs of Wall Street*. New York: Morrow,
     1962. 241 pages.

Written at the time of the Securities and Exchange Commission's
investigation of the securities markets (1962-63). Reviews role of
the SEC from its establishment in 1934 and presents various case
studies of the SEC's investigations. Includes an interview with
Ferdinand Pecora, counsel for the Senate Bank and Currency
Committee and one of the original Securities and Exchange
Commissioners. The final chapter explains why the SEC is
conducting the 1962-63 investigations. With bibliographic citations.

284. Brooks, John. *The Go-Go Years*. New York: Weybright and
     Talley, 1973. 375 pages.

In-depth study of Wall Street during the 1960s. "Go-go" refers
to a method of rapid in-and-out trading of huge blocks of stock for
the purpose of fast, large profits; the term was used with specific
application to operation of certain mutual funds. Studies
contributions of key individuals: Henry Ross Perot; Edward M.
Gilbert; William Lucius Carey, chairman of the SEC; William
McChesney Martin, former NYSE Chairman; Gerald Tsai, Jr.;
Meshulam Riklis; Charles Bluhdorn; and Bernard L. Lasker, NYSE
Chairman. Reviews various SEC investigations and legislation.
Studies ramifications of 1970 Crash. Research based on personal
accounts of participants and observers as well as periodical,
newspaper, and book materials. Includes bibliographical references.

285. Cary, William L. and Walter Werner. "Outlook for Securities Markets." *Harvard Business Review* 49 (July 1971): 16-18.

Describes securities markets' conditions during the late 1960s-early 1970s. Pinpoints recent problems of the markets as: the unprecedented and unplanned rise in trading activity volume on the NYSE; the increase in trade in mutual funds and pension funds; fragmention of the central market; a progressive shorter measure of investment performance; operating problems among broker-dealers due to increased volume; fragile capital structures of many broker-dealer firms; and fixed commission rates structure among the exchanges. Current market trends described by the authors are: technological developments; the possibility of a future single central market; institutional membership; competitive commission rates; changes in the nature of broker-dealer units; and industry concentration. Also examines recent SEC actions and changes made at the NYSE by its President Haack. With bibliographic citations.

286. Commerce Clearing House. *Securities Acts Amendments of 1964, with explanation, as signed by the President, August 20, 1964; Public law 88-467.* Chicago: Commerce Clearing House, 1964. 94 pages.

Text plus explanation of the Securities Acts Amendments of 1965. The stated purpose of the Amendments was "to amend the Securities Act of 1933, as amended, and the Securities Exchange Act of 1934, as amended, to extend disclosure requirements to the issuers of additional publicly traded securities, to provide for an improved qualification and disciplinary procedures for registered brokers and dealers, and for other purposes." The Amendments were designed to strengthen the protection afforded to the investing public by various securities laws. The Amendments stem from recommendations offered in the SEC's *Special Study of the Securities Industry.*

287. Conference on Securities Regulation. Duke University, 1964. *Conference on Securities Regulation: Conference at Durham, North Carolina, November 6-7, 1964.* Edited by Robert H.

Mundheim. New York: Commerce Clearing House, 1965. 232 pages.

Proceedings of a two-day Conference on Securities Regulation. Contents: "Broker-Dealer Regulation at the Federal Level," by Manuel F. Cohen; "State Regulation of Broker-Dealers," by Charles E. Rickerhauser, Jr.; "Self-Regulation," by Marc A. White; "Critique of the Three-Pronged System of Regulation," by Richard W. Jennings; "The Boiler-Shop Cases and the Reasonable Basis Rule," by Harry Heller; "Suitability," by Thomas A. O'Boyle; "The Broker-Dealer Looks at the Regulatory Scheme and Content," by Donald T. Regan; "The Economic Impact of Securities Regulation," by Dr. Irwin Friend; "Institutional Investors in the Equity Market," by Gordon D. Henderson; "Trust Companies and Banks as Institutional Investors," by Charles W. Buek; "Relation of the Individual Investor to the Institutional Investor," by Leon T. Kendall; "The Third Market," by Frank Weeden; "The Life Insurance Company as an Institutional Investor," by Frank J. Hoenemeyer, Jr.; "Impact of Institutional Investor on Equity Financing," by Dr. Roger F. Murray; and "The Institutional Investor as Shareholder," by Fred E. Brown. Includes essays on the effect of SEC recommendations and legislation on the NYSE.

288. *Crouse-Hind Company Listing* [film] New York: New York Stock Exchange, 1966. 16mm, b & w print, silent, 3 min.

Produced on the occasion of the listing of Crouse-Hind Company (CHI) manufacturer of the electrical conduit fittings, outdoor lighting equipment and traffic control systems. With shots of Federal Hall, the NYSE facade, Broad and Wall Streets, brokers and others at Post 4 on the NYSE floor.

289. Doede, Robert William. "The Monopoly Power of the New York Stock Exchange." Ph.D. Dissertation. University of Chicago, 1967. 104 pages.

Examines and analyzes the NYSE's characteristics as "a cartel in an otherwise competitive industry" (p. 4) and its concomitant role as the dominant firm in the organized securities exchanges industry. Describes the history of the NYSE as an organized monopoly, presents evidence demonstrating that the successful maintenance of the monopoly is due to economies of scale; and presents a model to measure extent of the NYSE's monopoly power. Concludes that the NYSE is without question a natural monopoly and indicates that exchanges represent an important area for future economic research. Studies economic implications of NYSE's fixed commission rate schedule. Includes a table, "History of Stock Exchanges in New York City: 1792-1935, containing names of exchanges and their years of existence. With statistical tables and bibliographical references.

* Ehrlich, Judith Ramsey and Barry J. Rehfeld. *The New Crowd: The Changing of the Jewish Guard on Wall Street.* see item 34 above.

290. *Eleventh Billion Share* [film] New York: New York Stock Exchange, 1967. 16mm, b & W, sound, 1 min.

Report on the listing of Northeast Utilities, marking the eleventh billion share listed on the NYSE. Also discusses the various industries represented on the NYSE.

291. Elias, Christopher. *Fleecing the Lambs.* Chicago: Henry Regnery, 1971. 246 pages.

An inside look at the NYSE by a former employee. Profiles various individuals at the Exchange including Presidents Robert W. Haack and G. Keith Funston. Presents a critical analysis of the NYSE specialist system. Relates past history of Wall Street and the NYSE describing such events as the Gold Corner, the Erie Railroad War, and the Richard Whitney case. Studies role of the Securities and Exchange Commission regarding Wall Street reforms. Expresses concern for the plight and the needs of the individual investor. Calls for major reforms on the NYSE.

292. Freund, William C. "A New World at the New York Stock Exchange." *Journal of Accounting, Auditing & Finance* 1 (Winter 1986): 83-86.

Describes major trends and changes in the NYSE and other securities markets. Discussed are: the transformation of the NYSE from a private club to a competitive and innovative institution which operates in the public interest; the inclusion of trading in options and futures; automation of trading; and development of international trading links.

293. Friend, Irwin and Marshall E. Blume. *The Consequences of Competitive Commissions on the New York Stock Exchange.* Philadelphia, Pa.: University of Pennsylvania. The Wharton School, April 1972. 143 pages.

Examines probable impact of competitive commission rates on all major sectors, most likely to be affected among which are broker-dealers, investors, and the markets for outstanding and new stock issues. Years of statistical study are: 1965-1970. Concludes that consequences of competitive NYSE commission rate structure would be beneficial, improving the efficiency of the stock market. With statistical tables and bibliographical references.

*   Galbraith, John Kenneth. "The Great Crash," see item 212 above.

294. Gardner, Deborah S. "Trading at the New York Stock Exchange." *NAHO* 13 (Spring-Summer 1981): 59-61.

Prepared by an archivist of the NYSE. Describes history of the NYSE from the Buttonwood Agreement in 1792 to the development of automated systems. Discusses structures of NYSE headquarters over the years to the building of its present location in 1903. With the installation of new trading posts on the NYSE, the old horseshoe posts have been removed and installed as exhibits at universities and museums including New York Metropolis Hall at the State Museum.

295. Gimlin, Hoyt. "Wall Street: 40 Years After the Crash," *Editorial Research Reports* No. 14, Vol. 2 (1969): 755-772.

Compares and contrasts the problems of the NYSE in 1969 with conditions during the 1929 Crash. Also provides brief histories of the Securities and Exchange Commission and the NYSE. Analyzes: the decline of stock prices in 1969; the effect of the decline on brokerage houses; the impact of institutional investors on the stock market; effects of automation; the Great Bull Market of the 1920s; the causes and effects of the 1929 crash; and regulation of the securities business and the role of the SEC.

*   Glynn, Lenny. "Arthur Cashin, Floor Broker, New York Stock Exchange." see item 40 above.

296. *Home Show* [film] New York: WNBC TV, 195?. 16mm, b & w, optical print, 12 min.

Excerpt from *Home Show*, April 17, 195-, hosted by Hugh Downs. Segment on the NYSE with Howard Whitman includes shots on the trading floor. Catherine Whittemore explains trading floor procedures. Features discussion of NYSE membership, the Buttonwood Agreement Story, the Tontine Coffee House, and the early history of the Exchange. Also explains the trading post, stock tickers, and how to read the ticker tape.

297. Jennings, Richard W. "The New York Stock Exchange and the Commission Rate Struggle." *The Business Lawyer 21* (November 1965): 159-183.

Analysis of the commission system on the NYSE and the proposed changes for the rate structure. The NYSE commission rate structure is designed to safeguard the commission system and prevent price cutting. The recent challenges to the rate structure are from two sources: nonmember professionals and institutional investors. Describes business practices that erode the "commission rate fortress"; these are: a) the "end run"; b) the give-up or directed split; and c) the Third Market conducted by securities dealers who are not members of any exchange and are free of Exchange restrictions including off-board trading and minimum commissions. Discusses the SEC's *Special Study* and the role of the SEC in the commission rate issue. Cites and reviews court cases dealing with the commission rate structure. Calls for concentrated study of the commission rate structure to analyze improvements needed.

298. Laderman, Jeffrey M. and Bruce Nussbaum. "The Big Board's Crusade Against Program Trading." *Business Week* Issue 2990 (March 23, 1987): 134-138.

Reports that NYSE Chairman John J. Phelan, Jr. will announce the appointment of the head for a study sponsored by NYSE concerning program trading. NYSE study will examine problems of program trading including destabilizing effects in the market and the potential for manipulation.

299. Macaulay, Frederick Robertson, in collaboration with David Durand. *Short Selling on the New York Stock Exchange.* New York: Twentieth Century Fund, 1951. 66 leaves.

Study of the effects of short selling on the NYSE, with statistical analysis of the time period 1929-1948. Records early history of short selling, describes basic characteristics of short selling on the NYSE, and motives of short sellers and their methods of operation.

* Marion, Larry. "John Phelan, Jr., Chairman and Chief Executive Officer, New York Stock Exchange." see item 62 above.

300. *Market in Motion* [film] s.l.: Vision Associates, 1970. 16mm color print, 13 min., optical sound.

Filmed in live action and graphic animation, explains NYSE functions, listed corporations, shareownership, member firm services, investment analysis and research, trading floor automation, and plans for a new NYSE building.

301. Martin, Ralph G. and Morton D. Stone. *Money, Money, Money: Wall Street in Words and Pictures*. Chicago: Rand McNally, 1960. 223 pages.

Chiefly photographs of activity in the Wall Street area. With section, "The Big Board," a series of photographs of the New York Stock Exchange, the building and a series of views of the trading floor, including activities of specialists. Also contains photographs of the American Stock Exchange, various brokerage houses, and investment clubs.

302. Martin, William McChesney, Jr. *The Securities Markets: A Report, with Recommendations*. Submitted to the Board of Governors of the New York Stock Exchange, August 5, 1971. New York: New York Stock Exchange, 1971. 26 pages.

Written by former President of the NYSE (1938-1941) who was commissioned to write a thorough study of the Constitution, rules, and procedures of the Exchange. Also, examines the securities industry as a whole. Considers the public interest as prime consideration in appraising the issues. Discusses implications of the crisis in the securities industry during the late 1960 - early 1970s marked by failure of some member firms. Presents recommendations to be implemented by the New York Stock Exchange alone; these are: reorganization of the NYSE; continuous review of member firms for financial soundness; additional regulation and improvement of the role of specialists and block positioners; prohibition of institutional membership as well as of member firm management of mutual funds; prohibition of crediting commissions against any fee charged for investment advice; and greater use of modern communication systems. Recommendations to be implemented by Congress, the SEC, and other Exchanges either acting alone or in concert with the NYSE are: development of a national exchange system providing a national auction market for each listed security; consideration of increased requirements for entry into securities business by broker-dealers; adoption of appropriate segregation requirements with respect to free-credit balances; resolution of differences which result in unequal regulation and elimination of the third market, preferably through development of national exchange system; additional time to the experiment with negotiated rates before implementing any further change; enactment of legislation granting anti-trust exemption to exchanges coexistent with SEC oversight; a coordinated effort to eliminate the stock certificate; and development of a consolidated exchange tape. Calls for cooperation from the exchanges, the SEC, the National Association of Securities Dealers, and Congress.

*   Marton, Andrew. "James Needham, Former Chairman, New York Stock Exchange." see item 63 above.

*   Marton, Andrew. "William Batten, Former Chairman, New York Stock Exchange." see item 64 above.

303. Mayer, Martin. *Wall Street: Men and Money.* Rev. ed. New York: Collier Books, 1962. 254 pages.

Study of Wall Street's financial markets: the New York Stock Exchange, the American Stock Exchange, the Over-the-Counter Exchange, money managers, etc. Defines key terms such as stocks and bonds, how they are issued, and how they are traded. Describes the NYSE's organization and events on the trading floor. Features interviews with key individuals, including G. Keith Funston, President of the New York Stock Exchange (1952).

*   Morgello, Clem. "Robert Haack, Former President, New York Stock Exchange." see item 66 above.

304. Murray, Roger F. "Urgent Questions about the Stock Market." *Harvard Business Review* 42 (September-October 1964): 53-59.

Studies ramifications of the SEC's *Special Study* of 1963. Four

central issues examined are: if the investing public are receiving
fair treatment in the securities markets; if the stock market's
behavior is exerting a healthy influence on the economy; are market
mechanisms able to make accurate verdicts on quality of managerial
performance?; and are markets dictating the cost and availability of
new equity capital effectively? States goal of regulation to assure
superior performance in the stock markets. Specific topics addressed
in the *Special Study* include: conflicts of interest; operations of
auction markets on the exchanges; selling practices; and availability
of information for investment decisions. Includes bibliographical
references.

305. New York Stock Exchange. *Board of Directors Meeting* [film]
New York: NYSE, 1972. 16mm. color print, optical sound, 4
minutes.

Photo session and introductory remarks of NYSE Chairman
Ralph D. Di Nunzio at the first meeting of the new Board of
Directors, July 13, 1972.

*   New York Stock Exchange. *The Exchange.* see item 267 above.

306. New York Stock Exchange. *International Competitiveness:
Perception and Reality.* New York: New York Stock Exchange,
August 1984. 62 pages.

Prepared and written by NYSE Senior Economist Mel
Colchamiro under direction of NYSE Chief Economist and Senior
Vice-President, Dr. William C. Freund. Analyzes economic trends,
with projections to 1995, for the international economy, including
employment, top occupations, exports, etc. With tables, charts, and
bibliographical references.

*   New York Stock Exchange. *Shareownership, 1952-* see item 455
below.

307. New York Stock Exchange. *The Stock Market Under Stress*. New York: New York Stock Exchange, March 1963. 60 pages.

Research study concerns the time period May 28 - May 31, 1962 when the market experienced sharp price declines and recoveries. Investigates: who was buying and who was selling; what were the characteristics of participating investors; and the activity of the Exchange's member organizations in response for the public's great demand for service. Compares and contrasts 1962 market break with the Stock Market Crash of 1929. Preface by NYSE President, G. Keith Funston. With statistical tables and charts, plus a detailed chronology of May 28 - 31, 1962.

308. New York Stock Exchange. Committee to Study the Stock Allocation System. *Report of the Committee to Study the Stock Allocation System*. New York: New York Stock Exchange, 1976. 2 vols.

Results of study is comprised of two volumes: V. 1: Findings, Conclusions, and Recommendations and V. 2: Supporting Documentation and Exhibits. The Committee was established by the NYSE Board of Directors by a resolution of May 23, 1974 in response to criticism of the allocation system voiced to the Floor Committee by certain floor members. Committee, under direction of William M. Batten, began active work in October 1974 and the report was distributed on January 27, 1976. Reviews, evaluates, and makes recommendations concerning allocation of stocks to specialist units, with specialist performance as a major factor in allocation decisions. Exhibits include: "The Origin, Development and Present Operations of the Exchange's Specialist System"; "The Origin, Development, and Present Operations of the Exchange's Stock Allocation System"; "History of the Exchange's Specialist Surveillance Programs"; "The Investigatory and Disciplinary Processes of the Exchange"; and "Automation and the Specialist." With statistical data on NYSE market activity and specialist statistical data. Lists criteria for stocks traded on the NYSE.

309. New York Stock Exchange. Office of Economic Research. *The Financial Health of U.S. Corporations: An Update.* New York: New York Stock Exchange, 1985. 23 pages.

Prepared and written by Senior Economist Mel Colchamiro under the direction of NYSE Chief Economist and Senior Vice-President, Dr. William C. Freund. Focuses attention on the state of United States corporate finances and the role that equity finance can play in strengthening corporate balance sheets. With charts and tables.

310. New York Stock Exchange. Office of Economic Research. *The Financial Health of U.S. Corporations: Current Assessment and Future Prospects.* New York: New York Stock Exchange, March 1983. 19 pages.

Prepared by NYSE Senior Economist, Mel Colchamiro under the direction of NYSE Chief Economist and Senior Vice-President, Dr. William C. Freund. Analyzes financial conditions of United States corporations. With tables and charts.

311. New York Stock Exchange. Quality of Markets Committee. *Report.*, New York: NYSE, 1981-

Annual report of the NYSE's Quality of Markets Committee whose chief responsibility is to provide high level focus on the quality of the market place. Members of the Committee prepare an annual report on market performance and make recommendations to strengthen the capabilities of NYSE's market system. Studied in reports are: market performance, Exchange systems such as ITS and DOT, and Exchange professionals. Includes statistical charts.

312. *New York Stock Exchange, 175th Anniversary, 1792-1967.* The Exchange, V. 28, no. 6, May 17, 1967. New York: New York Stock Exchange, 1967. 32 pages.

Special issue of the *Exchange* (see item 267 above) is dedicated to the NYSE on the 175th Anniversary of the signing of the Buttonwood Agreement. Features the articles: "The Dynamics of the New York Stock Exchange," by Keith Funston, President of the NYSE; "How Doth the Busy Little Woman: An Inquiry into the Financial Habits of Females, with Especial Reference to Investments and Husbands," by Emily Kimbrough; "The New York Stock Exchange Today: The People who use The Market, The Securities Traded, The People who make The Market," by John S. Tompkins; "Financial News: Meeting the 'Explosive Demand,'" by Edward W. Barrett; "Reflections of a Public Governor," by Jack I. Straus; "The Early Days," by Adolph Suehsdorf; "Vignettes..." a series of quotes about the NYSE and stock markets; "Half a Century on the Trading Floor," by Jack A. Coleman; "Tomorrow's Communicating World," by David Sarnoff; "The Investment World and the Future: The Next 25 Years," by Clem Morgello; and "Own Your Share of Colonial Business," a poem about the history of the NYSE, by Ogden Nash. With a photograph of the original Buttonwood Agreement and illustrations of: the signing of the Agreement; the floor of the NYSE; and the Tontine Coffee House.

313. Ney, Richard. *The Wall Street Jungle.* New York: Grove Press, 1970. 348 pages.

Study offers criticism of the New York Stock Exchange and American Stock Exchange and concentrates on their specialist systems. Analyzes the Securities and Exchange Commission's *Report of the Special Study of Securities Markets* (1963). With list of "Stock Symbols and Specialists," which was from the New York Stock Exchange publication, *Stocks and Specialists* (1969). Includes bibliographic notes and statistical charts.

314. *The One-Man Band that went to Wall Street.* [film] New York: New York Stock Exchange, 1973. 16mm, color, 16 min, optical sound.

Cartoon feature tells story of Fred Fugue, a one-man band to head of an entertainment conglomerate. Fugue incorporates his company, issues stocks, and lists on the NYSE. Examines history of NYSE, listing requirements, and discusses fluctuations in the market for Fugue's company.

315. Phelan, John J., Jr. "In Pursuit of Insider Traders." *Bankers Magazine* 169 (November/December 1986): 51-54.

Reports development at the NYSE of the automation of its audit and surveillance systems to monitor trades and expose unethical activities. The NYSE participates in an intermarket surveillance group. Additionally, approximately 2000 professionals in NYSE member firms examine trading that begins within their firms. Stresses that lack of integrity within the markets places the economic system at risk. Shareholders must be assured of a fair and honest market. Written by the Chairman of the New York Stock Exchange.

316. Platt, Gordon. "Big Board and Big Bang." *InterMarket* 4 (February 1987): 7-12.

Reports developments at the NYSE in light of the deregulation of London's financial market. Discusses difficulties of the NYSE maintaining its position as the world's largest exchange due to: competition from the Over-the-Counter market; automated trading systems; triple witching hours; commoditization of securities markets; increase in new financial instruments; and deregulation and globalization of markets. Recommends that the NYSE consider: electronic reporting facilities for off-hour trading designed to provide adequate protection for the individual investor and adequate service for institutional investors; investigation of international linkages; reform of its specialist system; and change in "one-share, one-vote" rule.

317. Regan, Donald T. *A View from the Street.* New York: New American Library, 1972. 220 pages.

Written by Chairman of the Board of Merrill Lynch, Pierce, Fenner & Smith. Recounts events on Wall Street during 1970-71, presents possible future on Wall Street, and includes detailed definitions of key terms and jargon. Analyzes market decline during May 25, 26, and 27, 1970 and what led up to it. Provides case studies of brokerage houses caught up in a paperwork crunch and reasons for failure of these brokerage houses. Studies the situation at Merrill Lynch during the early 1970s. Cross-references to definitions of terms are included in text; the letter "G" appearing after a word in the text indicates it is a term in the Glossary. Among definitions are: "Central Certificate Service of the New York Stock Exchange"; "Clearing Corporation (of the New York Stock Exchange)"; "Floor Broker"; "Gong"; "Haircutting"; "New York Stock Exchange Composite Index"; "New York Stock Exchange Revenues"; and "Specialist--Specialist's Post." Includes statistical charts and tables.

318. Robbins, Sidney. *The Securities Markets: Operations and Issues.* New York: Free Press, 1966. 303 pages.

Written by the Chief Economist for the Securities and Exchange Commission's *Special Study of the Securities Markets.* Discusses the securities markets in light of the *Special Study,* the Securities Acts Amendments of 1964, recent rules of the SEC, and changes adopted by self-regulatory agencies such as the NYSE. Provides in-depth coverage of organization of the NYSE and changes in its governance and structure throughout its history. Studies impact on securities markets of: the Securities Act of 1933; the Securities Exchange Act of 1934; the 1938 reorganization of the NYSE; the *Special Study*; and the Securities Acts Amendments of 1964. Includes bibliography.

319. Robinson, Ronald I. and Robert Bartett, Jr. "Uneasy Partnership: SEC/NYSE." *Harvard Business Review* 43 (January-February 1965): 76-88.

Studies key issues raised by the SEC's *Report of Special Study of Securities Markets* with emphasis on the questions: Is self regulation of the NYSE and other organized exchanges proving to be responsive to changing needs of investors?; Are the NYSE and other exchanges proving themselves capable of enough rigorous self-examination? and Has the SEC proved as creative as it might have been in seeking change? Discusses historical background of SEC from 1934 to the time of the *Special Study*. Focuses primarily on the NYSE in areas of floor trading, the role of the specialist, odd-lot transactions, short selling, and commission rates.

320. *Securities Acts Amendments of 1964.* Thomas G. Meeker, Reporter with an introduction by Philip A. Loomis, General Counsel, Securities and Exchange Commission. Philadelphia, Pa.: Joint Committee on American Legal Education, American Law Institute and the American Bar Association, 1964. 162 pages.

Outlines and analyzes the Securities Acts Amendments of 1964; studies the historical background of the Amendments; reviews provisions of the SEC's *Special Study*; and details revisions in the Securities Act of 1933 and the Securities Exchange Act of 1934 brought about in the Amendments. Covers topics of unlisted companies, proxy regulation, insiders' liability, regulation of entry into the securities business, accounting aspects, etc. Appendix includes copies of forms 10, 10-K, 11-K, 8-K, 9-K, Form 3, and Form 4. With bibliographical references and case citations.
See also item 286 above.

321. Seligman, Joel. *The SEC and the Future of Finance.* New York: Praeger, 1985. 378 pages.

Second part of Seligman's history of the SEC. First part is *The Transformation of Wall Street* (item 245). Covers the years 1977-1985, concentrating on securities and corporate law (enacted and proposed) involving: a national market system for stock trading; the options market; corporate disclosure; municipal disclosure; and regulation of banks as they enter securities and insurance fields. The author makes recommendations concerning legislation and stresses the fact that the SEC should place greater reliance on competition in securities regulation. Studies: implications, for securities markets, of the Securities Acts Amendments of 1975; developments at the NYSE, including the Consolidated Tape, ITS, DOT, and SuperDOT systems; and NYSE's plan to initiate trading in listed stock options. With bibliographical references.

322. Shultz, Birl E. *The Securities Market--and How it Works*. Rev.
     ed. Edited by Albert P. Squier. New York: Harper & Row,
     1963. 372 pages.

     Concerns primarily the NYSE, its history, functions,
     administration, listing of securities, trading, the role of the
     specialist, short selling, margin regulations, clearance and delivery
     of securities, etc. With sample forms, case studies, statistical tables,
     and bibliographical references.

*   *Securities Investor Protection Act of 1970*, see item 482 below.

*   Seligman, Joel. *The Transformation of Wall Street: A History of
     the Securities and Exchange Commission and Modern Corporate
     Finance*. see item 247 above.

323. Silberman, Lee. "Critical Examination of SEC Proposals."
     Harvard Business Review 42 (November-December 1964): 121-
     132.

     Analyzes the SEC's *Special Study of Securities Markets* with
     specific reference to its proposals regarding specialists, the "third
     market," brokerage house commissions, handling of odd-logs, floor
     trading, and organization of the NYSE. Reports NYSE President
     G. Keith Funston's reactions to the SEC's *Special Study* who stated
     that its recommendations would be reviewed "as though they had
     been made by management consultants engaged by us." (p. 121).
     A disagreement, however, developed between the SEC and NYSE
     regarding floor trading. Discusses: reasons for the SEC's
     investigation, developments on the NYSE since the release of the
     Special Study, and enactment of the Securities Acts Amendments of
     1964. Concludes that the *Special Study* offers constructive
     comments regarding the securities markets.

324. Sloane, Leonard. *The Anatomy of the Floor: The Trillion Dollar Market at the New York Stock Exchange.* Garden City, N.Y.: Doubleday, 1980. 228 pages.

Describes organization of the NYSE, projects future trends for the 1980s and relates activities on the floor of the Exchange. Some of research based on interviews with members and officers of the NYSE. Provides brief history of the NYSE from 1792 to 1980. Reviews contributions of those with major role in the NYSE's history, among which are Jacob Little, Jay Cooke, Jay Gould, and J.P. Morgan. Presents biographical profiles of NYSE Presidents and Chairmen: Richard Whitney, William McChesney Martin, Jr., Emil Schram, G. Keith Funston, Robert W. Haack, James J. Needham, and William M. Batten. Discusses activities of contemporary NYSE members including John J. Phelan, Jr. and Muriel Siebert. With bibliographical references.

325. Sobel, Robert. *The Last Bull Market: Wall Street in the 1960s.* New York: Norton, 1980. 242 pages.

History of the markets from the late 1940s to 1969. Explains causes of bull market and how it ended. Examines political and economic events of this time period. Studies roles of key people in the bull market: James Ling, Harold Geneen, Bernard Cornfeld, and Charles Bluhdorn. Includes bibliography.

*   Sobel, Robert. *N.Y.S.E.: A History of the New York Stock Exchange, 1935-1975.* see item 272 above.

326. Spray, David Eugene, ed. *The Principal Stock Exchanges of the World--Their Operation, Structure, and Development.* Washington, D.C.: International Economic Publishers, Inc., 1964. 428 pages.

Guide to international exchanges, with a section about the New York Stock Exchange, by Francis Higginson Philip, Investment Department, Empire Trust Co. Presents information on the NYSE's history, early regulation, significant dates, structure, constitution, trading procedures, listing requirements, commission rates, etc.

327. Stevens, Mark. *The Insiders: The Truth Behind the Scandal Rocking Wall Street*. Researched by Carol Bloom Stevens. New York: Putnam's, 1987. 256 pages.

Concerns insider trading scandals, notably those involving Dennis Levine and Ivan Boesky. Provides transcripts of key Securities and Exchange Commission testimony. Describes how insider traders were detected by the SEC. Studies possible prevention of future scandals.

328. Stoll, Hans R. *The Stock Exchange Specialist System: An Economic Analysis*. Monograph Series in Finance and Economics; monograph 1985-2. New York: Salomon Brothers Center for the Study of Financial Institutions/New York University. Graduate School of Business Administration, 1985. 53 pages.

Examines the stock exchange specialist system, emphasizing the New York Stock Exchange specialist. Studies role of specialist in historical context and in view of recent automated trading. Concludes that specialist system is central to operation of the NYSE. With bibliographical references and statistical tables.

329. Stone, James M. *One Way for Wall Street: A View of the Future of the Securities Industry*. Boston: Little, Brown, 1975. 187 pages.

Concerns future of the securities industry in light of developments during the late 1960s through the mid-1970s. Analyzes implications of the back office problem of investment firms during the late 1960s and the 1975 SEC ruling ending fixed commission rates. Discusses operations on the floor of the NYSE and presents a brief history of the NYSE, including a reprint of the Buttonwood Tree Agreement. With case studies and tables.

Appendix A is "The Size and Composition of the Securities Industry and Appendix B, "A Simulation Model of Liquidity in the Stock Market."

330. Taub, Stephen. "The Big Board: New Vigor." *Financial World* 155 (September 16, 1986): 78-80.

Describes recent changes at the NYSE including the SuperDOT 250 computer system which handles approximately 500 million shares per day. Among proposed changes are: twenty-four hour, seven day trading in 200-300 widely traded stocks and an increase in listings. Includes graphs.

331. *Today Show, May 17, 1967* [film] New York: WNBC, 1967. 16mm color print, optical sound, 11 min. copy available at New York Stock Exchange Archives.

Segment of *Today Show* with Paul Cunningham was filmed from the NYSE trading floor gallery to commemorate the 175th anniversary of the Buttonwood Agreement. Explains trading floor procedures and features an interview with G. Keith Funston, President of the Exchange. Funston discusses the growth of sales, listed securities, shareowners investor protection, and his outlook for the future.

332. *Trading Floor Film* [film]. New York: New York Stock Exchange, 1974? 16mm, color, 1 min., optical sound.

Record of trading floor activity. No narration.

333. United States. Congress. House. Committee on Interstate and Foreign Commerce. *Securities Markets Investigation: Hearings before a subcommittee of the Committtee on Interstate and Foreign Commerce, House of Representatives, Eighty-seventh Congress, first session, on H.J. Res. 438, joint resolution to amend the Securities Exchange Act of 1934 so as to authorize and*

*direct the Securities and Exchange Commission to conduct a
study and investigation of the adequacy, for the protection of
investors, of the rules of the national securities exchanges and
national securities associations...* Washington, D.C.: U.S.
Government Printing Office, 1961. 178 pages.

Hearings concern House Joint Resolution 438, a resolution
directing the SEC to make a study and investigation of adequacy of
rules of stock exchanges and the National Association of Securities
Dealers for protection of investors. Contains historical review of
legislative history of securities regulation. Among statements are
those of William L. Cary, Chairman of the SEC and of Keith
Funston, President of the NYSE. Funston presents overview of
current NYSE rules. A reprint of the New York Stock Exchange's
"Disciplinary Procedures" is included.

334. United States. Congress. Senate. Committee on Banking and
Currency. *Factors Affecting the Stock Market.* 84th Congress, 1st
session staff Report to the Committee on Banking and Currency.
Washington, D.C.: U.S. Government Printing Office, 1955. 201
pages.

Text of a study on major factors affecting the stock market,
including operations and regulations of exchanges and the over-
the-counter market. Study was distributed to members of the
Committee on Banking and Currency at the beginning of the
hearings on March 3, 1955. Staff who prepared the study were:
Robert A. Wallace, staff director; Dr. Asher Achinstern,
economist; Meyer Feldman, counsel; and Amherst E. Huson,
financial analyst. Topics covered are: stock price movements; stock
prices and general business fluctuations; credit and the stock
market; tax policies and the stock market; individual and
institutional investment in stocks; the stock exchanges; government
and the stock market; and the over-the-counter market. For the
New York Stock Exchange, covers its history, organizations,
policies, and memberships. Provides an organizational chart of the
NYSE, covering the time period January 1955. With list of charts
and tables.

335. United States. Congress. Senate. Committee on Banking and
   Currency. *Stock Market Study: Hearings before the Committee on
   Banking and Currency, United States Senate, 84th Congress, 1st
   session on Factors Affecting the Buying and Selling of Equity
   Securities, March 3,4,7,8,9,10,11,14,15,16,17,18,21,22, and
   23, 1955.* Washington, D.C.: U.S. Government Printing Office,
   1955. 1022 pages.

   Hearings concern conditions at the Stock Market in 1953-54.
   From September 1953 to November 1954 when the level of stock
   prices rose phenomenally and at a time when other economic
   sectors were shrinking and tightening. In November and December
   1954, a sudden change in the market took place, with stock prices
   reaching heights above those right before the 1929 Crash. The
   question was whether or not a new market crash was to take place.
   Hearings compare and contrast conditions in 1955 with 1929. Basic
   issues examined by the Hearings are: whether stock prices are too
   high, whether they can safely go higher, or whether they should be
   driven down. Key witnesses who provided testimonies during the
   Hearings were: G. Keith Funston, President of the NYSE; John
   Kenneth Galbraith, Professor of Economics, Harvard University;
   Bernard M. Baruch; Harold W. Scott, Chairman of the Board,
   NYSE; John A. Coleman, former Chairman of the Board and a
   member, NYSE; and George M. Humphrey, Secretary of the
   Treasury. With statistical charts and tables. Funston provides a
   detailed description of the NYSE, including its: history and
   composition; membership; and relationship to the national
   economy. Galbraith discusses the 1929 Crash, its effects, and how
   another Crash may be prevented.

336. United States. Congress. Senate. Committee on Banking, Housing
   and Urban Affairs. Subcommittee on Securities. *Securities Acts
   Amendments of 1975: Hearings before the Subcommittee on
   Securities of the Committee on Banking, Housing and Urban
   Affairs, United States Senate, Ninety-Fourth Congress, First
   Session on S. 249, To Amend the Securities Exchange Act of
   1934, and for other purposes, February 19, 20, and 21, 1975.*
   Washington, D.C.: U.S. Government Printing Office, 1975. 525
   pages.

The objectives of the Securities Acts Amendments are to clarify operational direction and regulatory posture of securities industry, to promote a national market system, and to assure increased competition through competitive commission rates in the securities industry. With witnesses: Ray Garrett, Jr., Chairman of the Securities and Exchange Commission; James J. Needham, Chairman, New York Stock Exchange; Donald L. Calvin, Vice-President, NYSE; William C. Freund, Vice-President and Chief Economist, NYSE; H. Virgil Sherrill, Chairman, Board of Directors, Securities Industry Association, etc. Needham describes the possible ramifications of the Securities Acts Amendments and proposes changes in S. 249. Among additional statements and data: reprints of February 1975 *New York Times* articles by Robert Metz; Letters to Senator Williams from James J. Needham; "the Securities Industry: and Myth vs. Reality--and a Proposal," a reprint of a paper by Frank A. Weil.

337. United States. Congress. Senate. Committee on Banking, Housing, and Urban Affairs. Subcommittee on Securities. *Stock Exchange Commission Rates: Hearings before the Subcommittee on Securities of the Committee on Banking, Housing and Urban Affairs, United States Senate, Ninety-second Congress, second session on S. 3169, A bill to amend the Securities Exchange Act of 1934 to Prohibit Certain Minimum Commission Rates, and for Other Purposes, March 22, 23, and 24, 1972.* Washington, D.C.: U.S. Government Printing Office, 1972. 527 pages.

Hearings on S. 3169, a bill to provide for competitive commission rates. With reprint of bill and testimony of witnesses: William J. Casey, Chairman, Securities and Exchange Commission, accompanied by High F. Owens, James J. Needham, A. Sydney Herlong, Jr. and Philip Loomis, Jr., Commissioners; Dr. William C. Freund, Vice President and Chief Economist, New York Stock Exchange; Prof. Paul A. Samuelson, Massachusetts Institute of Technology; Alan Greenspan, Townsend-Greenspan & Co.; and Donald T. Regan, Chairman, Merrill Lynch, Pierce, Fenner & Smith, Inc. Among Additional Statements and Data are: *The Monopoly Power of the New York Stock Exchange*, a dissertation by Robert William Doede; "Martin's Monopoly," by Paul A.

Samuelson, an article from *Newsweek*, January 17, 1972; reprint of Irwin Friend's and Marshall E. Bloom's 1972 Study, *The Consequences of Competititive Commissions on the New York Stock Exchange*; reprints of articles from *Barron's, Wall Street Journal* and the *New York Times*; New York Stock Exchange's Analysis of commission rate discounts; NYSE's Analysis of negotiated rates, fourth quarter, 1971; and NYSE's negotiated rates and market liquidity. Hearings include analysis of William McChesney Martin, Jr.'s report: *The Securities Markets*. With statistical tables and bibliographical references.

338. United States. Securities and Exchange Commission. *Report of the Special Study of the Securities Industry of the Securities and Exchange Commission.* 88th Congress, 1st session. House document no. 95. Washington, D.C.: Government Printing Office, 1963-64. 6 vols.

Studies adequacy of investor protection in the securities markets. The examination and preparation of the report was conducted by a separate group established in the SEC and designated the Special Study of Securities Markets, supervised by Milton H. Cohen, Director. Contents: Part 1: Chapter I. Introduction; Chapter II. Qualifications of Persons in the Securities Industry; Chapter III. Broker-Dealers, Investment Advisers and Their Customers-- Activities and Reponsibilities; Chapter IV. Primary and Secondary Distributions to the Public; Part 2: Chapter V. Trading Markets- -Introduction; Chapter VI. Exchange Markets; Chapter VII. Over-the-Counter Markets; Chapter VIII. Trading Markets-- Interrelationships; Part 3: Chapter IX. Obligations of Issuers of Publicly Held Securities; Part 4: Chapter X. Security Credit; Chapter IX. Open-End Investment Companies (Mutual Funds); Chapter XII. The Regulatory Pattern; Chapter XIII. The Market Break of May 1962; Part V: Letters of Transmittal from the SEC Chairman, Letters of Transmittal from the Special Study of Securities Markets, and Summaries, Conclusions and Recommendations of Parts 1-4; and Part 6: Index. Regarding the New York Stock Exchange, the *Study* provides in-depth analysis and makes recommendations regarding: commission rate structure; need for automation; short selling; floor traders; odd-lot dealers;

specialist system; competition with other markets; surveillance techniques; and organizational structure. Also discusses historical background of the structure of the NYSE as a self-regulatory institution.

*   *Wall Street and Regulation.* Edited by Samuel L. Hayes, III. see item 252 above.

339. Welles, Chris. *The Last Days of the Club.* New York: Dutton, 1975. 460 pages.

The changes at the NYSE, whose membership is referred to as "The Club," during the 1970s and culminating on May 1, 1975. On "Mayday," brokerage commission rates were no longer fixed by the NYSE for purchase and sale of stocks listed on the NYSE. A second key event was the signing of the Securities Acts Amendments of 1975 which calls for a central market system for securities trading. After the law was signed, the NYSE introduced a new consolidated ticker tape, which lists trades executed both on and off the floor of the Exchange. Indicates there is a trend toward dominance on Wall Street by the powerful institutional investors, mostly banks. Features case studies of members of "the Club." With a bibliography.

340. West, Richard R. and Seha M. Tinic. *The Economics of the Stock Exchange.* New York: Praeger, 1971. 222 pages.

Topic of study is the market for corporate common stock, focusing on processes and institutions that bring buyers and sellers together. Seeks answers to: what economic functions brokers and dealers perform; why some stocks trade on an exchange while others trade over-the-counter; why there are only two major stock exchanges; and what factors influence size of spread between bid and asked prices for stock; and how institutional investors influence the structure of the stock market. Also examines the relationship between the NYSE and other exchanges and reasons why the NYSE has maintained a dominant position in the stock exchange industry for nearly 200 years. Uses economic models and provides statistical tables. With bibliographical references.

341. Wise, T.A. "Wall Street's Main Event: SEC vs. the Specialist." *Fortune* 69 (May 1964): 149-152, 203-204.

Reports dispute between the NYSE and the Securities and Exchange Commission regarding the SEC proposal to restrict and possibly ban floor trading (defined as trading for profit on the floor of the NYSE by members, who can trade without paying brokers' commissions). The larger issue, contends the author, is not the future of the floor trader but rather the specialist. Reasons for the specialists fighting for floor trading is: many of the specialists do some floor trading themselves; full-time floor traders often prove useful to specialists as sources of capital; and, most importantly, specialists realize they themselves are a target for SEC regulators. Relates history of the specialist system on the NYSE and the present roles of specialists.

342. *Your Share in Tomorrow* [film] s.l.: International Film Foundation, Knickerbocker Productions, Inc., 1957. 16mm, 27 min. Script available.

Briefly covers the NYSE's early history. Explains NYSE functions, trading floor mechanics, and reports on a brokerage firm in Easton, Pennsylvania for a discussion of member firm services and an analysis of investors. Offers projections for future industrial and technological developments. With foreign language editions available in German, Japanese, Russian, and Spanish.

343. Zahorchak, Michael G. *Favorable Executions: The Wall Street Specialist and the Auction Market.* New York: Van Nostrand Reinhold Co., 1974. 189 pages

Subjects of work are the stock exchange specialists and stock auction process. Examines operations and organization of the American Stock Exchange and the New York Stock Exchange.

CHAPTER XV
OCTOBER 1987 CRASH

The Crash of 1987 is the subject of numerous government reports, monographs, journal and newspaper articles, and audiovisual media. Most of these materials analyze causes and results of Black Monday and recommend measures for preventing a future Crash. Some studies compare and contrast events of 1987 with those of 1929. Studies of the Crash were prepared by the President's Task Force or the Brady Commission, the Securities and Exchange Commission, the Commodity Futures Trading Commission (CFTC), the New York Stock Exchange, the Chicago Mercantile Exchange, and the General Accounting Office. The New York Stock Exchange has reviewed and recommended changes, notably in its program trading practices and its specialist system.

This chapter contains a listing of representative sources on the Crash of 1987 including the special reports listed above. Additional sources of information may be found by scanning periodical and newspaper indexes, government publications indexes, and business databases.

344. Abken, Peter A. "Stock Market Activity in October 1987: The

Brady,CFTC & SEC Reports." Book Review. *Economic Review. Federal Reserve Bank of Atlanta* 73 (May/June 1988): 36-43.

Reviews three key reports: *Report of the Presidential Task Force on Market Mechanisms* (the Brady Report); *Final Report on Stock Index Futures and Cash Market during October 1987 to the U.S. Commodity Futures Trading Commission* (the CFTC Report); and *The October 1987 Market Break* (the Securities and Exchange Commission Report). Concentrates on what role program trading played in market decline and, if anything, what should be done about program trading. Examines trading activities on the New York Stock Exchange and the Chicago Mercantile Exchange. Studies recommendations of each report and presents a chart which reviews the basic findings of each.

345. Arbel, Avner and Albert E. Kaff. *Crash: Ten Days in October...Will It Strike Again?* Chicago, Illinois: Longman Financial Services, 1989. 212 pages.

Describes events of Black Monday, October 19, 1987 and events in the days before and after the Crash. Analyzes causes and possible consequences of the Crash. Amidst their factual account, the authors have added, in italics, fictional accounts of disastrous events that did not take place during this time period. Appendix provides statistics including, "Share Volume for All NYSE Stocks, October 29, 1987," "Survey of Factors That Caused the Crash," "NYSE Specialist Performance," "Dow Jones Industrial One Minute Chart, Monday, October 19, 1987," and "The Crash Around the World." Authors urge review, by government officials and legislators and financial professionals, of possible measures to prevent future crises and minimize damage caused by Crash of 1987.

346. Arbel, Avner, Steven Carvell and Erik Postnieks. "The Smart Crash of October 19th." *Harvard Business Review* 66 (May/June 1988): 124-136.

Maintains that October 19, 1987 Crash was not what many

analysts, investors, and observers believe it to be. Studies Crash as representing a restoration of credibility in the market pricing mechanism. Contends that portfolio insurance and program trading did not worsen Crash, but curtailed its duration. Tests various stock market theories concerning investor behavior, market pricing mechanisms, valuation, risk, rational markets, and fluctuations under conditions of the October 1987 Crash. Indicates that analysts, mutual funds, leading market indicators, and insiders were not effective in predicting the Crash. Finds that a value-based investment formula devised by Benjamin Graham predicted the drop in prices which occurred during the Crash. Recommends further study of the possibility that economic models and other theories in social science work better under catastrophic conditions. With bibliographical references and statistical tables.

347. *Black Monday & Beyond* [videorecording] Written, produced, and directed by Jim Auker: made in cooperation with: National Association of Investors Corporation; the major stock, futures, and options exchanges; and The Nightly Business Report. Narrated by Leon McNew. Birmingham, MI.: Yukon Video, 1988. 100 min., color.

Hour by hour account of October 19 and 20, 1987. Explains key terms and discusses events leading up to the Crash. Explains and analyzes: program trading, portfolio insurance, risk arbitrage, futures, and options. Includes scenes of events on the trading floors of the New York Stock Exchange, the Chicago Board Options Exchange, the Chicago Mercantile Exchange, the Tokyo Stock Exchange, etc. Features interviews with: Ken Brandt, First Vice President, Shearson. Lehman Hutton; Kirk Love, Vice President, Prudential Bache; David Ruder, Chair, Securities and Exchange Commission; Charles Henry, President, Chicago Board Options Exchange; William Brodsky, President, Chicago Mercantile Exchange; and John Phelan, Jr., Chairman and CEO, New York Stock Exchange. Also provides investment strategies in light of the changing picture of the market and events of Black Monday.

348. *Black Monday and the Future of Financial Markets.* By Robert J.
     Barro and others, Edited by Robert W. Kampuis, Jr. and others.
     Homewood, Illinois: Dow Jones-Irwin/Chicago, Illinois: Mid
     American Institute for Public Policy Research, 1989. 396 pages.

   Series of essays on the Crash of October 19, 1987. Reports
   findings of the Mid America Institute for Public Policy Research's
   (MAI) Task Force on Black Monday and the Future of Financial
   Markets. Six research scholars representing fields of finance,
   macroeconomics, market structure, and regulation analyze events
   of October 1987, causes and effects of the Crash, and
   recommendations. Divided into two parts: Part I contains the Task
   Force Papers and Part II consists of excerpts from other reports on
   the Crash. Contents of Part I: "Overview," by Allan H. Meltzer;
   "The International Crash of October 1987, by Richard W. Roll;
   "Perspectives on October 1987, or What Did We Learn From the
   Crash, by Eugene F. Fama; "The Stock Market and The Macro
   Economy: Implications of the October 1987 Crash," by Robert J.
   Barro; "October 1987 and the Structure of Financial Markets: An
   Exorcism of Demons," by Lester G. Telser; and "Should One
   Agency Regulate Financial Markets?" by Daniel R. Fischel. Part
   II provides excerpts from: Brady: "The Report of the Presidential
   Task Force on Market Mechanisms"; Miller: "Preliminary and
   Final Reports of the Committee of Inquiry Convened by the
   Chicago   Mercantile   Exchange";   Britain: "Report   of   the
   International Stock Exchange of London"; CFTC: "The Final
   Report of the Division of Market Regulation, Securities, and
   Exchange Commission"; and GAO: Preliminary Observations of the
   Crash, U.S. General Accounting Office." With statistical tables.

349. Blitzer, David M. "After the Crash: Slowdown Probable,
     Depression Unlikely." *Standard & Poor's Industry Surveys.*
     Trends and Projections 155 (November 12, 1987): 1-6.

   Explains causes and consequences of Black Monday, projects
   economic outlook for 1988. States that, although the damage
   caused by 1987 Crash exceeded that of 1929 Crash in terms of
   dollar value and percentage decline in equity prices, the economy
   will not experience the severity of the Great Depression.

Includes statistical tables on current and projected economic indicators.

350. Bose, Mihir. *Crash! A New Money Crisis?* Illustrated by Ron Hayward Associates. Issues..Issues..Issues.   New York: Gloucester Press, 1989. 32 pages.

Relates what happened in 1987 Crash and its significance for the world's money system and individual investors. Compares 1929 and 1987 Stock Market Crashes. Provides glossary of terms among which are "stock," "inflation," "currency," "interest rate," "capitalism," "Communism," and "reserves." Part of Issues..Issues..Issues, a series for young adults designed to discuss notable and current issues.

351. Bose, Mihir. *The Crash: The Fundamental Flaws Which Caused the 1987-88 World Stock Market Slump--and What They Mean for Future Financial Stability.* London: Bloomsbury, 1988. 180 pages.

Analyzes international implications and magnitude of the 1987 Crash. Discusses events of October 19-20 and their causes and effects. Relates what happened from the perspectives of the New York Stock Exchange, the Chicago Mercantile Exchange, the Chicago Board of Trade as well as Exchanges overseas including London, Tokyo, Hong Kong, and Sydney. Compares 1929 and 1987 Stock Market Crashes. Among statistical charts: "World Stock Market Movements, 12 - 23 October 1987," "1929/1987 U.S. Share Price Comparison," "U.S. Budget Deficit 1982 - October 1987," and "International Share Price Index Movements 1975 - October 1987." With a bibliography of books, newspapers, magazines, and reports.

*   Bowsher, Charles A., Comptroller General of the United States, General Accounting Office. *Financial Markets: Preliminary Observations on the October 1987 Crash.* January, 1988. see item 393

*   *Brady Commission Report.* see item 402 below.

352. Buckley, Mark J. *The Stock Market Crash of October 19, 1987: Was the Market Overvalued?* Chester, Pennsylvania: Widener University. School of Management, 1988. 46 pages.

A paper submitted in partial fulfillment of the requirements of Management 700 Seminar leading to the degree, Master of Business Administration. Investigates notion that stock market was overvalued prior to Crash. Investigative method used is to determine intrinsic values of Dow Jones Industrial stocks and compare them to their market values right before the October 19th Crash. Results indicate market values of stocks investigated were overvalued. Also surveys literature written on causes or contributing factors of Crash, which include: portfolio insurance, stock index arbitrage, program trading, margin requirements, Federal deficits, and market overvaluation. With bibliography and statistical tables.

353. Cardiff, Gray Emerson. *Panic-Proof Investing and How to Profit from the Crash of '87.* New York: Prentice-Hall, 1988. 241 pages.

Guide to strategies for investing in the stock market, precious metals, and real estate. Examines the stock market cycles including a historical perspective of bull and bear markets and panics. Studies "supercycles," or movement of the market in broad cycles of fortune and failure. Discusses implications of Crash of 1987 for present and future investment strategies. With statistical charts and bibliographical notes.

354. Chicago Mercantile Exchange. *Findings of the Committee of Inquiry: Examining the Events Surrounding October 19, 1987; Final Report: Spring 1988; Preliminary Report: December 22, 1987.* Committee of Inquiry Members: Merton Miller, Chairman; John D. Hawke, Burton Malkiel, Myron Scholes. Chicago: Chicago Mercantile Exchange, 1988. 1 vol. (various

pagings).

Studies performance of the Chicago Mercantile Exchange's futures market during the Stock Market Crash, October 1987. Recommends changes in CME's contracts or procedures that might improve functioning of the market particularly under conditions of great stress. Recommends: the Securities and Exchange Commission and the Commodity Futures Trading Commission undertake a thorough examination of their policies on position limits for index options and futures; equalization of margins called for by the Brady Commission Report be undertaken in the most direct way possible, specifically through turning over to the private sector those remaining parts of the stock margin process still administered by the Federal Reserve System; and an examination of capital markets and their regulation from a perspective broader than that of a single day or week with a concern beyond that of the individual investor. Appendix A of the *Final Report* consists of a study, "The Price Pressure Effects from Portfolio Insurance and Arbitrage Activity During the October Crash," by Mark S. Rzepczynski. The *Preliminary Report* provides the following: Appendix A. Appointment of the Committee of Inquiry; Appendix B. Chronology of Wire Service Reports; Appendix C. Price Data; Appendix D. CME Emergency Authority; Appendix E. Margin Requirements; and Appendix F. Glossary. With bibliographical footnotes and statistical tables and figures.

355. Cole, Robert J. "Wall Street Point Man: John J. Phelan Jr." *New York Times*, 21 October 1987, D17.

Profiles John Phelan, Jr., Chairman and Chief Executive Officer of NYSE. Provides perspectives on Black Monday from Phelan's point of view.

356. Coll, Steve. "Crisis Chronology: The Day Wall Street Went Wild." *The Washington Post*, 25 October 1987, A1+

Describes events of Black Monday from the opening of the futures market in Chicago to the end of the day's trading at the

New York Stock Exchange. Outlines causes of Crash among which are structural weaknesses in the financial markets and economic problems. Records reactions of John J. Phelan, Jr. to Crash.

*   *Crashes and Panics: The Lessons from History.* see item 96 above.

357. Crossen, Cynthia and others. "Anguish Abroad: Foreign Ardor Cools Toward U.S. Stocks after Market's Dive; Mass Exodus Seems Unlikely, but Share Buying Abates and Japanese are 'scared'; Europe fears U.S. Recession." *Wall Street Journal* 210 (October 26, 1987): 1+

Reaction, internationally, to Black Monday, October 19, 1987.

358. Dunn, Ruben J. and John Morris. *The Crash Put Simply: October 1987.* New York: Praeger, 1988. 179 pages.

First published in French in 1987 by Louis Courteau Editrice, Inc. Guide to the economy and to the stock markets as a background to learning the meaning of the events and causes of Black Monday, October 19 and Terrible Tuesday, October 20. Explains basic concepts of supply and demand, money, recessions, expansions, inflation, panics, etc. Recommends investment strategy that is cautious and flexible in view of recent economic and financial events. Includes glossary, statistical tables, and a bibliography.

359. Edwards, Franklin R. "Studies of the 1987 Stock Market Crash: Review and Appraisal." *Journal of Financial Services Research* 1 (1988): 231-251.

Examines conclusions and analyses of the Crash by: the Brady Commission, the Commodity Futures Trading Commission, the Securities and Exchange Commission, the General Accounting Office, the New York Stock Exchange, and the Chicago Mercantile Exchange. Compares and contrasts the six studies in regard to causes of the Crash, margins and trading halts, and the role of stock index futures. Recommends initiating a constructive dialogue between stock and futures exchanges on every aspect of trading and operations. With bibliographical references.

360. Farney, Dennis. "Different Worlds: Main Street's View of the Crash is Far Different from Wall Street's." *Wall Street Journal*, 30 December 1987, 1+

Reactions to the Crash from the perspectives of the financial community and the rest of America, including small investors. The financial community is recovering from the Crash's damages. Among the after-effects are out of work traders and investment bankers. For the rest of the country, the view seems to be one of detachment. Polls have indicated that few small investors sold stocks during the Crash or in the weeks immediately following.

361. Feinberg, Andrew. "Blown Away by Black Monday." *The New York Times Magazine*, 20 December 1987, 38; 66-69.

Story of Warren R. "Pete" Haas, managing partner of A.B. Tompane & Co. and one of the New York Stock Exchange's specialist, and his experiences on Black Monday. Examines the effects of the Crash on NYSE's specialist system.

362. Ferguson, Robert. "On Crashes." *Financial Analysts Journal 45* (March/April 1989): 42-52.

Studies Crash and causes using economic models and principles of behavioral psychology. Stresses importance of psychological factors, among which is escape behavior. With bibliographical footnotes and statistical figures.

363. *Financial Market Volatility: A Symposium.* Sponsored by the Federal Reserve Bank of Kansas City, Jackson Hole, Wyoming, August 17-19, 1988. Kansas City, 1988. 261 pages.

Offers answers to the questions: "What are the sources of
financial market volatility?" "What impact does it have on domestic
and international economies?" "What public policies should be
adopted in response?" Examines issue of volatility in equity
markets, credit markets, commodity markets and foreign exchange
in light of the stock market decline of October 19, 1987. The first
section studies sources of financial market volatility; the second
section explores consequences of financial market volatility; the
third section describes possible policy responses; and the fourth
section summarizes remarks of overview panel. Contributors:
Franklin R. Edwards, Professor, Columbia University; Jacob A.
Frenkel, Economic Counsellor and Director of Research,
International Monetary Fund; Mark Gertler, Associate Professor,
University of Wisconsin; Morris Goldstein, Deputy Director,
Research Department, International Monetary Fund; Charles A.E.
Goodhart, Professor, London School of Economics; David D.
Hale, First Vice President and Chief Economist, Kemper Financial
Services, Inc.: Robert E. Hall, Professor, Stanford University;
Robert D. Hormats, Vice Chairman, Goldman Sachs International
Corporation; R. Glenn Hubbard, Professor, Columbia University;
Paul Krugman, Professor, Massachusetts Institute of Technology;
Alexandre Lamfalussy, General Manager, Bank for International
Settlements; Louis I. Margolis, Managing Director, Salomon
Brothers Inc.; Frederic S. Mishkin, Professor, Columbia
University; Michael Mussa, Member, U.S. Council of Economic
Advisers; Brian Quinn, Executive Director, Bank of England;
Robert V. Roosa, Partner, Brown Brothers Harriman and
Company; Robert J. Shiller, Professor, Yale University; Lawrence
H. Summers, Professor, Yale University; and James Tobin,
Professor, Yale University. The Moderators: Robert Eisner,
Professor, Northwestern University and Lyle Gramley, Senior Staff
Vice President and Chief Vice Economist, Mortgage Bankers
Association. Foreword by Roger Guffey, President of the Federal
Reserve Bank of Kansas City.

364. Gammill, James F., Jr. and Terry A. Marsh. "Trading Activity
    and Price Behavior in the Stock and Stock Index Futures Markets
    in October 1987." *Journal of Economic Perspectives* 2 (Summer
    1988): 25-44.

Describes events of October 1987 Crash and days immediately before with analysis of how several categories of market participants behaved during time period of October 15 - October 20. Refers to findings of the Presidential Task Force and reports of the Securities and Exchange Commission and the Commodity Futures Trading Commission. Concentrates on trading activity at the NYSE and the S & P 500 stock index futures contract traded on the Chicago Mercantile Exchange. Reviews key concepts such as "program trading," "portolio insurance," "stock index futures," and "index arbitrage." With bibliographical references and statistical figures. Written by staff members with the Presidential Task Force on Market Mechanisms.

365. Geller, Jeffrey A. "A Response to the Brady Report." *Financial Analysts Journal* (March/April 1988): 4-6.

Examines role of derivatives in Crash of 1987 with focus on portfolio insurer's role as a large seller. Calls for better ways to disseminate information in securities markets so investors can respond appropriately.

366. Gelman, Eric. "Does 1987 Equal 1929?" *New York Times*, 20 October 1987, 1 +

Offers answer to question of whether or not aftershocks of Black Monday would be as devastating as those of the 1929 Crash. According to many economists the answer is no, since there are many safeguards to prevent another cascading financial collapse that characterized the 1929 Crash. Provides commentaries by economists John Kenneth Galbraith, Geoffrey H. Moore, and Robert A. Kavesh.

367. Glazer, Sarah. "Spotlight on Wall Street." *Editorial Research Reports* , 18 December 1987, 658-671.

Studies causes and effects of Crash and measures taken to prevent it happening again. Reviews role in Crash of program trading, the

NYSE specialist system, portfolio insurance, index arbitrage, etc. Summarizes roles of the following agencies which are preparing reports concerning the Crash: the President's Task Force (Brady Commission), Securities and Exchange Commission, Commodity Futures Trading Commission, the New York Stock Exchange, Chicago Mercantile Exchange, Chicago Board of Trade, and the Committee on Investments of Employee Benefit Assets. Provides definitions of key terms, a comparative analysis of the Crashes of 1929 and 1987, and statistical charts. The "Recommended Reading" section is an annotated guide to books, articles, and reports and studies.

368. Greenwald, Bruce and Jeremy Stein. "The Task Force Report: The Reasoning Behind the Recommendations." *Journal of Economic Perspectives* 2 (Summer 1988): 3-24.

Provides framework for considering recommendations of the Presidential Commission on Market Mechanisms (the Brady Commission). Describes aspects of Crash that emphasize it as a unique crisis event. Appendix to article consists of brief introductory guide to instruments, marketplaces and trading strategies among which are: "Stocks, Futures Contracts and Options Contracts," "Exchanges and Market Making," "Regulation," and "Margin." With bibliographical references and statistical tables. Written by staff economists with the Presidential Task Force on Market Mechanisms.

369. Hall, Gordon. *The Crash of 1987.* Olathe, Kansas: Johnson County Publishers, 1987. 247 pages.

Chronicles events and causes of Crash in historical context. Describes reactions to Crash of fictional characters: Tom Franke, a financial newsletter publisher; Janice Davenport, a stockbroker; and John Robertson, president of a small manufacturing company in Oklahoma. Also relates effects of Crash on Co-conspirators X, Y, and Z. Provides excerpts from press reports and articles published before, during, after the Crash. Offers predictions for economic, political, and international events through the early

1990s. Includes statistical tables.

370. Jahnke, William W. "The Crash of '87." *Financial Analysts Journal 43* (November/December 1987, pp. 6-9.

Offers answers to questions about Crash, including: who or what was to blame for the decline?; was it the twin deficits, international tensions, or program trading?; had the 1980s bull market pushed stock prices to unrealistic heights?; could investors have anticipated the Crash?; and what can we learn from the Crash? With bibliographical references and statistical tables.

371. Katzenbach, Nicholas deB. *An Overview of Program Trading and Its Impact on Current Market Practices.* A Study Commissioned by the New York Stock Exchange. New York: December 1987. 40 pages.

Study of program trading which is broadly defined as "nothing more than buying or selling several stocks simultaneously on a stock exchange. Moreover, computers are now programmed to specify the stocks to be bought or sold at 'market' price, and the various exchange members can use their computers to execute the trade through the NYSE's Designated Order Turnaround System ('DOT')." (p. 10) Reviews events of Black Monday and offers preliminary observations as events relate to program trading. Discusses program trading in relation to historical overview of Federal regulation of financial markets; stock index futures and index options; stock market volatility and market manipulation; and public confidence. Offers conclusions and recommendations for changes at the New York Stock Exchange; in index and options futures; and in regulatory authority. Includes statistical figures and bibliographical references.

372. McClain, David. *Apocalypse on Wall Street.* Homewood, Illinois: Dow Jones-Irwin, 1988. 187 pages.

Analyzes the 1987 Crash, its causes and effects. Covers:

development of the great global bull market of the 1980s; the
transfer of leadership from Paul Volker to Alan Greenspan as
Federal Reserve chairman and the effect on the economy and the
market; and the events of October 19-20, 1987. Compares events
of the 1987 with those of 1929 and 1893. Discusses role of the new
financial technology as a factor in the 1987 Crash. Offers
recommendations of what needs to be done with regard to national
macroeconomic policies and to financial market microstructure.
Examines recommendations of the Brady Commission Report, the
General Accounting Office, the New York Stock Exchange, the
Securities and Exchange Commission, and the Commodity Futures
Trading Commission. Includes statistical tables and bibliographical references.

373. Mackay, Robert J., ed. *After the Crash: Linkages Between Stocks
     and Futures.* Lanham, Maryland: American Enterprise Institute,
     1988. 100 pages.

     Series of essays by informed market participants, regulators, and
     academics assess Crash, its causes, and resulting proposed
     regulatory reforms. Analyzes reports produced by the Brady
     Commission, the Securities and Exchange Commission, the
     Commodity Futures Trading Commission, and the exchanges.

374. Magnet, Myron. "1987 Need Not Become 1929." *Fortune* 116
     (November 23, 1987): 46-48.

     Describes the 1987 Crash as the first stock market panic
     unfolding on camera and instantly communicated around the world.
     Discusses causes, economic effects, and measures that should be
     taken to prevent a recession. Analyzes mistakes of policymakers
     after 1929 Crash and cautions today's policymakers against making
     the same mistakes. Contends 1929 Crash did not make the Great
     Depression of the 1930s inevitable.

375. Markham, Jerry W. and Rita McCloy Stephanz. "The Stock
     Market Crash of 1987--the United States Looks at New

Recommendations." *Georgetown Law Review* 76 (August 1988): 1993-2043.

Analyzes: commodity futures trading; the regulatory history of securities and commodity futures trading; the reports of regulatory agencies, trading exchanges, and financial institutions; the jurisdictional clashes and regulatory differences between the Securities and Exchange Commission and the Commodity Futures Trading Commission; and controversial proposals to raise margin requirements on commodity futures contracts and to impose government regulation of commodity futures margin requirements. Reports studied are those of: the Brady Commission, the Securities and Exchange Commission, the Commodity Futures Trading Commission, the General Accounting Office, Wells Fargo, the New York Stock Exchange, the Chicago Mercantile Exchange, the Bank of England, and the International Stock Exchange. With bibliographical references.

376. Mayer, Martin. *Markets: Who Plays, Who Risks, Who Gains, Who Loses*. New York: Norton, 1988. 303 pages.

Part of Mayer's study of international securities markets consists of a description of events of October 19 and 20, 1987, their causes and effects. Analyzes implications of events for international markets and for NYSE operations. With a glossary and bibliographical notes.

377. Mayer, Martin. "Some Watchdog! How the SEC Helped Set the Stage for Black Monday." *Barron's* 67 (December 28, 1987): 18-19.

Studies index arbitrage and portfolio insurance as factors in the October 1987 Crash. Approximately one year before the Crash, John Phelan had predicted that index arbitrage and portfolio insurance when combined could produce a chain reaction. Prior to December 1986, the Securities and Exchange Commission had a rule against selling short into a decline; the potential damage created by a combination of portfolio insurance and index arbitrage was limited by this rule. The Securities & Exchange Commission had withdrawn the restriction on for brokers and dealers in certain circumstances. In the interest of improving brokers and dealers, indications are that the SEC was remiss in protecting the public.

378. Metz, Tim. *Black Monday: The Catastrophe of October 19, 1987 and Beyond.* New York: Morrow, 1988. 264 pages.

Story of events of Black Monday from perspectives of John Phelan, chairman of the New York Stock Exchange; E. Gerald Corrigan, President of the Federal Reserve Bank of New York; Paul E. Steiger, one of the two deputy managing editors of *The Wall Street Journal*; Scott Serfling, trader on the Chicago Mercantile Exchange; and Donald Stone, a specialist trader and vice chairman of the New York Stock Exchange. Analyzes causes, effects, and reports findings of the Brady Commission and of the Securities and Exchange Commission. Includes bibliography.

379. Metz, Tim, et al. "The Crash of '87: Stocks Plunge 508 Amid Panicky Selling." *Wall Street Journal*, 20 October, 1987, 1+

Reports the events of Black Monday when the Dow Jones Industrial Average fell 508 points or 22.6% to 1738,74. The drop was greater than the 12.8% decline of October 29, 1929. Five factors leading to Black Monday were described by NYSE Chairman, John Phelan as: the market had gone five years without a large correction; fears of inflation; rising interest rates; the U.S.-Iran conflict; and volatility caused by derivative instruments including stock index options and futures. Reports reactions of President Ronald Reagan, government officials, securities analysts, traders, and money managers.

380. Miller, Jeffrey D., with Mara Miller and Peter J. Brennan. *Program Trading: The New Age of Investing.* New York: J.K. Lasser Institute, 1989. 212 pages.

Studies program trading in view of the 1987 Crash. Examines the new stock market strategies such as portfolio insurance and index arbitrage which use program trading techniques. Reviews findings of the Brady Commission and the Securities and Exchange Commission. Calls for acceptance of program trading as a factor in investment strategy and stock market practice.

*   Miller, Merton H., John D. Hawke, Jr., Burton Malkiel, and Myron Scholes. *Preliminary Report of the Committee of Inquiry Appointed by the Chicago Mercantile Exchange to Examine the Events Surrounding October 19, 1987.* See item 354 above.

381. Nagarajan, K.V. *The Stock Market Crash of October 1987: A Bibliography.* Public Administration Series: Bibliography No. P 2855. Monticello, Illinois: Vance Bibliographies, 1990. 7 pages.

List of material on the 1987 Stock Market Crash include: Official Reports; Stock Exchange Releases; Books; Articles; Unpublished Papers; Conferences and Symposia; and Computer Searches.

382. New York Stock Exchange. *New York Stock Exchange Initiatives to Handle Excess Market Volatility and Enhance Investor Confidence.* Facts Sheet. New York: NYSE, September 1990. 7 leaves.

Describes initiatives undertaken by NYSE since the October 1987 market break. These initiatives are designed to handle effectively excessive market volatility and to enhance investor confidence. The following are reviewed: circuit-breakers, program trading measures, technological and operational improvements, regulatory changes, arbitration process improvements, appointment of market volatility and investor confidence panel, work of various NYSE advisory committees, and coordination of procedures between the NYSE and the Chicago Mercantile Exchange (CME).

383. Norton, Robert E. "The Battle Over Stock Market Reform." *Fortune* 117 (February 1, 1988): 18-26.

Studies Brady Commission and its report. Discusses reports still to come from the Securities and Exchange Commission, Commodity Futures Trading Commission, General Accounting Office, various Congressional Committees, and academics. Reviews NYSE's study of program trading by former Attorney General Katzenbach.

384. Perry, James M. and David Shribman. "Taking Stock: Changes Since the Crash Can't Prevent a Repeat but Might Soften One; New Circuit Breakers are Set, Speculative Excess Abates; Yet Many Reforms Lag." *Wall Street Journal* 17 October 1988, 1+

Provides annotated chart reviewing how existing and proposed circuit breakers would be implemented in the event of a market crash.

385. Sanger, David E. "Limits Set on Program Trades." *New York Times*, 21 October 1987, D17.

Reports NYSE's placement of restrictions on program trading as result of October 19 market drop. Includes illustrated explanation, "How Program Trading Works."

386. Santoni, G.J. "The October Crash: Some Evidence on the Cascade Theory." *Economic Review. Federal Reserve Bank of St. Louis* 70 (May/June 1988): 18-33.

Studies the Cascade Theory which was described by the Brady Commission report as an explanation for the Crash. Examines minute-by-minute price data from cash and futures market for stocks from October 15-23 to determine if data are best explained by the Cascade Theory or different trading rules in the two markets. Analyzes the specialist system on the New York Stock Exchange and rules of the Commodity Futures Trading Commission. Explains trading strategies, "portfolio insurance" and "index arbitrage." Includes series of quotations on Crash of 1987 from articles published in the *New York Times* and the *Christian*

Science Monitor. With statistical charts and bibliographical references.

387. Shiller, Robert J. *Market Volatility.* Cambridge, Massachusetts: MIT Press, 1989. 464 pages.

Concerns sources of volatility in prices of speculative assets including corporate stocks, bonds, etc. Presents evidence of author, from his own work and his work with coauthors, on importance of economic fundamentals and changes in opinion or psychology to speculative price movements. Some essays are reprints from articles written by author and coauthors. Comprised of: Part I. Basic Issues and Alternative Models; Part II. the Stock Market; Part III. the Bond Market; Part IV. the Real Estate Market; Part V. the Aggregate Economy; and Part VI. Popular Models and Investor Behavior. Part VI analyzes the Crash of 1987 and reviews findings of the Brady Commission, Chicago Mercantile Exchange, Commodity Futures Trading Commission, and the Securities and Exchange Commission. With bibliographical references and statistical figures.

388. Smith, Randall, Steve Swartz, and George Anders. "Black Monday: What Really Ignited the Market's Collapse after Its Long Climb." *Wall Street Journal* 16 December 1987, 1+

Reviews causes of Black Monday's events and indicates that weak links within financial markets allowed early sell-off to go out of control. Among the stresses playing crucial roles: portfolio insurance remained unchecked throughout the day; index arbitrage was abandoned when computerized execution system was clogged by small retail orders; Fidelity Investments, the largest U.S. mutual fund operator, was forced to unload close to $1 billion in equities; fears of trading halt by the Securities and Exchange Commission; and NYSE specialists were overwhelmed by sell orders. With statistical chart: "The Market Meltdown (DJIA Every Five Minutes on October 19)."

389. Stern, R.L. and Allan Sloan. "The Day the Brokers Picked Their Own Pockets," *Forbes 140* (November 16, 1987): 32-33.

Contends that changes in Wall Street including program trading and portfolio insurance are only part of larger problem. Describes conflict of interest that pits brokerage house interest against those of house's customers and against interest of market. Stresses need for public confidence in the market.

390. Stewart, James B. and Daniel Hertzberg. "Before the Fall: Speculative Fever Ran High in the 10 Months Prior to Black Monday." *Wall Street Journal,* 11 December 1987, 1+

Reviews and analyzes events leading up to the Crash, beginning with the bull market in the early 1980s. Contends that this bull market had some elements of a speculative craze. Studies growth of the stock-index futures market and increasing popularity of program-trading strategies such as portolio insurance and index arbitrage.

391. Stewart, James B. and Daniel Hertzberg. "Market Medicine: Brady Panel Proposals Underscore Worries '87 Crash Could Recur; Its Call for Radical Changes is Spurred by Finding System Neared Collapse; Friday's 140-point nosedive." *Wall Street Journal,* 11 January 1988, 1+

Reports on recommendations of the Task Force chaired by Nicholas F. Brady to study the October 19, 1987 Stock Market Crash. Also discusses stock market nosedive on January 8, 1988.

392. *The Stock Market Crash of 1987: Causes and Effects* [videorecording] Produced for Random House by Contemporary Media Productions. *The New York Times* Current Affairs Series. Westminster, Maryland: Random House Media, 1988. 23 min., color, with accompanying brochure, "Videogram."

Chronicles events of the October 1987 Crash. Explains causes, effects, and impact on the economy. Studies similarities and differences between 1929 and 1987 Stock Market Crashes. Reviews recommendations of the Brady Commission, the General Accounting Office, the Securities and Exchange Commission, the Commodity Futures Trading Commission, the New York Stock Exchange, and the Chicago Mercantile Exchange. Defines key concepts and terms among which are: "Dow Jones Industrial Average," "Bull Market," "Bear Market," and "Stocks." Features an interview with Dr. Vincent Misarro, senior economist of The Conference Board. With accompanying guide, "Videogram," which includes a synopsis of the video, a discussion guide, and a bibliography.

393. *The Stock Market Crash of October 1987: Federal Documents and Materials on the Volatility of the Stock Market and Stock Index Futures Market.* Compiled by Bernard D. Reams, Jr. Federal Legislative Histories of Laws and Legislation on Economics, Monetary Policy, and Stock Market Regulation. Buffalo, N.Y.: William S. Hein, 1988. 2 volumes.

Series of documents, chronologically arranged, on the Crash. Contents: Document No. 1: *Impact of the Stock Market Drop and Related Economic Developments on Interest Rates, Banking, Monetary Policy and Economic Stability.* Before the Committee on Banking, Finance, and Urban Affairs of the House, 100th Cong., 1st Sess. (October 29, 1987); Document No. 2: *Review of Recent Volatility in the Stock Market and the Stock Index Futures Markets.* Before the Subcommittee on Conservation, Credit, and Rural Development of the Committee on Agriculture of the House, 100th Cong., 1st Sess. (November 4, 1987); Document No. 3: *Volatility and Panic in the Nation's Financial Markets.* Before the Committee on Banking, Housing, and Urban Affairs of the Senate, 100th Cong., 1st Sess. (November 4, 1987); Document No. 4: *Role of Commodity Prices in the International Coordination of Economic Policies and in the Conduct of Monetary Policy.* Before the Subcommittee on Domestic Monetary Policy and the Subcommittee on International Finance, Trade, and Monetary Policy of the Committee on Banking, Finance and Urban Affairs of the Senate, 100th Cong., 1st Sess. (November 5, 17, and December 18, 1987); Document No. 5: Commodity Futures Trading Commission,

Division of Trading Markets. *Analysis of Trading in the Chicago Board of Trade's Major Market Index Futures Contract on October 20, 1987* (January 4, 1988); Document No. 6: *Report of the Presidential Task Force on Market Mechanisms* (January 1988); Document No. 7: U.S. General Accounting Office. *Financial Markets: Preliminary Observations on the October 1987 Crash* (January 1988); Document No. 8: U.S. Securities and Exchange Commission, Division of Market Regulation. *The October 1987 Market Break* (February 1988); and Document No. 9: Working Group on Financial Markets. *Interim Report of the Working Group on Financial Markets* (May 1988). With a selected chronological bibliography.

394. Swartz, Steve and Bryan Burrough. "The Aftermath: Crash Could Weaken Wall Street's Grip on Corporate America." *Wall Street Journal*, 29 December 1987, 1+

Indicates Stock Market Crash is changing Wall Street's relationship with thousands of companies. Possible effects are: slowdowns in takeover activity; decrease in available money for start-up companies; commercial banks may regain some of market share lost to Wall Street; and companies may have to raise funds by turning to debt rather than selling stocks.

395. United States. Commodity Futures Trading Commission. Division of Economic Analysis. Division of Trading and Markets. *Final Report on Stock Index Futures and Cash Market Activity During October 1987 to the U.S. Commodity Futures Trading Commission.* Washington, D.C.: The Commission, 1988. 1 volume (various pagings)

Studies events of October 1987 with specific reference to futures markets and related stock market activity, including program trading. Updates the Commission's *Interim Report* of November 9, 1987 and the *Follow-up Report* of January 6, 1988. Examines floor activities of futures exchange members in handling and executing customer orders, futures regulatory programs, etc. Defines key concepts and refers to other reports on October 1987 including, reports by the Brady Commission and by the New York Stock Exchange. Recommends: clarification of legal relationships between clearing organizations and clearing banks; availability of FEDWIRE in exigent market conditions; settlement banks' access to financial data; development of central computerized financial database; intraday margin calls; enhancement of financial surveillance data systems; FCM collection of customer margins; financial adequacy of margin levels; use of continuous intermarket trade data for financial surveillance; continuous input of trade data; and mechanisms for ongoing evaluation. Includes statistical charts.

396. United States. Congress. House. Committee on Agriculture. Subcommittee on Conservation, Credit, and Rural Development. *Review of Recent Volatility in the Stock Market and the Stock Index Futures Markets: Hearing before the Subcommittee on Conservation, Credit, and Rural Development of the Committee on Agriculture, House of Representatives, One Hundredth Congress, First Session, November 4, 1987.* Washington, D.C.: Committee on Agriculture; For sale by the Superintendent of Documents, U.S. Government Printing Office, 1988. 87 pages.

Reports of representatives from the Commodity Futures Trading Commission (CFTC) regarding volatility in the stock market and the stock index futures markets. The CFTC regulates all trading in futures contracts, including contracts on the Standard & Poor's 500 Index, which is traded on the Chicago Mercantile Exchange; the Composite Index, traded on the New York Futures Exchange; the Major Market Index, traded on the Chicago Board of Trade; and the Value Line Index, traded on the Kansas City Board of Trade. Witnesses, all from the CFTC, are: Kalo A. Hineman, Acting Chairman; Robert R. Davis, Commissioner; William E. Seale, Commissioner; and Fowler C. West, Commissioner. Reviews events of the Stock Market Crash. See also item 269.

397. United States. Congress. House. Committee on Banking, Housing, and Urban Affairs. *Impact of the Stock Market Drop and Related Economic Developments on Interest Rates, Banking, Monetary Policy and Economic Stability: Hearing Before the Committee on*

*Banking, Finance and Urban Affairs, House of Representatives,
One-Hundredth Congress, First Session, October 29, 1987.*
Washington, D.C.: Committee on Banking, Housing, and Urban
Affairs; For sale by the Superintendent of Documents, U.S.
Government Printing Office, 1988. 137 pages.

Examines implications of the Stock Market Crash and its effect
on the U.S. economy. Includes statements by: Dr. John Kenneth
Galbraith, Department of Economics, Harvard University; Dr.
Allen Sinai, chief economist and managing director, Shearson
Lehman Brothers; Dr. Herbert Stein, senior fellow, American
Enterprise Institute; and Martin Feldstein, president, National
Bureau of Economic Research. Appendix contains: "The Stock
Market Decline and Economic Policy," by Martin Feldstein;
"Opening Statement by Rep. Chalmers P. Wylie; "The 1929
Parallel," by John Kenneth Galbraith (reprint of an article from the
Atlantic Monthly, January 1987); "Economic Impacts, Financial
Market Consequences, and Policy Prescriptions from the 'Crash of
'87,'" by Allen Sinai; "Statement of Herbert Stein"; "The Setting
of Margin Requirements for Financial Futures," by Edward
Rensaw; "Some Lessons from History," by Edward Renshaw;
"Letters of Invitation"; and "Opening Statement," by Rep. Mary
Rose Oakar.

398. United States. Congress. Senate. Committee on Banking, Housing,
and Urban Affairs. *"Black Monday," The Stock Market Crash of
October 19, 1987: Hearings Before the Committee on Banking,
Housing, and Urban Affairs, United States Senate, One
Hundredth Congress, Second Session on the Turbulence in the
Financial Markets last October, the Functioning of Our Financial
Markets During that Period, and Proposals for Structural and
Regulatory Reforms, February 2, 3, 4, and 5, 1988.* Washington,
D.C.: Committee on Banking, Housing, and Urban Affairs; For
Sale by the Superintendent of Documents, U.S. Government
Printing Office, 1988. 604 pages.

Transcript of four days of hearings on Black Monday, Terrible
Tuesday, and consequences of the Stock Market Crash. Examines
findings and recommendations of Brady Commission and of the

Securities and Exchange Commission as well as those of the
Commodity Futures Trading Commission, the Chicago Mercantile
Exchange, New York Stock Exchange, U.S. General Accounting
Office, etc. Provides statements by Nicholas F. Brady, Chairman,
Presidential Task Force on Market Mechanisms; Alan Greenspan,
Chairman, Board of Governors, Federal Reserve System; David S.
Ruder, Chairman, Securities and Exchange Commission; Kalo
Hineman, Acting Chairman, Commodity Futures Trading
Commission; William J. Brodsky, President and CEO, Chicago
Mercantile Exchange; Joseph R. Hardiman, President National
Association of Securities Dealers; Steven L. Hammerman,
Chairman of the NASD Board of Governors; Frank J. Wilson,
NASD Executive Vice President and General Counsel; Kenneth R.
Leibler, President, American Stock Exchange; Karsten Mahlmann,
Chairman, Chicago, Board of Trade; John J. Phelan, Chairman and
CEO, New York Stock Exchange; and Richard L. Fogel, Assistant
Comptroller, General Accounting Office. Phelan discusses Brady
Commission Report, the SEC Report, the General Accounting
Office's preliminary observations, the organization of NYSE and
effects of the October market break. Includes copy of *An Overview
of Program Trading and Its Impact on Current Market Practices*,
by Nicholas deB Katzenbach, A study commissioned by the New
York Stock Exchange, December 21, 1987, a description of
NYSE's SuperDOT System, and a copy of NYSE specialist job
description.

399. United States. Congress. Senate. Committee on Banking, Housing,
and Urban Affairs. *The Conclusions and Recommendations of
The President's "Working Group on Financial Markets:" Hearing
Before the Committee on Banking, Housing, and Urban Affairs,
United States Senate, One Hundredth Congress, Second Session
on Actions Recommended to Enhance the Integrity, Efficiency,
Orderliness, and Competitiveness of Our Nation's Financial
Markets and to Maintain the Confidence of Investors, Both Large
and Small, May 24, 1988.* Washington, D.C: Committee on
Banking, Housing, and Urban Affairs; For sale by the
Superintendent of Documents, U.S. Government Printing Office,
1988, 183 pages.

Interim report on President's Working Group on Financial Markets which describes changes already implemented by agencies and self-regulatory organizations as a result of October 1987 stock market crash. Working Group recommends more changes to enhance market stability. Testimony is by Witnesses: George D. Gould, Under Secretary for Finance, Department of the Treasury and Chairman of the Working Group; Alan Greenspan, Chairman, Board of Governors, Federal Reserve System; David S. Ruder, Chairman, Securities and Exchange Commission; and Dr. Wendy Gramm, Chairman, Commodity Futures Trading Commission.

400. United States. Congress. Senate. Committee on Banking, Housing, and Urban Affairs. *Volatility and Panic in the Nation's Financial markets: Hearing Before the Committee on Banking, Housing, and Urban Affairs, United States Senate, One Hundredth Congress, First Session on the Recent Turbulence in the Stock Market (Black Monday, October 19, 1987) and to Examine the Causes of the Market's Steep Decline, November 4, 1987.* Washington, D.C.: Committee on Banking, Housing, and Urban Affairs; For sale by the Superintendent of Documents, U.S. Government Printing Office, 1988. 121 pages.

Studies stock market turbulence of October 1987 and analyzes possible causes. Features testimony of David S. Ruder, Chairman of the Securities and Exchange Commission, who describes events of October 1987; reports monitoring functions of the SEC during this time; reviews consultation activities with the New York Stock Exchange and other major securities exchanges, the Commodity Futures Trading Commission and other governmental agencies, etc.; and discusses the SEC's study of the Crash. Also includes the document: "On the Efficiency of the Financial System," by James Tobin.

401. United States. General Accounting Office. *Stock Market Crash of October 1987: GAO Preliminary Report to Congress.* Commodity Futures Law Reports; no. 322, pt. 2. Chicago: Commerce Clearing House, 1988. 103 pages.

Report undertaken by General Accounting Office at request of several Congressional Committees. Addresses questions of: what happened, why, and what could be done, if anything, to prevent a recurrence. Considers legislative or regulatory actions that might be needed. Studies: events of October 1987 and the broad new trading interests and strategies that have evolved in capital markets. Calls for: improvement by regulators of intermarket data sharing and communication; trading and information systems should be reevaluated and improved by the markets to ensure that they are capable of handling the new trading pressures placed on them; self- and federal regulatory agencies should develop intermarket contingency plans to deal with market breaks; and strong leadership exerted to develop appropriate intermarket regulatory structure to deal with: intermarket products and strategies, provision of adequate liquidity in normal times and emergencies, and growth in linkages across international financial markets. Discusses the performance during the Crash of automated trading systems for the New York Stock Exchange. Reviews measures implemented by NYSE to improve these trading systems. Summarizes regulatory responses to Crash by: the Securities and Exchange Commission, the Commodity Futures Trading Commission, the New York Stock Exchange, the Chicago Mercantile Exchange, etc. See also item 393.

402. United States. Presidential Task Force on Market Mechanisms. *Report of the Presidential Task Force on Market Mechanisms.* New York: The Task Force, For Sale by the Superintendent of Documents, U.S. Government Printing Office, Washington, D.C., 1988. 1 vol. (various pagings)

The Brady Commission Report, submitted to the President of the United States, the Secretary of the Treasury, and the Chairman of the Federal Reserve Board. Prepared by Task Force members: Nicholas F. Brady, Chairman; James C. Cotting; Robert G. Kirby; John R. Opel; Howard M. Stein; and Prof. Robert R. Glauber, Executive Director. The Task Force on Market Mechanisms was established by President Reagan to "...review relevant analyses of the current and long-term financial condition of the Nation's securities markets; identify problems that may threaten the short-term liquidity or long-term solvency of such markets; analyze potential solutions to such problems that will both assure the continued functioning of free, fair, and competitive securities markets and maintain investor confidence in such markets; and provide appropriate recommendations..." (p.1) Analyzes events of Crash, why it happened, and how such an event may be avoided in future. Based on information from U.S. agencies, various exchanges, clearinghouses, market participants, and regulatory officials. Consists of two parts: part one contains discussion of findings, conclusions, and recommendations; part two contains staff studies with detailed information considered by Task Force on the global bull market, events of October 14-20, 1987; historical perspectives, comparison of 1929 and 1987, surveys of market participants and other interested parties, etc. Brady Commission recommends: coordination by one agency of a few critical regulatory issues which have an impact across related market segments and affect the entire financial system; unified clearing systems across marketplaces to reduce financial risk; margins should be consistent across marketplaces as a means of controlling speculation and financial leverage; circuit breaker mechanisms, including price limits and trading halts, should be formulated and implemented; and information systems established to monitor transactions and conditions in related markets. Includes statistical tables.

403. United States. Securities and Exchange Commission. Division of Market Regulation. *The October 1987 Market Break.* Washington, D.C.: The Commission; For sale by the Superintendent of Documents, U.S. Government Printing Office, 1988. 1 volume (various pagings).

Report by SEC's Division of Market Regulation of the causes, effects and regulatory ramifications of the October 1987 market break. Study conducted in conjunction with other reports, including those of the Presidential Task Force on Market Mechanisms and the Commodity Futures Trading Commission. This report "is designed to provide an independent factual basis to enable the Commission to determine the most appropriate regulatory responses to ensure the soundness of the nation's securities markets and the protection of investors." (p. xi). This Report "attempts to reconstruct the trading activity during the October market break and analyze how the trading systems for stock and its derivatives (i.e. options and futures) may have contributed to the rapidity and depth of the market decline" (p. xi). Fundamental assumption in report that extreme price volatility, which was part of the October market break, is undesirable. Studies index-related trading strategies: asset re-allocation and hedging, portfolio insurance, and index arbitrage and the use of automated stock order-routing systems for trading strategies listed above. Discusses: automated order routing and execution systems, including NYSE's DOT System; specialist performance, international securities markets and performance during October 1987, and complaints received by SEC during market break. Examines long-term effects of market break and possible preventive measures for future occurrences. Includes charts and graphs providing statistics for October 1987. Provides glossary of key terms and acronyms used in Report.

404. Winch, Kevin F. *The Stock Market "Crash" of 1987: The Early Response of Regulators.* CRS Report for Congress. Washington, D.C.: Congressional Research Service, 1987. 16 pages.

Reviews roles of regulatory agencies: the Securities and Exchange Commission and the Commodity Futures Trading Commission. Describes proposed (as of December 1987) studies dealing with October 1987 Crash, notably those by the SEC, the Brady Task Force, the Commodity Futures Trading Commission, and the General Accounting Office. Discusses immediate responses to the Crash, among which are daily price limits (futures and options), daily price limits (stocks), and index options trading halt. With bibliographical references.

405. Witryol, Faith. "The Stock Market Crash of 1987." M.S. Thesis. Massachusetts Institute of Technology, 1988. 160 leaves.

Analyzes the Crash, its causes and consequences. Studies market, regulatory and investment community participation in and its response to the drop in the Dow Jones Industrial Average and futures markets declines. Examines portfolio insurance and index arbitrage as factors in the Crash. Describes regulatory responses to the Crash among which are reports by the Brady Commission, the Securities and Exchange Commission, the Commodity Futures Trading Commission (CFTC), and the U.S. General Accounting Office. Compares events of 1987 with those of the 1929 Crash. Bibliographic references listed consist of: Public Documents; Books and Journals; and Magazines and Newspapers. With statistical charts and tables.

406. Working Group on Financial Markets. *Interim Report of the Working Group on Financial Markets.* Washington, D.C.: U.S. Government Printing Office, 1988. 38 pages.

Interim Report of the Presidential Working Group on Financial Markets, created pursuant to Executive Order, March 18, 1988. Recommendations include: coordinated circuit breakers; improvement of operation of credit, clearing, and settlement system;current minimum margin requirements provide adequate level of protection to the financial system; and contingency planning, including continuation of the Working Group. Reviews automated systems capacity enhancements by the New York Stock Exchange, the American Stock Exchange, and the National Association of Securities Dealers. With the Appendices: A. Coordinated Trading Halts and Reopenings; B. Adequacy of Prudential Margin Requirements; C. Report of Staff Subgroup on Credit, Payment and Settlement System Issues; D. Clearing and Settlement Recommendations; E. Market Report Actions Taken (or Planned) by Federal Agencies, Self-Regulatory Organizations, Clearing Agencies, and Market Participants as of May 16, 1988; and F. Working Group Participants. See also item 269.

407. Zweig, Philip L. "*FW*'s Man of the Year: NYSE Chairman John Phelan," *Financial World 156* (December 29, 1987): 22-25.

Interview with John J. Phelan Jr. concerning causes and effects of the Crash. Phelan discusses: the roles of program trading and the specialist system during the Crash. Phelan considered most difficult part of Crash ordeal was making decision to keep the NYSE open. He warns that the possibility exists for a future, more serious Crash. He considers real underlying problem for the financial markets to be the fact that equity markets are financing grossly overleveraged traders, speculators, and dealmakers.

CHAPTER XVI
1988-1991

During the time after the 1987 Crash, the New York Stock Exchange examined methods of preventing another Black Monday, studied and developed technological innovations, and planned for the possibility of twenty-four hour trading.

Material included in this chapter are the New York Stock Exchange's report, *Market Volatility and Investor Confidence;* Federal legislation; Securities Reforms of 1990; and secondary sources discussing developments at the NYSE and on Wall Street. The secondary sources cover topics which include the insider trading scandal of the 1980s and technological innovations at the New York Stock Exchange.

408. Commerce Clearing House. *Securities Reforms of 1990.* Chicago, Commerce Clearing House, 1990. 247 pages.

Contents: *Securities Enforcement Remedies and Penny Stock Reform Act of 1990* (As of October 15, 1990, P.L. 101-429, 104 Stat. 931); *Market Reform Act of 1990* (Act of October 16, 1990, P.L. 101-432, 104 Stat. 963); and *Securities Acts Amendments of 1990* (Act of November 15, 1990, P.L. 101-550, 104 Stat. 2713). Presents the laws and explanations as well as portions of Congressional Committee and Conference Reports. The Securities Enforcement provides additional flexibility and enforcement power to the SEC. The Penny Stock Reform Act is designed to curb fraud and manipulation in the penny stock market. The Market Reform Act of 1990 aims to provide additional authority to the SEC to prevent disruptions to the securities markets and to improve the clearance and settlement of securities transactions. The Securities Acts Amendments concern: authorizations of appropriations for fiscal years 1990 and 1991; granting additional authority to the SEC to improve coordination of national enforcement efforts; improvement of communications between mutual funds and their shareholders; and the updating of the law concerning public issuance of debt securities. With a topical index.

*   Ehrlich, Judith Ramsey and Barry J. Rehfeld. *The New Crowd: The Changing of the Jewish Guard on Wall Street.* see item 34 above.

409. *Electronic Bulls and Bears: U.S. Securities Markets and Information Technology.* Washington, D.C.: Congress of the U.S., Office of Technology Assessment; For sale by the Superintendent of Documents, U.S. Government Printing Office, 1990. 205 pages.

Assesses the role that communication and information technologies play in the securities markets. Report written at requests by the House Committee on Energy and Commerce and the House Committee on Government Operations. Written in light of findings of the *Securities Exchange Act Amendments* which presented goals for an electronically integrated "national market system." Topics covered are: public policy and securities markets; functions of securities markets; operations of stock, futures, and options markets; domestic clearing and settlement; technology and the securities markets; market fraud; and the regulatory structure. For the NYSE studies: the specialist system; the effects of the 1987 Stock Market Crash; the SuperDOT system; and self-regulatory functions. With an Appendix, "Clearing and Settlement in the United States." With an "Acronyms and Glossary" section and bibliographical references. Includes tables and illustrative figures.

410. Gambee, Robert. *Wall Street Christmas*. New York: Norton, 1990. 272 pages.

Contains color photographs of the financial district around the Christmas holidays. Among photographs: The New York Stock Exchange building; the floor of the New York Stock Exchange; upstairs at the New York Stock Exchange; pediment sculpture on the New York Stock Exchange; Broad and Wall Streets; Nassau Street; Fraunces Tavern; and a Wall Street snowstorm. Each photograph is accompanied by descriptive material.

411. Goodman, Ann. "Can Technology Save the New York Stock Exchange?" *Wall Street Computer Review* 8 (June 1991): 28-38.

Describes competition between NYSE and foreign markets, NASDAQ Market, Instinet, etc. Chairman William Donaldson is calling for Congressional support of the NYSE. Plans and priorities for the NYSE designed to compete effectively with other markets are: implementation of twenty-four hour trading by end of the 1990s; mid-1992 completion of MetroTech, a backup center for all NYSE's systems; improvement of implementation of technology on the trading floor for brokers and specialists; and contingency planning so the NYSE will always be able to trade.

412. Lowenstein, Louis. *What's Wrong with Wall Street: Short-Term Gain and the Absentee Shareholder*. Reading, Massachusetts: Addison-Wesley, 1988. 268 pages.

Study of Wall Street describes: evolution of the modern stock market; the nature of the stock market; takeover bids; role of shareholder within corporation; legislation; and trend toward institutionalization of the market (i.e. ownership of larger share of publicly traded stocks by pension funds, etc.). Examines New York Stock Exchange's history since the turn of the century, covering the Crash of 1929, the Securities Act of 1933, the Securities Exchange Act of 1934, and the 1987 Crash. With bibliographical notes and glossary.

413. *Market Volatility and Investor Confidence: A Report to the Board of Directors of the New York Stock Exchange, Inc.* New York: New York Stock Exchange. Market Volatility and Investor Confidence Panel, June 7, 1990. 1 vol. (various pagings).

Report of the Market Volatility and Investor Confidence Panel, a group created by the NYSE to address concerns about the impact of market volatility and to make recommendations to help maintain a strong market. The Panel's findings were: equity and equity derivative markets are essentially stable and sound, though market fluctuations are inevitable; a need exists to increase public understanding of these markets due in large part to events of October 1987 and October 1989; during the past twenty years, U.S. financial markets have experienced changes which include development of index derivative products and increased trading of portfolios of stocks; investors have been concerned with large one-day price changes in U.S. equity markets that have occurred in recent years; arbitrage is not, in itself undesirable and is a natural feature of linkage between equity and equity derivative markets; individual investors are concerned that markets are operated fairly and honestly; corporate financial executives, retail brokers, and professional investors have greater concerns than individual investors about volatility and program trading; and U.S. markets linkage with markets in the rest of the world have made less predictable the consequences of restricting certain trading practices. Their recommendations are: coordinated and mandatory circuit breakers should be established across all domestic markets to halt trading during times of market stress; Liquidity should be enhanced in times of market stress. Measures to increase liquidity should include the SEC's easing of existing constraints of corporations to repurchase their own common stock; exchanges and market professionals should work with the media to educate the public concerning program trading, index arbitrage, etc.; new products should be developed designed to enable individual investors to protect themselves from extremes of intraday price swings; exchanges and their regulators should work toward improving their capabilities to detect intermarket trading abuses; one federal agency should regulate authority over U.S. equity and equity derivative markets; and margin requirements should be set by the exchanges, with government oversight consolidated in one federal agency.

414. Nussbaum, Bruce. "Applause for John Phelan is Dying Out Fast."
Business Week Issue 3037 (February 8, 1988): 78-80.

Reviews problems faced by Phelan after the 1987 Crash and in
view of the planned Congressional Hearings on the Crash. Criticism
regarding Crash is directed toward Phelan and the NYSE's
automated system. Phelan is working on forming a consensus on
curbing market swings. Phelan must attempt to reconcile two major
factions exist in the securities industry: one contending that
unlimited liquidity cannot exist and the other maintaining that
portfolio managers should be permitted to hedge their investments
by unrestricted use of stock-index futures and options.

415. Salwen, Keith G. and Torres, Craig. "Big Board Sets Out on the
Path to Late Trading." *Wall Street Journal* 216 (February 16,
1990): C1, C15.

Reports the NYSE is taking first steps toward an after-hours
trading system. President Richard Grasso commented that an after-
hours trading system will eventually be put into place, with a
possible, eventual 24-hour trading system. Discusses effect such a
system would have on the NYSE specialist system.

416. Sheeline, William E. "Who Needs the Stock Exchange." *Fortune*
122 (November 19, 1990): 119-124.

Examines role of the NYSE in view of developments in
electronic trading systems and competition from other markets.
Discusses Steven Wunsch's competing electronic auction system,
the first system to offer price discovery dependent of the NYSE's
last trade. Describes Phelan's tenure as Chairman of the NYSE
(1984-1990) during which the NYSE spent more than $200 million
on computers to expedite order delivery, execution, reporting, and
monitoring. Incoming Chairman, William Donaldson faces
challenges regarding competition and must work to bring together
interests of specialists, floor brokers, brokerage firms, listed
companies, institutional investors, and individual investors.
Provides biographical information on Donaldson, detailing his work

as a Governor of the NYSE; his work as Under Secretary of State for Henry Kissinger; Dean of the Yale School of Organization and Management; and founding, with Dan Lufkin and Richard Jenrette, Donaldson Lufkin and Jenrette.

417. Siconolfi, Michael and William Power. "Donaldson Named Big Board's Chief; Cost Cuts a Priority." *Wall Street Journal* 16 (August 10, 1990): C8.

NYSE ended its six-month search for a new Chairman by naming William H. Donaldson for the job; he succeeds John J. Phelan, Jr. who retires at the end of 1990. Donaldson is a former NYSE director and founder of securities firm of Donaldson, Lufkin, & Jenrette, Inc. Richard A. Grasso has been named as its Executive Vice-President when Richard R. Shinn retires at the end of 1990. Among challenges faced by Donaldson are: using new trading technologies, developing new investment products, and addressing increasing internationalization of financial markets. Donaldson cited cost cuts at the NYSE as a major priority.

418. Smith, Randall. "October Rerun? Stock Market Braces for a Crucial Test After Friday's Plunge." *Wall Street Journal* 214 (October 16, 1989): 1, 6.

Reports events of October 13, 1989, when the market fell 190.58 points. The great speed with which the market dropped was demonstrated by its fall of 154 points in 65 minutes. Compares conditions of 1989 drop with events of October 1987's crash. Evaluates possible causes of market drop including the collapse of the buyout of UAL Corp., parent company of United Airlines.

419. Stewart, James B. *Den of Thieves*. New York: Simon & Schuster, 1991. 493 pages.

Story of the insider trading scandal of the 1980s involving: Dennis Levine, Ivan Boesky, Martin Siegel, and Michael R. Milken. Analyzes effects on the Wall Street financial community.

Provides biographical information for the four men. Describes role of the SEC in detecting the trades and tracking down the participants. Discusses conditions on Wall Street during the 1980s, including Black Monday and its effects. Research based on interviews and review of key documents including grand jury transcipts. The Epilogue updates information on Levine, Boesky, Siegel, and Milken. With bibliographical references, a chronology of events, and photographs.

420. "Stock Markets Mount Biting Campaigns." *Wall Street Journal* 215 (May 4, 1990): B5.

Reports plan of the three major U.S. stock markets, the NYSE, the American Stock Exchange, and the Nasdaq Over-the-Counter Market, to run large advertising campaigns. Each exchange will boast about themselves and, at the same time, belittle the competition. This type of advertising occurs for the first time in history.

421. Sturc, John H., et al. "The Securities Enforcement Remedies and Penny Stock Reform Act of 1990." *Review of Securities and Commodities Regulation* 24 (April 17, 1991): 79-86.

Addresses the SEC's new authority under the Remedies Act. Discusses reasons for promulgation of the Remedies Act. The SEC is given much greater administrative powers and provides much stiffer penalties in area of civil enforcement.

422. United States. Congress. House. Committee on Energy and Commerce. Subcommittee on Telecommunications and Finance. *Stock Market Reform: Hearings before the Subcommittee on Telecommunications and Finance of the Committee on Energy and Commerce, House of Representatives, 101st Congress, 1st session on H.R. 1609, A Bill to Amend the Securities Exchange Act of 1934 to provide additional authorities to prevent disruptions to the nation's securities markets, July 27, September 28, October 25, and November 9, 1989.* Washington, D.C.: U.S.

Government Printing Office, 1990. 479 pages.

Concerns H.R. 1609, the Stock Market Reform Act of 1989 which: grants the Securities and Exchange Commission the authority to halt trading in a market emergency; directs the SEC to implement large trading reporting; authorizes the SEC to assess the financial health of holding companies associated with brokered dealers; and directs the SEC to facilitate coordinated clearing and settlement. Includes text of H.R. 1609; testimonies; and correspondence. Among those providing testimonies: Richard C. Breeden, Chairman, Securities and Exchange Commission; William J. Brodsky, President, Chicago Mercantile Exchange; Richard A. Grasso, President, New York Stock Exchange; Joseph R. Hardiman, President, National Association of Securities Dealers, Inc.; Kenneth R. Leibler, President, American Stock Exchange; Edward I. O'Brien, President, Securities Industry Association; and William J. O'Neil, Chairman, Investor's Daily. Grasso, President of the NYSE summarizes the Exchange's views of the Stock Reform Act and reviews major initiatives undertaken since the October 1987 market break.

423. United States. Congress. Senate. Committee on Banking, Housing, and Urban Affairs. *The Market Reform Act of 1990: Report of the Committee on Banking, Housing, and Urban Affairs, United States Senate To Accompany S. 648 together with Additional Views*. Washington, D.C.: Committee on Banking, Housing, and Urban Affairs; For sale by the Superintendent of Documents, U.S. Government Printing Office, 1990. 107 pages.

Text of Market Reform Act of 1990 (S.648) and accompanying report of the Senate Committee on Banking, Housing, and Urban Affairs. Describes history and background of legislation: the 1987 Market Crash; Studies of the Market Crash, including those of the Brady Commission and the SEC; and the market disturbance on October 13-14, 1989. The Market Reform Act, a bill to amend the Securities Exchange Act of 1934, is designed to strengthen the regulatory oversight over the U.S. securities market, improve the supervision of financial market participants, and to promote coordination among market regulators. The Act clarifies and broadens authority by the SEC to take appropriate actions in the event of market emergencies; to establish an information-gathering and reporting system to monitor and assess activities of large traders and to detect illegal trading activity; to give SEC authority to identify and assess risks to brokers and dealers that result from financial activities of their affiliates; and to coordinate and strengthen coordination among U.S. financial regulators.

424. United States. Congress. Senate. Committee on Banking, Housing, and Urban Affairs. Subcommittee on Securities. *Definition of Insider Trading: Hearings Before the Subcommittee on Securities of the Committee on Banking, Housing, and Urban Affairs, United States Senate, One Hundredth Congress First Session on Proposed Legislation to Clarify the Law on Insider Trading Which Will Provide Every Professional and Firm Engaging in the Securities Business, as well as Everyone Else, With a Single Statute to Determine What the Law is and What Their Liability is in the Area. Prosecution will be Easier and Punishment Will Be Tougher When the Law is Clear, Part I, June 17, 19, 1987.* Washington, D.C.: Committee on Banking, Housing, and Urban Affairs; For Sale by the Superintendent of Documents, U.S. Government Printing Office, 1987. 195 pages.

Report of first two of the three hearings on proposed legislation (S. 1380, "The Insider Trading Proscriptions Act of 1987") to clarify the law on insider trading. Witnesses include: Charles Cox, Commissioner, Securities and Exchange Commission; Thomas G. Moore, member, Council of Economic Advisers; Gary L. Tidwell, Associate Professor of Business Administration, College of Charleston, Charleston, South Carolina; James F. Olson, Partner, Gibson, Dunn and Crutcher; and Harvey L. Pitt, partner, Fried, Frank, Harris, Shriver, and Jacobson.

425. United States. Congress. Senate. Committee on Banking, Housing, and Urban Affairs. Subcommittee on Securities. *Definition of Insider Trading...Part II, August 7, 1987.* Washington, D.C.: U.S. Government Printing Office; For sale by the Superintendent of Documents, U.S. Government Printing Office, 1987. 123

pages.

Third hearing on statutory approach to clarify and define law on insider trading. Witnesses are: Charles C. Cox, Acting Chairman, Securities and Exchange Commission; Harvey L. Pitt, Esq.; John F. Olson, Esq.; Theodore A. Levine, Esq.; and Richard M. Phillips, Esq., on behalf of the New York Stock Exchange Legal Advisory Committee.

426. United States. Congress. Senate. Committee on Banking, Housing, and Urban Affairs. Subcommittee on Securities. *The Market Reform Act of 1989: Joint Hearings before the Subcommittee on Securities and the Committee on Banking, Housing, and Urban Affairs, United States Senate. 101st Congress, 1st Session on S. 648, to amend the Securities Exchange Act of 1934, May 18 and October 26, 1989.* Washington, D.C.: U.S. Government Printing Office, 1989. 426 pages.

Hearings regarding legislation aimed at responding to the October 1987 Crash. The four provisions of the Market Reform Act as requested by the SEC are: emergency powers, large trade reporting, risk assessment, and coordinated clearing. Witnesses include: John Phelan, Chairman and Chief Executive Officer, New York Stock Exchange; Joseph Hardiman, President, National Association of Securities Dealers; Leo Melamed, Chairman, Executive Committee, Chicago Mercantile Exchange; Jeffrey B. Lane, President and Chief Operating Officer, Shearson Lehman Hutton, Inc.; and George S. Bissell, Chief Executive Officer, Keystone Massachusetts Group. Among material supplied for the record: Opinion Research Corp., Form 19b-4, proposed rule change by the New York Stock Exchange. Phelan, in his testimony on May 18, 1989, discusses the philosophy and strengths of the NYSE market system; initiatives instituted by the NYSE since the October 1987 market break; and comments on the proposed Market Reform Act.

*   Weiss, Gary. "William Donaldson." see item 86 above.

427. Welles, Chris. "Putting the Market Back on Track." *Business Week* Issue 3034 (January 18, 1988): 20-21.

Studies possible causes of the 1987 Crash and examines possible reform measures for the NYSE and other markets. The reforms are: devising an electronic trading system with equal access by all buyers and sellers, among which are market makers and public investors; expediting order flow through upgraded back-office machinery; reconciling present rules covering price-change limits between the New York and Chicago markets; and increasing margin requirements for speculators in financial futures and options. States that many experts contend that reforms may be ineffective due to effect on market of uncontrollable economic events.

CHAPTER XVII
STATISTICS SOURCES

The following materials contain statistics concerning NYSE: stock prices, Dow Jones averages, bond and option trading, the NYSE composite index, volume, etc. Depending on the source, statistics can be presented on a daily, weekly, or monthly basis and some materials offer historical data. All sources listed are in paper and/or microform, with notes as to whether they are available in online or CD-ROM formats. Full descriptions of online systems and CD-ROM products which offer statistical data are provided in Appendix VI.

It should be noted that not all newspapers which include NYSE data are presented here. Other major daily newspapers such as the *Washington Post, Newsday,* and the *Boston Globe* feature a financial section with data on securities.

Also included here is the New York Stock Exchange's *Shareownership*, a statistical guide to characteristics of NYSE's shareholders.

428. *American Statistics Index (ASI): A Comprehensive Guide and Index to Statistical Publications of the U.S. Government.* Bethesda, Maryland: Congressional Information Service, V. 1 - 1974- Monthly index and abstracts issues, plus annual cumulation of indexes and abstracts. Available in paper, online database, and CD-ROM formats.

Guide and index to statistical publications of the U.S. Government covers periodicals, series, special reports, annuals, etc. Issued in two sections, one for the Index, and the other for Abstracts, with description of the statistical publication. Relevant publications may be retrieved in Government Documents depository libraries or by ordering diazo microfiche and paper copies from the Congressional Information Service. *ASI* is available online through ORBIT Information Technologies and DIALOG. Additionally, *ASI* is accessible through CIS's CD-ROM product, Statistical Masterfile.

429. *Bank and Quotation Record.* Arlington, Massachusetts: National News Services. Monthly.

Features stock market quotations from various exchanges, including the New York Stock Exchange, the American Exchange, Boston, etc.

430. *Barron's National Business and Financial Weekly.* Chicopee Falls, Massachusetts: Barron's Publishing Company, 1921- Weekly.

Features investment statistics with articles of interest to investors. With a "Review and Preview: An Investor's Almanac," consisting of the week's statistics for Dow Industrials, 30-Year Treasury Bonds, 3-Month Treasury Bills, etc. and a summary of the week's economic and financial events. "Barron's Market Week" presents data for the past week including: the New York Stock Exchange Composite List; Bonds/New York Exchange; Options Trading; Commodities Futures; NYSE Most Active Stocks; NYSE Biggest % Movers; Dow Jones Industrials; New York Stock Exchange Composite; NYSE volume; NYSE Odd-Lot Trading; and New York Stock Exchange Monthly Statistics. Also reports new listings on the NYSE and name changes for companies whose stocks are traded on the NYSE.

431. Berlin, Howard M. *Handbook of Financial Market Indexes, Averages, and Indicators.* Homewood, Illinois: Dow Jones-

Irwin, 1990. 416 pages.

Guide to international major financial market averages and indexes. Explains statistics and how they are derived.

432. *The Business One Irwin Business and Investment Almanac.* (Former titles: *Dow Jones-Irwin Business Almanac,* 1971-1981 and *The Dow Jones-Irwin Business and Investment Almanac,* 1982-1990). Homewood, Illinois: Dow Jones-Irwin, 1991- Annual.

Reviews the year's events in business and economics and provides current and historical statistics. Section, "Stock Market: U.S. and Foreign" furnishes data on the major stock exchanges; Cash Dividends on NYSE Listed Common Stocks; Stock Market Averages by Industry Group; Dow Jones Industrial Average; How to Read NYSE and AMEX Quotations; Securities Markets: Notable Dates; Investment and Financial Terms, etc.

433. *Business One Irwin Investor's Handbook* (formerly *Dow Jones Investor's Handbook,* 1982-1990). Homewood, Illinois: Business One Irwin, 1991- Annual.

Presents statistics covering: Dow Jones Averages, including changes in Dow Jones Industrials from 1928 to present; Yearly highs and lows of Dow Jones Averages from 1913 to present; a list of Dow Jones Industry Groups; Barron's Confidence Index; New York Stock Exchange Composite Stock Index; New York Stock Exchange's numbers of listed stock; NYSE's daily reported stock volume; NYSE's cash dividends and yields on common stocks; and the year's NYSE composite, listing stocks and bonds, their sales, high and low prices, net change, etc. Also provides statistics for the American Stock Exchange, Over-the-Counter Exchange, mutual funds, and selected foreign markets. Explains how key statistical indicators are tabulated.

434. *Business Week.* New York: McGraw-Hill, 1929- Weekly.

Articles and features with a section, "Investment Figures of the Week," consisting of statistics with commentary of securities market activities for the week. Among statistics presented are latest Dow Jones Industrials as well as stock and bond prices.

435. Chapman, Karen. *Investment Statistics Locator*. Phoenix: Oryx Press, 1988. 182 pages.

Index to where investment statistics may be found. To use this source, first check the general category needed, find the name of source in abbreviated form, scan the list of abbreviations, and consult the source.   Twenty-two titles are used as sources of investment statistics. The "Sources Guide" section is an annotated listing; among titles in this section are: *Commercial and Financial Chronicle, Daily Stock Price Record, Wall Street Journal, New York Stock Exchange Fact Book,* and *Value Line.* Among statistics indexed are: "New York Stock Exchange Beta Index," "New York Stock Exchange--Common Stock," and "New York Stock Exchange--Short sales." Frequency of statistics (i.e. daily, weekly, monthly, etc.) may be scanned in the index.

436. *Commercial & Financial Chronicle.* Daytona, Florida: The Commercial & Financial Chronicle, Inc., weekly.

Contains weekly stock market statistics with daily opening, high, low, and closing prices and/or bid and asked quotations for all markets including the NYSE.

437. *Daily Graphs: New York Stock Exchange.* Los Angeles, California: William O'Neil & Co., Inc., 1972- Weekly. (Formerly: *Daily Graphs. N.Y.S.E. - OTC*)

Daily graphs representing statistics on the NYSE regarding volume, averages, prices, etc.

438. *Directory of Publicly Traded Bonds.* comp. by National Quotation

Bureau. New York: Facts on File, 1989-   Semiannual, with monthly updates.

Lists approximately 16,500 publicly traded bonds with data on coupon rate, maturity, and interest rates, etc.

439. *Directory of Publicly Traded Stocks*. comp. by National Quotation Bureau. New York: Facts on File, 1989- Semiannual, with monthly updates.

Lists approximately 23,000 publicly traded securities, with information on shares outstanding, new issues, stock price range, par value, dividend data, mergers and acquisitions, etc.

440. *The Dow Jones Averages, 1885-1970*. Edited by Phyllis S. Pierce. Homewood, Illinois: Business One Irwin, 1991. 1 vol. (various pagings)

Presents daily statistics for the Dow Jones Averages from 1885-1990. Provides an introduction, "Market Volatility and the Dow," an analysis of the Dow and the markets during the 1980s. With a chronology of the history of Dow Jones Averages from 1884 through 1990. Daily statistics include the high, low, and closing Dow Averages, plus daily stock sales and bond averages. Includes a chart: "The Dow Jones Industrials, Monthly Average, 1940-1990."

*   *Dow Jones Investor's Handbook*, see item 433 above.

*   *Dow Jones-Irwin Business Almanac*. see item 432 above.

441. Fisher, Kenneth L. *The Wall Street Waltz: 90 Visual Perspectives, Illustrated Lessons from Financial Cycles and Trends*. Chicago: Contemporary Books, 1987. 210 pages.

Series of charts, with explanations and commentaries. Charts are from books, magazines, brokerage firm materials, newsletters, research services, etc. Consists of three sections: the first concerns the stock market; the second, interest rates, inflation, commodity pricing, and real estate; and the third, general business conditions. Time period covered ranges from the 1700s through 1986. Among charts: "Sears, Roebuck & Company's Stock Price, 1926-1955"; "Railroad Stock and Bonds, 1860-1935"; "British Stocks vs. Dow Jones Industrials, 1958-1977"; "Stock Indexes in Seven Countries"; "The Dow Jones Industrial Average as Adjusted for Inflation, 1920-1985"; "Stocks vs. News Items, 1949-1968"; and "Stock Price Indexes, 1927-1929."

442. Frumkin, Norman. *Guide to Economic Indicators.* Armonk, New York: M.E. Sharpe, 1990. 242 pages.

Presents concise descriptions of over fifty economic indicators, both foreign and domestic. The section, "Stock Market Price Indexes and Dividend Yields" describes and provides statistics for: the New York Stock Exchange Composite Index, the Dow Jones Industrial Average, Standard & Poor's 500 Composite Price Index, the Wilshire 5000 Equity Index, the New York Stock Exchange Composite Dividend Yield, the Dow Jones Industrial Average Dividend Yield, the Standard & Poor's 500 Composite Dividend Yield, and the Wilshire 5000 Equity Dividend Yield. Section includes bibliographical references.

443. *Investor's Business Daily.* Los Angeles, California: Investor's Business Daily, Inc., 1991- (Formerly: *Investor's Daily*, V. 1, 1984 - V. 8, no. 110, September 13, 1991)

Articles and statistics: 60 NYSE Stocks with Greatest % Rise in Volume; NYSE Stocks in the News; Dow Jones Industrials; NYSE Volume; NYSE Stock Prices; Futures; NYSE Bonds; NYSE Insider Selling, etc.

444. Moody's Investors Service. *Moody's Bond Record and Annual*

Bond Record. New York: Moody's Investors Service. monthly, with annual volume.

Provides statistics on bonds, with facts relating to market position, date or dates of maturity, high and low sales for all listed issues, etc.   Covers corporate bonds, municipal bonds, U.S. Treasury bonds, etc. With Moody's Corporate ratings for bonds, ranging from Aaa, the best quality to C, the lowest rated class.

445. Moody's Investors Service. *Moody's Bond Survey.* New York: Moody's Investors Service. weekly.

Provides statistics and ratings for bonds as well as preferred stock. With an an economic overview and descriptions of recent and prospective offerings.

446. Moody's Investors Service. *Moody's Dividend Record.* New York: Moody's Investors Service. weekly, with monthly and annual supplements.

Reports dividend payments for securities traded in the United States and Canada. Covers approximately 18,000 stocks.

HG 4905 .M815

447. Moody's Investors Service. *Moody's Handbook of Common Stocks.* New York: Moody's Investors Service, Inc. quarterly.

Furnishes financial and business information on over 900 stocks with high investor interest. Contains the following sections: a guide to using the publication; a feature article highlighting a specific industry; analysis of stock price movements by company; industry price charts which compare the New York Stock Exchange Composite Index with specific industry groups; classification of companies by industry; the Dow Jones Industrial Average; Moody's Utilities Index; New York Stock Exchange Index; American Stock Exchange Index; Moody's Daily Commodity Price Index; companies added and dropped; recent and pending stock dividends and splits; recent dividend changes; recent and pending name changes; changes in company quality grade; latest earnings; latest developments; and company reports. The section on company reports consists of full-page information for selected companies listed on the NYSE, the American Stock Exchange, and the Over-the-Counter Market; condensed statistical information for NYSE companies for which there is no full page coverage; and long-term stock price charts for 90 NYSE companies for which there is no full page coverage. Each full page section presents information on: where the company is traded; the company ticker symbol; the short-term price score; long-term price score; long-term price chart; Moody's comment, which evaluates grade (quality) of the company's common stock and provides a concise statement on important characteristics of the company; dividend information; recent price; capitalization; interim earnings; company background; recent developments; prospects; ten-year comparative statistics and ratios (i.e. net income, revenues, return on equity, etc.); number of stockholders; company name and address; names of officers; year and place of incorporation; annual shareholders' meeting date; transfer agents; registrars; and institutional holdings.

448. *The National Stock Summary.* Jersey City, N.J.: National
     Quotation Bureau, Inc., 1913-   semi-annual.

Contains a summarization of market quotations which have appeared in National Daily Services or have been supplied by dealers on special lists. Each entry contains: name of company, its address, state of incorporation, par value, where traded, transfer agent, number of shares outstanding, dividends, convertibles, etc.

449. New York Stock Exchange. *Annual Report.* New York: NYSE,
     1933-

The year's statistical and financial highlights, plus narrative information on developments at the NYSE by officers, including the Chairman and President. Among statistics featured are share volume, revenues from operations and investment, consolidated statement of cash flows, etc. With a Chairman's Letter and a President's Letter. The section, "Basic Guide to the World's Most

Advanced Financial Market" discusses such topics as Specialists, NYSE Member Firms, Listed Companies, Market Surveillance, and Enforcement. With names and group photographs of the NYSE Board of Directors and rosters of NYSE Committees.

450. New York Stock Exchange, Inc. *NYSE Bond Report*. New York: New York Stock Exchange. Daily.

Presents individual transactions of all NYSE bond issues, by bond symbol and time of trade. Contains separate closing quote section, detailing call or flat conditions, yields on closing quotes, CUSIP designations, etc. Prepared overnight for availability the next morning, it is available in printed and microfiche formats.

451. New York Stock Exchange, Inc. *NYSE Daily Sales Reports*. New York: New York Stock Exchange. Daily.

Provides data on individual transactions of all NYSE listed issues by security symbol, time of trade, from all markets. Contains separate block trading section, all closing quotes, etc. Produced overnight for availability the next morning, it is available on microfiche and printed report formats or through direct computer transmission.

452. New York Stock Exchange, Inc. *NYSE Indexes*. New York: New York Stock Exchange. Daily.

Presents daily closings of the NYSE Indexes: Composite, Industrial, Transportation, Utility, and Financial. Retrospectively records NYSE indexes from January 1966 on, with weekly closings from January 1939 on Composite only.

453. New York Stock Exchange, Inc. *NYSE Member Firm Sales Networks--As of Year-End 1988*. New York: New York Stock Exchange, 1989.

Surveys numbers and geographic distribution of sales officers and the working registered representatives of New York Stock Exchange member firms that deal with the public.

454. New York Stock Exchange, Inc. *New York Stock Exchange Fact Book*. New York: New York Stock Exchange, Inc., 1956- Annual.

Statistical reference manual for the NYSE offers a narrative of the year in review and presents historical data for the Exchange. The "Stock Market Activity" section provides data for: Selected Historical Record Highs; Stock Volume, Round Lots; Stock Volume, Odd Lots; Stock Volume, Average and Trading Days; Distribution of Round-Lot Volume; Reported Trades; Most Active Stocks on the NYSE; NYSE Member Trading; Intermarket Trading System Activity, etc. The "Stock Market Activity" section also presents definitions and data for: Exchange Systems: SuperDOT; Opening Automated Report Service (OARS); Market Order System; Limit Order System; Electronic Display Book System; Booth Program; Post Trade System; Intermarket Trading System (ITS), etc. The "Listed Companies" section describes the qualifications for listing on the NYSE; a list of the year's top fifty NYSE-listed companies in terms of largest numbers of common stockholders-of-record; common stocks added or deleted during the year; stocks of foreign corporate issuers listed geographic region for the year; the year's common stock splits; longevity records including annual dividend records since the eighteenth and nineteenth centuries; etc. The "Bonds" section provides data on the year's most active bonds; the year's largest bond listings; a list of new Automated Bond System (ABS) Subscribers; etc. The "Futures" section includes statistics for the New York Futures Exchange, a wholly-owned subsidiary of the NYSE. The "Options" section provides data on the year's NYSE Composite Index and Equity Options Trading, NYSE Equity Options Reported Volume, and Contract Specifications for Stock Index Options. "Stock Price Trends" includes statistics concerning the NYSE Composite Index, including its monthly range of components, daily closings, yield and P/E Ratio, and Growth Rates. "Securities Market Credit" contains data on Short Sales, Short Interest, the Federal Reserve Board's Initial margin requirements, and Securities market credit. "The Investing Public analyzes characteristics and geographic distribution of shareholders of public corporations. "The Exchange Community" presents data on Exchange Membership, Member Organizations, and Securities Industry personnel. "Foreign Markets" includes statistics for international transactions in stocks. The "Historical Section" contains historical data for a number of statistical series as well as a chronology of significant historical dates in NYSE's history. Among statistical data presented in this section are: "Daily Reported Share Volume: Average, High and Low Days; NYSE Large Block Transactions; Odd-lot Volume; Bond Volume; NYSE Composite Index; Cash Dividends on NYSE Listed Common Stocks; Membership Prices; and NYSE Market Data Services. With an index and annotated listing of current NYSE publications.

455. New York Stock Exchange. *Shareownership, 1952-* New York: New York Stock Exchange, 1953-   irregular.

Series of NYSE publications providing results of surveys of individual shareowners with statistics concerning age, sex, occupation, geographic distribution, income, portfolio size, etc. Includes results of an attitudinal survey as well as statistical charts.

456. *The New York Times*. New York: the New York Times Company, 1851-

Part of each day's *New York Times* is its Business Day section which, in addition to articles and features, lists statistics for New York Stock Exchange issues as well as charts for the S & P 500 Index and NYSE volume. Also contains data for Dow Jones industrials, most active NYSE stocks, odd-lot trading.

457. O'Hara, Frederick M. and Robert Sicignano. *Handbook of United States Economic and Financial Indicators*. Westport, Connecticut: Greenwood Press, 1985. 224 pages.

Reference data on major economic financial indicators for the

United States. Arranged alphabetically by indicator with cross references included. Each entry consists of: name of indicator, description, derivation, use, publisher, where and when announced, and where to find additional information. Among indicators listed: Dow Jones Industrial Average, Dow Jones Composite Average, New York Stock Exchange Composite Index, New York Stock Exchange Advance-Decline Line, New York Stock Exchange Big Block Activity, New York Stock Exchange Firms' Free Credit Balance, New York Stock Exchange Firms' Margin Accounts, New York Stock Exchange Members' Short Sells Ratio, New York Stock Exchange Nonmembers' Short Sells Ratio, New York Stock Exchange Odd-Lot Index, New York Stock Exchange Odd-Lot Sales and Purchase Index, New York Stock Exchange Odd-Lot Short Sales, New York Stock Exchange Price-Earnings Ratio, New York Stock Exchange Seat Sales, New York Stock Exchange Short Interest Ratio, New York Stock Exchange Volume, New York Stock Exchange Volume Momentum, etc. Appendixes contain an Abbreviations List and Guide to Sources as well as a List of Compilers of Indicators. Includes index.

458. *SEC Monthly Statistical Review.* Washington, D.C.: Securities and Exchange Commission; for sale by the Superintendent of Documents, U.S. Government Printing Office, 1942- Monthly. Former title: *Statistical Bulletin*

Includes securities market statistics among which are Dow Jones Averages, NYSE stock and bonds data, etc.

459. Standard & Poor's Corporation. *Analyst's Handbook.* New York: Standard & Poor's, 1964- Annual, with monthly supplements.

Provides approximately 20 financial statistics on a per share basis for various industry categories contained in the Standard & Poor's 500. Designed to enable users to compare vital per share data and financial statistics for the S & P Industrial Stocks with the 71 industries comprising the index.

460. Standard & Poor's Corporation. *Bond Guide.* New York: Standard
     & Poor's. Monthly. paper and microfiche formats.

     Provides information for more than 6100 corporate bonds, 625
     convertibles and over 300 Canadian and international issues.
     With expanded S & P debt rating presentation and data to help
     assess an issuer's degree of leverage: capitalization and debt to
     capital ratio.

*   Standard & Poor's Corporation. *Chart Guide.* see Standard &
     Poor's Corporation. *Trendline's Chart Guide.*

461. Standard & Poor's Corporation. *Daily Action Stock Charts.* New
     York: Trendline Division of Standard & Poor's. weekly.

     Covers over 750 stocks showing 12 months of price action
     plotted on a daily basis. Each entry includes: name; ticker symbol;
     where traded; basic business of company; daily high, low, and
     closing prices; 10-30 week moving averages; quarterly and annual
     earnings; book value; S & P earnings estimate; dividends; relative
     strength, etc.

462. Standard & Poor's Corporation. *Daily Stock Price Records.* New
     York Stock Exchange. New York:Standard & Poor's, 1962-
     quarterly. (Former title: Standard & Poor's *I S L Daily Stock
     Price Index. New York Stock Exchange*)

     Available in microfiche and paper copy formats. Each quarterly
     book divided into two parts: Part I. "Major Technical Indicators of
     the Stock Market" and Part II. "Daily and Weekly Stock Action."
     Part I consists of statistics and how they are derived; among these
     statistics are the Standard & Poor's Industrial Stock Price Index,
     Standard & Poor's Utility Stock Price Index, Standard & Poor's
     Transportation Stock Price Index, Standard & Poor's Financial
     Stock Price Index, Standard & Poor's "500" Composite Stock Price
     Index, Dow-Jones Industrial Average, Dow-Jones Transportation
     Average, Dow-Jones Utility Average, NYSE Volume, Average

Price of Ten Most Active Stocks, Barron's Confidence Index, and Odd-Lot Indexes. Part II contains the daily and weekly record of NYSE stocks. Each entry in Part II includes ticker symbol; shares outstanding; volume; high, low, and closing prices; relative strength; dividends; and 30-week moving averages of individual stock prices.

463. Standard & Poor's Corporation. *Dividend Record.* New York: Standard & Poor's, daily with weekly, quarterly, and annual cumulations.

Available on microfiche and paper copy formats. Dividend information on over 10,000 common and preferred stock.

464. Standard & Poor's Corporation. *Earnings Forecaster.* New York: Standard & Poor's, weekly.

Per share earnings estimates for companies for current year and makes projections for the following year.

465. Standard & Poor's Corporation. *Earnings Guide.* New York: Standard & Poor's, 1991- monthly.

Provides Wall Street consensus of earnings estimates. Furnishes the high and low estimate and computes a mean estimate for each of the next two years. Estimates in the *Guide* are compiled by over 1600 financial analysts representing more than 130 individual brokerage firms nationwide. Also contains data on book value, cash flow, estimated five-year projected earnings growth rate, and annual revenue. Ranking system for common stocks range from A+ to C, with D meaning "In Reorganization" and NR, not rated.

466. Standard & Poor's Corporation. *The Outlook.* New York: Standard & Poor's, 1937- Weekly.

Studies the outlook for financial and economic trends as well as

investment opportunities. Evaluates stocks for their investment
potentials. Provides the past week's statistics for Daily Stock Price
Indexes and Weekly Bond Yields % as well as Dow Jones and
Standard & Poor's Indexes. Also presents Monthly Stock Price
Indexes.

467. Standard & Poor's Corporation. *S & P 500 Directory*. New York:
Standard & Poor's, Annual.

500 is comprised of a representative sample of common stocks
that trade on the New York Stock Exchange, the American Stock
Exchange, and the Over-the-Counter market. The 500 is a basket
of a weighted average of stock prices and common shares
outstanding. Explains calculation methodology and total return
methodology. Provides an alphabetical list of the 500 companies
that comprise the S & P's 500 Composite Price Index. For each
company listed, the entry includes the ticker symbol, the S & P
industry group, and a summary.

468. Standard & Poor's Corporation. *S & P 500 Information Bulletin*.
New York: Standard & Poor's. Monthly.

Each issue contains: performance data including daily dividend
and total return information for the index; a list of stocks in the S
& P 500 with their shares, price, market value, etc.; news reports
of events that have a bearing on the index, including acquisitions
and mergers; and market commentary and analysis.

469. Standard & Poor's Corporation. *Statistical Service*. New York:
Standard & Poor's, 1978-   One volume looseleaf service with
monthly supplements.

Data for indexes developed by Standard & Poor's as well as the
Dow Jones averages. Includes the Security Price Index Record,
published every two years, which contains information to help
determine the performance history of particular stock groups during
recessions, recovery periods, or periods of increasing or declining

interest rates. Also presents comparative sales volume and price performance of stocks and bonds during periods of inflation; performance/activity indicators such as price/earnings ratios, earnings, and dividends. The Current Statistics section provides 40 to 50 pages of new and revised statistics on indicators listed above, plus new data on S & P stock price indexes.

470. Standard & Poor's Corporation. *Stock Guide.* New York: Standard & Poor's, 1943 - Monthly.

Gives pertinent financial data on over 5200 common and preferred stock plus 650 mutual fund issues. Includes stocks traded on the New York Stock Exchange, the American Stock Exchange, Over-the-Counter, Philadelphia, London, etc. Data presented for: ticker symbol, name of company, where traded, par value, common stock ranking (by S & P), preferred stock rating (by S & P), dividends, financial position, principal business, price range, annual earnings, etc. Each issue features economic and industrial profiles.

471. Standard & Poor's Corporation. *Stock Market Encyclopedia.* New York: Standard & Poor's. Published in February and March of each year.

Features: S & P Stock Reports on approximately 750 companies; S & P Common Stock Ranking; a profile of the S & P 500 Index; charts of the S & P Stock Indexes; articles on topics of interest to investors; listings showing leading companies and companies with highest yields; summary of companies' yearly stock price ranges, etc.

472. Standard & Poor's Corporation. *Stock Reports, New York Stock Exchange.* New York: Standard & Poor's.

Reports for stocks listed on the NYSE provide data on: name, address, officers, price, dividend yield, S & P ranking, beta, business summary, per share data, income data, balance sheet data, net asset value per share, dividend data, finances, capitalization, etc. The Index section lists companies covered in the S & P NYSE, ASE, and OTC Reports; a glossary of terms; and an explanation of the S & P Common Stock Ranking System.

473. Standard & Poor's Corporation. *Trendline's Chart Guide.* New York: Standard & Poor's, 1991-   monthly.

Gives price action charts and comparative data for 4,428 stocks listed on various exchanges, including the NYSE, as well as the NASDAQ. Each chart covers a full year of market action, with weekly high, low, close, and volume. Also plotted on each chart is a 30 week moving average of prices. Information also available for each chart is: industry group, exchange where traded, ticker symbol, number of shares outstanding, latest 12 month earnings, dividend rate, S & P earnings/dividend ranking and relative price performance comparisons for the last 52, 13, and 4 weeks. Additionally publication includes charts for the stock market averages, Dow-Jones Industrial Average, Standard & Poor's Composite Index of 500 Stocks, New York Stock Exchange volume; and Advance-Decline line; NYSE Composite Index; Trendline's Market Barometer, etc.

474. *Statistical Reference Index (SRI).* Bethesda, Maryland: Congressional Information Service, Inc. V. 1 -   1980- Issued in two parts: an Abstracts and an Index volume. Monthly, with annual cumulations. Available in paper and on CD-ROM.

Indexes statistics from publications available from sources other than Federal Government Agencies. Statistical sources are associations and institutes, business and commercial publishers, state government agencies, research centers, and universities. Indexes are by Subjects and Names, Category, Issuing Source, and Publication Title. The accompanying Abstracts volume provides bibliographic citations and addresses of publications as well as summary of the statistics source. An optional companion is the SRI Microfiche Library, containing over 90 percent of titles indexed in SRI. Available on CD-ROM through CIS's Statistical Masterfile.

475. *United & Babson Investment Report.* Wellesley Hills, Massachusetts: Babson-United Investment Advisors, Inc. Weekly.

Analyzes current economic and financial indicators; recommends stocks; projects trends in the market; and profiles selected companies.

476. *Value Line Investment Survey.* New York: Value Line, Inc. weekly. available on microfiche, paper, and software. 1931-

Weekly, investment advisory service registered with the United States Securities and Exchange Commission. The service consists of three sections: Summary and Index, a weekly, alphabetical catalog of 1700 stocks at their most recent prices and their current rankings for Timeliness and Safety; Selection & Opinion, which analyzes the outlook of the stock; and Ratings and Reports which presents a full page report on each of the 1700 stocks. Data provided for each stock include: recent price; dividend yield; highest and lowest prices of the year; number of shares traded monthly; where traded; quarterly dividends paid; quarterly earnings; and capital structure. Statistics presented in the Selection & Opinion section include the Dow Jones Industrial Average; Gross National Product; Consumer Price Index; and Value Line Composite.

477. *Wall Street Journal.* New York: Dow Jones, 1889- Five times per week.

Features news stories on current events worldwide and in business and finance. The "Money and Investing" section includes: articles about the securities markets and investing; "The Markets Diary," consisting of statistical charts for the Dow Jones Industrial Average, Commodities CRB Futures Index, Lehman Brothers T-Bond Index, etc.; a "Stock Market Data Bank," a statistical chart with the trading day's major indexes among which are the Dow Jones Averages, the New York Stock Exchange Composite, NYSE Industrials, NYSE Utilities, NYSE Transportation, NYSE Finance, Standard & Poor's Indexes, the Most Active Stocks on the NYSE;

Price Percentage Gainers and Losers on the NYSE, Breakdown of Trading in NYSE Stocks; and Volume Percentage Leaders in NYSE Stocks; "New York Stock Exchange Composite Transactions," a list of the trading day's stock quotations, including high, low, and closing prices; "Listed Options Quotations"; "NYSE Composite Index (New York Futures Exchange)"; and "New York Exchange Bonds."

CHAPTER XVIII
DIRECTORIES

Directories described range from directories of: international exchanges; brokerage firms; and the New York Stock Exchange. Commerce Clearing House publishes a directory that is updated monthly of the NYSE; the directory lists NYSE members, companies traded on the NYSE, and its Constitution and Bylaws.

478. *Directory of World Stock Exchanges.* Compiled by The Economist Publications. Baltimore, Maryland: Johns Hopkins University Press, 1988. 469 pages.

Directory of international stock exchanges. Entry for the New York Stock Exchange consists of: name, address, telephone number, Telex, Members of board of directors, categories of memberships, cost and qualifications for membership, functions of governing body, regulatory regime, registration and transfer procedure, investor protection, types of securities dealt in, types of market, method of quotation and market-making, ordering and settlement procedure, price publication procedure, new issues procedure, affiliated broking firms, history, technical publications, etc.

479. *Handbook of World Stock and Commodity Exchanges.* Cambridge, Massachusetts: Basil Blackwell, 1991. 482 pages.

Directory of world stock and commodity exchanges reports, for each exchange: name and address; telephone, fax, and telex numbers; opening hours; types of shares traded; daily price limits; brief history, etc. Foreword is by Leo Malamed, Chairman, Executive Committee, Chicago Mercantile Exchange and George Hayter, Managing Director, Trading Markets Division, the International Stock Exchange, London. Entry for the NYSE provides: name, address, and telephone number; principal officers; overseas offices; brief history; structure; official opening hours; number of companies listed as of December 31, 1989; number of issues listed as of December 31, 1989; number of foreign companies listed as of December 31, 1989; number of foreign issues listed as of December 31, 1989; market capitalization as of December 31, 1989; main indices; securities traded; description of trading system; settling and clearing; commission rates and other client costs; taxation and regulations affecting foreign investors; investor protection details; prospective developments; and option contracts. Also presents an entry for the New York Futures Exchange (NYFE), incorporated on April 5, 1979 as a wholly owned subsidiary of the NYSE. Lists NYFE's address and telephone number; offices; history, structure, etc.

480. New York Stock Exchange. *Guide Reports.* New York: NYSE, 193?-

Directory of members, member firms, organizations, and listed securities.

481. New York Stock Exchange. *Ticker Symbol Abbreviations.* New York: Francis Emory Fitch, 1903-

Directory of ticker symbols, post locations, par values, and minimum commission rates.

482. *New York Stock Exchange Guide.* Chicago, Illinois: Commerce
     Clearing House, 1957-   Monthly.   3 vols. (loose-leaf service)

   The official publication of the New York Stock Exchange
contains its directory, Constitution, rules, and policies as well as
relevant Federal laws and regulations. Volume 1 consists of: a list
of all NYSE Officers, Members, and Member Organizations; Listed
Securities, a directory of stocks and bonds listed on the NYSE; a
Directory for Telephone Inquiries; and a Compendium of NYSE
Exchange Services. Volume 2 presents the NYSE's Constitution
and Rules, with an index and tables of contents. Volume 3 contains
related laws and regulations including texts of the Securities Act of
1933; the Securities Exchange Act of 1934; Securities Investor
Protection Act of 1970; Federal Reserve Board--Officials and
Regulations G, T, and U; and a Topical Index to Federal
requirements. The *Guide* is updated by loose-leaf reports that reflect
changes and new developments.

483. *Securities Industry Yearbook.* New York: Securities Industry
     Association, 1980-   Annual.

   Directory of the securities industry as represented by the
Securities Industry Association (SIA). The "Rankings" section ranks
securities industry companies by: capital, number of offices,
number of employees, and number of registered representatives.
"Tables" section lists member firms with publicly-traded stock
(listing where stocks are traded); member firms wholly owned by
outside organizations; member firms partially owned by outside
organizations; mergers & acquisitions involving SIA securities
firms for the year; and member firms that clear for others. The
"Directory of SIA Members" lists securities organizations; each
entry provides the organization's name, address, telephone number,
major subsidiaries, year founded, number of offices, number of
employees, number of customer accounts, number of registered
representatives, form of partnership, industry memberships
(including major exchanges), description of firm, senior
management, departments, capital position, and underwriting and
syndication. "Industry & Market Statistics" consists of statistical
tables and charts concerning: Revenues & Expenses of NYSE Firms

Doing a Public Business, Securities Industry Pre-Tax Profit Margin, Securities Industry Average Pre-Tax Return on Equity, Number of NYSE Member Firms Doing a Public Business, Market Activity-NYSE, etc. "Major Exchanges & Selected Entities" lists major exchanges and organizations with names, addresses, and officers. "Sources" is a buyers' guide to products and services related to the securities industry.

484. *Standard & Poor's Security Dealers of North America.* New York: Standard & Poor's. Semiannual.

Directory of brokerage firms in U.S. and Canada. Also lists names and addresses of U.S. and Canadian exchanges and associations, major foreign stock exchanges, etc.

CHRONOLOGY OF THE NEW YORK STOCK EXCHANGE

May 17, 1792 - Twenty-four brokers met beneath buttonwood tree (sycamore) in front of what is now 64 Wall Street. These brokers formed the first organized stock market in New York. Agreement is known as the Buttonwood Agreement or Buttonwood Tree Agreement.

1793 - The Buttonwood Agreement brokers moved operations indoors to the Tontine Coffee House at Wall and Water Streets. New rules adopted.

March 8, 1817 - First formal Constitution and name, "New York Stock and Exchange Board" adopted. First President was Anthony Stockholm.

April 8, 1817 - Moved operations to a second floor room at 40 Wall Street. Headquarters for the Exchange was subsequently moved some ten or twelve times before moving to present loccation at 18 Broad Street.

1820 - The New York Stock and Exchange Board revised their Constitution, established daily meetings, and a regular call of stocks.

March 16, 1830 - Dullest day in NYSE's history with only 31 shares traded.

1837 - First major panic.

1844 - First telegraph line.

1857 - Panic brought about by widespread speculation and overextension of credit. Called Banking Panic or "Western Blizzard."

April 7, 1861 - New York Stock and Exchange Board passed resolution which signified allegience to the Union during the Civil War.

1861 - Jay Gould began his career on Wall Street.

January 29, 1863 - The name "New York Stock and Exchange Board" changed to "New York Stock Exchange."

1866 - Beginning of series of conflicts for control over Erie Railroad or "Erie Wars."

October 1867 - Daniel Drew expelled from Erie Railroad.

November 15, 1867 - Stock tickers first introduced.

1868 - First NYSE Governing Committee elected.

March 10, 1868 - Panic on NYSE caused by dumping of 50,000 bogus shares of Erie Railroad stock by Jay Gould, Daniel Drew, and James Fisk, Jr. When Commodore Cornelius Vanderbilt failed to support price of stock, Erie fell from 83 to 78, closing at 71.

March 11, 1868 - Gould, Drew, and Fisk fled to Jersey City, N.J.

July 1868 - Jay Gould became President of Erie.

October 23, 1868 - Memberships in NYSE become salable. Previously, members had reserved seats in particular places, and had rights to seats for life.

February 1, 1869 - NYSE required that securities be registered by listed companies. Measure was designed to prevent over-issuance of stock which had happened in 1868 when bogus Erie shares were dumped on the market.

May 8, 1869 - NYSE and Open Board of Brokers adopted plan to consolidate. Revised Constitution and By-laws passed.

June 1869 - Jay Gould secretly began buying gold.

September 24, 1869 - "Black Friday" panic started when attempted gold corner by Jay Gould and Jim Fisk, Jr. failed when the United States Treasury placed $4 million in gold on the market to buy bonds. Subsequently, price of gold fell from 160 to 133.

November 1, 1871 - Revised Constitution and Bylaws.

September 18, 1873 - NYSE closed from September 18 through September 29 due to Panic of 1873. Failure of Jay Cooke & Co.

December 1, 1873 - Trading hours set from 10 A.M. to 3 P.M. and Saturdays from 10 A.M. to noon.

1874 - Arrangements made for odd-lot trading.

1875 - NYSE records of complete transactions begun. Prior to this, only sales on calls were reported.

November 13, 1878 - Telegraph and telephone lines installed at the New York Stock Exchange.

December 17, 1878 - Gold Exchange closed.

May 14, 1884 - A.S. Hatch, NYSE President, failed financially during Panic of 1884.

July 3, 1884 - Dow Jones & Co. started publishing average closing prices of representative, active stocks.

December 16, 1886 - NYSE's first million share day with 1,200,000 shares.

1889 - First issue of the *Wall Street Journal* published

1890 - *Poor's Handbook of Investment Securities* published information about industrial stocks.

May 17, 1892 - One hundredth anniversary of Buttonwood Agreement.

December 2, 1892 - Death of Jay Gould.

1892 - Method of conducting business at posts on trading floor started.

January 23, 1895 - The New York Stock Exchange recommended that traded or listed companies publish and distribute annual statements, with financial information, to shareholders.

1897 - Dow Jones Average divided into two sections: "Industrials" and "Rails."

1901 - Panic when Northern Pacific Railroad was cornered and its price rose to $1,000 a share.

April 23, 1903 - New building opened for NYSE at 18 Broad Street.

1906 - Beginning of "stock pyramiding" practice.

October 23, 1907 - Time of Panic of 1907.

October 24, 1907 - J.P. Morgan & Co. forestalled national financial crisis by using $25 million of funds to maintain solvency of key New York banks.

June 7, 1909 - Release of report on the securities market and the Panic of 1907 by the Hughes Committee.

March 31, 1910 - NYSE's Department of Unlisted Securities abolished.

February 20, 1913 - Release of report of Pujo Committee or "Money Trust."

March 31, 1913 - Death of J.P. Morgan. At time of his funeral, NYSE closed for a day.

December 23, 1913 - Federal Reserve System established.

July 31, 1914 - World War I - NYSE closed.

November 28, 1914 - NYSE reopened for bond trading under certain restrictions.

December 11, 1914 - NYSE reopened for stock trading under certain restrictions.

April 1, 1915 - All trading restrictions removed.

October 13, 1915 - The basis for quoting and trading in stocks changed from percent of par value to dollars.

August 4, 1917 - NYSE closed due to extremely hot weather conditions.

November 11, 1918 - Armistice day, World War I.

January 2, 1919 - Separate tickers for bond quotations installed.

April 26, 1920 - Stock Clearing Corporation established.

September 16, 1920 - Explosion on Wall Street outside J.P. Morgan & Co. Thirty people were killed and one hundred injured. NYSE closed for rest of day.

March 22, 1921 - Stock Clearing Corporation began clearance of loans for NYSE members.

October 2, 1922 - Formal opening of NYSE's offices at 11 Wall Street.

1924 - Beginning of Coolidge bull market.

October 30, 1924 - Sliding scale of commission rates adopted.

June 25, 1925 - Revised NYSE Constitution became effective.

January 3, 1927 - Trading started in inactive stocks on the basis of a 10-share unit of trading. Post 30 designated for "10 share unit" stock issues.

October 29, 1929 - Stock Market Crash; 16,410,000 shares traded.

1932-1934 - Senate Committee on Banking and Currency investigated securities markets; investigations later known as Pecora Hearings.

March 1, 1932 - Suicide of Ivar Kreuger, the "Match King."

March 4, 1933 - NYSE closed until March 14 for bank holiday.

May 27, 1933 - Enactment of Securities Act of 1933. Its purposes: to provide full disclosure to investors and to prohibit fraud in connection with sale of securities.

June 6, 1934 - Enactment of Securities Exchange Act of 1934. It established the Securities and Exchange Commission and provided for regulation of securities trading.

December 10, 1937 - NYSE President, Charles R. Gay appointed special committee to investigate organization and administration of the Exchange.

January 27, 1938 - Release of recommendations by Conway Committee, appointed by Charles R. Gay, for study of NYSE's organization and administration. Committee recommended: a salaried president; a chairman of the board to be chosen from members; reduction in size of the Governing Board; greater representation by the public on the Governing Board; and reduction of standing committees from 17 to 7.

March 17, 1938 - Former New York Stock Exchange President Richard Whitney expelled from NYSE for embezzlement. Approval by NYSE Governors of Conway Committee Recommendations.

May 17, 1938 - NYSE's new Constitution became effective.

June 30, 1938 - William McChesney Martin elected by Board of Governors as NYSE's first salaried President.

1938 - NYSE open to the public for tours.

1941 - 1945 - World War II.

September 29, 1952 - Trading hours changed to weekdays, 10. A.M.

to 3:30 P.M., with no Saturdays.

June 4, 1953 - Woodcock, Hess & Co. became first member corporation.

1963 - Release of *Report of Special Study of Securities Markets of the Securities and Exchange Commission.*

November 25, 1963 - United States securities exchanges closed for funeral of John F. Kennedy.

August 3, 1964 - New NYSE member classification: Registered Trader.

July 14, 1966 - New NYSE composite index inaugurated.

December 20, 1966 - Transmission of trade and quote data became fully automated.

May 17, 1967 - 175th Anniversary of founding of NYSE.

December 1967 - Muriel Siebert became first woman member of the NYSE

June 19, 1969 - NYSE appropriated $7.5 million for future automation projects.

March 26, 1970 - Public ownership of member firms approved.

February 18, 1971 - NYSE incorporated.

July 27, 1971 - First member organization: Merrill Lynch

May 1972 - NYSE reorganized and Chairman of Board became full-time, salaried Chief Executive Officer.

July 13, 1972 - Board of Directors, with ten public members, replaced Board of Governors.

August 1972 - James J. Needham began term of office as first full-time salaried Chairman and Chief Executive Officer.

August 5, 1971 - *The Securities Markets: A Report, with Recommendations* by William McChesney Martin, Jr. submitted to the Board of Governors of the New York Stock Exchange.

May 11, 1973 - Depository Trust Company succeeded Central Certificate Service.

October 1, 1974 - Trading hours extended to 4 P.M.

April 30, 1975 - Fixed commission system abolished.

May 1, 1975 - "May Day," first day without fixed commission system

June 16, 1975 - Introduction of full consolidated tape.

January 19, 1976 - New high-speed data line began transmitting market data at approximately 36,000 characters per minute.

March 1, 1976 - Designated Order Turnaround (DOT) system started.

March 4, 1976 - Adoption of alternative listing standards to accommodate major foreign corporations.

May 24, 1976 - Specialists began handling odd-lots.

February 3, 1977 - Foreign broker/dealers permitted to obtain membership.

April 17, 1978 - Inauguaration of Intermarket Trading System (ITS).

August 7, 1980 - New York Futures Exchange (NYFE) opened.

May 6, 1982 - Trading in NYSE Composite Index Futures initiated on the NYFE.

May 17, 1982 - Trading begun through experimental linkage between the NASD and the Intermarket Trading System (ITS), operated by NYSE and six other exchanges.

August 18, 1982 - First 100 million share day (132,681,120 shares).

January 28, 1983 - Trading in options on NYSE Composite Index Futures began on the NYFE.

September 23, 1983 - Trading began in options on NYSE Composite Index.

November 6, 1984 - NYSE open on a Presidential Election Day for first time in its history.

November 16, 1984 - NYSE inaugurated SuperDOT 250.

March 28, 1985 - President Ronald Reagan visited the NYSE, became first U.S. President to visit Exchange.

June 3, 1985 - NYSE began trading in options on three Over-the-Counter stocks.

September 30, 1985 - NYSE trading hours set at 9:30 A.M. to 4 P.M.

October 21, 1985 - NYSE began trading in options on two listed stocks.

June 5, 1986 - Board of Directors expanded to 24 outside directors: 12 public members; and 12 industry leaders.

September 21, 1987 - Highest price paid for NYSE membership: $1,150,000.

October 19, 1987 - "Black Monday," largest point drop in the Dow Jones Industrial Average at 508 points.

October 20, 1987 - Highest volume day: 608,148,720 shares.

October 19, 1988 - Securities and Exchange Commission approved a series of initiatives by the NYSE and Chicago Mercantile Exchange (CME). Initiatives are designed to coordinate procedures between the equities and futures markets, including coordinated circuit breakers; a joint effort against front running; inter-exchange communications; and shared audit trail and surveillance information.

November 7, 1988 - An office is opened by NYSE in London to assist European companies in gaining access to U.S. capital markets and becoming listed on the NYSE.

June 12, 1990 - Release of the NYSE Market Volatility and Investor Confidence Panel's results of their six-month study recommending initiatives whose purpose is to reduce market volatility and to enhance investor confidence.

August 6, 1990 - NYSE implemented a new rule requiring Trade Data + 1 (T + 1) completion of transactions effected on the NYSE.

September 11, 1990 - NYSE approved two crossing sessions which will extend trading hours to 5:15 P.M. The NYSE filed with the SEC to go forward with these trading hours in 1991.

May 17, 1992 - 200th Anniversary of the New York Stock Exchange.

APPENDIX II
PRESIDENTS AND CHAIRMEN OF
THE NEW YORK STOCK EXCHANGE

Presidents of the New York Stock Exchange. Under the amended Constitution of the NYSE, effective May 16, 1938, the Presidency became a salaried office. There was no President elected from May 1972 - May 1980. In May 1972, the Exchange was reorganized and the Chairman of the Board became a full-time, salaried Chief Executive Officer.

1817 - Anthony Stockholm
1818 - 23 - C.S. Mumford
1824 - 26 - Edward Lyde
1827 - 29 - James W. Bleecker
1830 - Russell H. Nevins
1831 - 33 - John Ward
1834 - R.D. Weeks
1835 - Edward Prime
1836 - R.D. Weeks
1837 - 51 - David Clarkson
1851 - 52 - Henry G. Stebbins
1852 - 55 - Charles R. Marvin
1855 - 57 - Charles R. Marvin
1857 - 58 - John H. Gourlie
1858 - 59 - Henry G. Stebbins
1858 - 61 - William H. Neilson
1861 - 62 - W.R. Vermilye
1862 - 63 - Abraham B. Baylis

1863 - 64 - Henry G. Stebbins
1864 - 65 - William Seymour, Jr.
1865 - 66 - R.L. Cutting
1866 - 67 - William Alexander Smith
1867 - 68 - John Warren
1868 - 69 - William Searls
1869 - 70 - William H. Neilson
1870 - 71 - William Seymour, Jr.
1871 - 72 - William B. Clerke
1872 - 73 - Edward King
1873 - 74 - Henry G. Chapman
1874 - 75 - George H. Brodhead
1875 - 76 - George W. McLean
1876 - 77 - Salem T. Russell
1877 - 78 - Henry Meigs
1878 - 80 - Brayton Ives
1880 - 82 - Donald Mackay
1882 - 83 - Frederick N. Lawrence
1883 - 84 - Alfrederick S. Hatch
1884 - 86 - J. Edward Simmons
1886 - 88 - James D. Smith
1888 - 90 - William L. Bull
1890 - 92 - Watson B. Dickerman
1892 - 94 - Frank K. Sturgis
1894 - 98 - Francis L. Eames
1898 - 1900 - Rudolph Keppler
1900 - 03 - Rudolph Keppler
1903 - 04 - Ransom H. Thomas
1904 - 05 - Henry K. Pomroy
1905 - 07 - Henry K. Pomroy
1907 - 12 - Ransom H. Thomas
1912 - 14 - James B. Mabon
1914 - 19 - Henry G.S. Noble
1919 - 21 - William R. Remick
1921 - 24 - Seymour L. Cromwell
1924 - 28 - Edward H.H. Simmons
1928 - 30 - Edward H.H. Simmons
1930 - 35 - Richard Whitney
1935 - 36 - Charles R. Gay
1936 - 38 - Charles R. Gay

1938 - 41 - William McChesney Martin, Jr.
1941 - 51 - Emil Schram
1951 - 67 - G. Keith Funston
1967 - 72 - Robert W. Haack
1980 - 84 - John J. Phelan, Jr.
1985 - 88 - Robert J. Birnbaum
1988 -   Richard A. Grasso

Chairmen, Board of Governors, 1938 - 1972

May 1938 - June 1938 - William McChesney Martin, Jr.
July 1938 - May 1940 - Edward E. Bartlett, Jr.
May 1940 - May 1941 - Charles B. Harding
May 1941 - May 1943 - Robert L. Stott
May 1943 - May 1947 - John A. Coleman
May 1947 - May 1951 - Robert P. Boylan
May 1951 - May 1954 - Richard M. Crooks
May 1954 - May 1956 - Harold W. Scott
May 1956 - May 1958 - James Crane Kellogg, III
May 1958 - May 1961 - Edward C. Werle
May 1961 - February 1962 - J. Truman Bidwell
February 1962 - May 1965 - Henry M. Watts, Jr.
May 1965 - May 1967 - Walter N. Frank
May 1967 - May 1969 - Gustave L. Levy
May 1969 - May 1971 - Bernard J. Lasker
May 1971 - August 1972 - Ralph D. DeNunzio

Chairmen, Board of Directors

August 1972 - May 1976 - James J. Needham
May 1976 - May 1984 - William M. Batten
May 1984 - December 1990 - John J. Phelan, Jr.
January 1991 -   William H. Donaldson

INFORMATION SERVICES OF THE NYSE ARCHIVES,
PUBLICATIONS DEPARTMENT, AND VISITORS' CENTER

I. NEW YORK STOCK EXCHANGE ARCHIVES

Archivist: Steven Wheeler
New York Stock Exchange
Archives and Corporate Research Center
22nd Floor
11 Wall Street
New York, N.Y.   10005
Tel. 212-656-2252

The New York Stock Exchange Archives has been referred to as "the keeper of the Exchange's corporate memory." The Archives provides research and reference services to NYSE staff, members, member organizations, listed companies, scholars, graduate students, and the general public. Researchers have access to key documents from the original copy of the 1792 Buttonwood Agreement to the current NYSE annual report. Housed in the Archives are artifacts such as early stock tickers, still photographs, a collection of books concerning NYSE history, periodicals, films, and special reports. Appointments may be made by writing or calling the Archivist.

Major collection groups housed in the Archives are:

Records of NYSE Committees and Departments (1817-Present): include minutes, stenographic transcripts of hearings, correspondence, reports and other records of about 150 committees and departments charged with carrying out the various administrative and regulatory duties of the Exchange.

Records of Various Subsidiary and Affiliate Companies: include minutes, correspondence, legal and financial records that document the many ancillary functions performed by the Exchange. Records of the Open Board of Stock Brokers (1863-1869) document the activities of a rival securities exchange born in the speculatively active years of the Civil War; it merged with the NYSE in 1869. Records of the New York Quotation Company (1889-1957) document the corporate and technological history of providing quotations over a network of stock tickers.

Listing Statements (1867-Present): are printed summaries of applications submitted by corporations wishing to have their securities traded at the NYSE. The statements include data on the business, history, organizational structure, capitalization and financial standing of a wide variety of American and foreign companies. A related record group, Listing Applications (1864-Present) provides even greater documentation on selected corporations.

The Publications Collection encompasses house organs such as annual reports, employee newsletters, statistical bulletins and investor's magazines, as well as marketing and informational booklets. Also included are reports and studies conducted by the Exchange and by outside organizations, as well as histories and memoirs of the securities industry.

The Graphics Collection consists of prints, drawings, photographs and motion pictures and provides a pictorial record of the Exchange's history. Included are scenes of Wall Street and the financial district, the NYSE trading floor, back offices, special events, and portraits of members.

Specific Records Groups include:

Records of the New York Stock and Exchange Board, 1817-1869

Records of the NYSE: Committee and Departmental Records, 1869-Present

Records of the Open Board of Stock Brokers, 1863-1869

Records of the NYSE Building Company, 1863-1945

Records of the NYSE Gratuity Fund, 1873-1962

Records of the New York Quotation Company, 1889-1957

Records of the NYSE Safe Deposit Company, 1913-1942

Records of the Stock Clearing Corporation, 1920-1956

Records of the 39 Broad Street Corp., 1933-1941

Records of the New Jersey Stock Exchange, 1933-1958

Records of the New York Futures Exchange, 1977-1982

NYSE Constitutions and Directories, 1865-1982

NYSE Sales and Quotations, 1818-1952

NYSE Listing Statements, 1867-1974

NYSE Listing Applications, 1864-Present

Motion Picture Films, 1923-1974 (N.B. Selections of specific films are listed in chapters of the main section of bibliography)

Papers of Alfrederick Smith Hatch, Stock Broker and NYSE President, 1883-1885

New York Stock Exchange Presidents and Officers Speeches, 1922-1984

United Financial Employees Union, Local 205, 1941-1971
Securities Exchange Commission (SEC) Hearings, 1968-1977

III. PUBLICATIONS OF THE NYSE

The New York Stock Exchange offers various monographs, pamphlets, kits, serials, etc. for sale. Some of these publications are its *Fact Book* (Annual), *Shareownership* (periodical publication), *Marketplace: A Brief History of the New York Stock Exchange*, and *Market Volatility and Investor Confidence*. Publications are separated into several categories: NYSE publications, Market data products reports, NYSE options publications, and New York Futures Exchange publications. For further information, addresses and telephone numbers for each category of publication are listed below:

NYSE Publications:

New York Stock Exchange, Inc.
11 Wall Street
New York, N.Y.   10005
Telephone: 212-656-5273

NYSE Market Data Products:

New York Stock Exchange, Inc.
Market Data Products
11 Wall Street
New York, N.Y.   10005
Telephone: 212-656-3800

NYSE Options Publications:

NYSE Options Marketing
11 Wall Street
New York, N.Y.   10005
Telephone: 212-656-8533 (inside New York State)
           800-6926973
New York Futures Exchange Publications:

New York Futures Exchange
20 Broad Street
10th Floor
New York, N.Y. 10005
Attention: Publications Department
Telephone: 212-656-6053

III. NEW YORK STOCK EXCHANGE VISITORS' CENTER

Free tickets to the NYSE Visitors' Center are distributed weekdays at 20 Broad Street. Visitors' Center telephone number is 212-656-5167. The Visitors' Center offers: access to a gallery overlooking the NYSE trading floor; a self-guided tour; various exhibits; and a media presentation.

DIRECTORY OF SELECTED SERIAL PUBLICATIONS

The following are selected serial publications with information on the NYSE, with names of publishers, addresses, frequency, prices, and where publication is indexed. Articles from some of the titles listed here are included as annotated entries; other titles have been presented in the chapter covering statistical sources. It should be noted that subscription prices are for 1991, and prices are subject to change. This is a selected list of serial publications; additional titles can be located by scanning indexes, abstracts, and databases.

Barron's National Business and Financial Weekly
Dow Jones & Co. Inc.
200 Liberty Street
New York, N.Y.   10281
V. 1, 1921- Weekly, $109 per year
Indexed in: *Business Periodicals Index, Business Index, Business Publications Index and Abstracts, Magazine Index, Popular Magazine Review, Trade and Industry Index.*

Business History Review
Harvard Business School
Soldiers Field
Boston, Massachusetts   02163
V. 1, 1926-   Quarterly, $25, individuals; $40, institutions
Indexed in: *Business Periodicals Index, Current Contents, PAIS,*

Historical Abstracts, Social Science Citation Index, Social Sciences Index, America: History and Life, Book Review Index, Business Index, Economic Abstracts, Trade and Industry Index, Work Related Abstracts, etc.

Business Week
McGraw-Hill Inc.
1221 Avenue of the Americas
New York, N.Y. 10020
V. 1, 1929- Weekly, $39.95 per year
Indexed in: *Business Periodicals Index, Chemical Abstracts, Oceanic Abstracts, Pollution Abstracts, Readers' Guide to Periodical Literature, Abridged Readers' Guide to Periodical Literature, Abstrax, BMT Abstracts, Business Publications Index and Abstracts, Banking Literature Index, Book Review Index, Business Index, Computer Business, Computer Industry Update, Computer Literature Index, Current Literature in Family Planning, Current Packaging Abstracts, Operations Research/Management Science, Future Survey, Higher Education Current Awareness Bulletin, Key to Economic Science, Management Contents, Microcomputer Index, Magazine Index, Popular Magazine Review, Personnel Literature, Resource Center Index, Management and Marketing Abstracts, Robomatix Reporter, Trade and Industry Index, Textile Technology Digest.* Also available online through MCGRAW-HILL PUBLICATIONS ONLINE, Dow Jones/News Retrieval, Mead Data Central.

Commercial and Financial Chronicle
National News Service, Inc.
Box 1839
Daytona Beach, Florida 32015-1839
V. 1, 1839- Weekly, $140 per year.
Indexed in: *Business Periodicals Index, PROMT*

Daily Graphs. N.Y.S.E.
William O'Neil & Co., Inc.
Box 24933
Los Angeles, California 90024

V. 1, 1972- Weekly, $379 per year.

Financial Analysts Journal
Association for Investment Management and Research
Box 3668
Charlottesville, Virginia   22903
V. 1, 1945- Bi-Monthly, $150 per year
Indexed in: *Business Periodicals Index, Business Index, Management Contents, World Bank Abstracts, PROMT, Business Publication Index and Abstracts, etc.*

Forbes
Forbes, Inc.
60 Fifth Avenue
New York, N.Y.   10011
V. 1, 1917- Fortnightly, $52 per year
Indexed in: *Business Periodicals Index, Chemical Abstracts, Data Processing Digest, Readers' Guide Abstracts, Business Publications Index and Abstracts, Banking Literature Index, Business Index, Computer Literature Index, Computer Business, Key to Economic Science, Magazine Index, Management Contents, PROMT, Rehabilitation Literature, Robomatix Reporter, Trade and Industry Index.* Also available online through DIALOG and Mead Data Central. Indexed online and on CD-ROM through database, ABI/INFORM.

Fortune Magazine
Time, Inc.
Time & Life Building
1271 Avenue of the Americas
New York, N.Y.   10020
Subscriptions to:
Fortune
Box 30604
Tampa, Florida   33630-0604
V. 1, 1930- Bi-Weekly, $49.95 per year
Indexed in: *Business Periodicals Index, Operations Research/Management Science, Excerpta Medica, International*

Management Information Business Digest, Executive Science Institute, PAIS, Readers' Guide to Periodical Literature, Science Abstracts, American Bibliography of Slavic and East European Studies, Institute of Paper Chemistry. Abstract Bulletin, BMT Abstracts, Business Publications Index and Abstracts, Business Index, Computer Industry Update, Computer Literature Index, Computer Business, Fuel and Energy Abstracts, International Aerospace Abstracts, Oceanic Abstracts, Key to Economic Science, Magazine Index, Pollution Abstracts, Management Contents, Management and Marketing Abstracts, Popular Magazine Review, PROMT, Resource Center Index, Robomatix Reporter, Selected Water Resource Abstracts, Work Related Abstracts, Textile Technology Digest, Trade and Industry Index. Also available online through VU/TEXT Information Services. Indexed and abstracted online and on CD-ROM through ABI/INFORM.

Futures: The Magazine of Commodities and Options
Oster Communications, Inc.
219 Parkade
Cedar Falls, Iowa   50613
V. 1, 1972-   Monthly. $39 per year (in North America); $92 (elsewhere)
Indexed in: *Business Periodicals Index, Business Publications Index and Abstracts, Educational Administration Abstracts, Trade & Industry Index.*

Harvard Business Review
Harvard University
Graduate Schoool of Business Administration
Soldiers Field Rd.
Boston, Massachusetts   02163
V. 1, 1922-   Bi-Monthly, $55 per year.
Indexed in: *Business Periodicals Index, Anbar, Current Contents, Excerpta Medica, Computing Reviews, Operations Research/Management Science, International Management Information Business Digest, PAIS, Psychological Abstracts, Readers' Guide to Periodical Literature, Social Science Citation Index, Science Abstracts, ASEAN Management Abstracts, Abstracts of Health Care Management Studies, ABI/Inform, Trade and Industry Index,* etc. Available online

through BRS, DIALOG, Data-Star, Mead Data Central, and Human Resources Information Network.

Institutional Investor: The Magazine for Finance and Investment
Institutional Investor, Inc.
Circulation Department
488 Madison Avenue
New York, N.Y.   10022
V. 1, 1967 -   Monthly, $265 per year
Indexed in *Business Periodicals Index, PAIS, Social Science Citation Index, Business Index, Trade and Industry Index, CAD/CAM Abstracts, Management Contents, Risk Abstracts, Key to Economic Science.* Accessible on CD-ROM through ABI/INFORM.

Investor's Business Daily (formerly *Investor's Daily*)
Box 25970
Los Angeles, California   90025
daily, $94 per year

Journal of Portfolio Management
Institutional Investor, Inc.
Circulation Department
488 Madison Avenue
15th Floor
New York, N.Y.   10022
V. 1, 1975-   Quarterly, $195 per year
Indexed in: *Business Periodicals Index, PAIS, Social Science Citation Index, Management Contents, Business Index, Risk Abstracts, Trade and Industry Index, Automatic Subject Citation.* Also indexed online and CD-ROM database, ABI/INFORM.

Market Signals
Northern Trust Company
Investment Management Services
50 LaSalle Street
Chicago, Illinois   60675

V. 1, 1986-   Semi-monthly, $225 per year

Moody's Bond Record and Annual Bond Record Service
Moody's Investors Service
99 Church Street
New York, N.Y.   10007
Monthly, $249 per year

Moody's Bond Survey
Moody's Investors Service
99 Church Street
New York, N.Y.   10007
Weekly, $1,175 per year.

Moody's Dividend Record and Annual Dividend Record
Moody's Investors Service
99 Church Street
New York, N.Y.   10007-0300
Semi-weekly, includes cumulative and annual supplements, $460 per year.

Moody's Handbook of Common Stocks
Moody's Investors Service
99 Church Street
New York, N.Y.   10007-0300
V. 1955-   Quarterly, $210 per year

New York Stock Exchange Guide
Commerce Clearing House, Inc.
4025 W. Peterson Avenue
Chicago, Illinois   60646
1957-   Monthly, $400 per year

National Stock Summary

National Quotation Bureau, Inc.
600 Plaza Three
Harborside Financial Center
Jersey City, N.J.   07311-3895
V. 1, 1913-   semi-annual, $170 per year

New York Stock Exchange Stock Reports
Standard & Poor's Corporation
25 Broadway
New York, N.Y.   10004
V. 1, 1933-   Weekly, looseleaf format; quarterly bound volume
available, $1280 per year

SEC News Digest
U.S. Securities and Exchange Commission
450 Fifth Street, N.W.
MISC-11
Washington, D.C.   20549
Distributed by:
Washington Service Bureau
1225 Connecticut Avenue, N.W.
Washington, D.C.   20036
Daily, $100 per year
Also available online through: Bureau of National Affairs, NewsNet.

Securities Week
McGraw-Hill, Inc.
Business Week Management Information Center
1221 Avenue of the Americas
36th Floor
New York, N.Y.   10020
V. 1, 1973-   Weekly, $1310 per year
Also available online through: DIALOG, Dow Jones/News Retrieval,
Mead Data Central, Mc Graw-Hill Publications Online

Standard & Poor's Analysts Handbook
Standard & Poor's Corporation

25 Broadway
New York, N.Y.   10004
1964-   Annual, with monthly updates, $795 per year.

Standard & Poor's Bond Guide
Standard & Poor's Corporation
25 Broadway
New York, N.Y.   10004
V. 1, 1938-   Monthly, $185 per year

Standard & Poor's Daily Stock Price Record. New York Stock Exchange
Standard & Poor's Corporation
25 Broadway
New York, N.Y.   10004
V. 1, 1962-   Quarterly, $345 per year

Standard & Poor's Dividend Record
Standard & Poor's Corporation
25 Broadway
New York, N.Y.   10004
Weekly, $420 per year

Standard & Poor's Outlook
Standard & Poor's Corporation
25 Broadway
New York, N.Y.   10004
Weekly, $280 per year

*Standard & Poor's Review of Securities, Commodities Regulation: An
Analysis of Current Laws, Regulations and Court Decisions Affecting
the Securities Index.*
Standard & Poor's Corporation
25 Broadway
New York, N.Y.   10004
V. 1, 1968-   Semi-monthly, $475 per year

Indexed in: *Current Law Index, Legal Resource Index*

Standard & Poor's Statistical Service
Standard & Poor's Corporation
25 Broadway
New York, N.Y.   10004
Monthly, $545 per year

Standard & Poor's Stock Guide
Standard & Poor's Corporation
25 Broadway
New York, N.Y.   10004
V. 1, 1943-   Monthly, $112 per year

Standard & Poor's Stock Market Encyclopedia
Standard & Poor's Corporation
25 Broadway
New York, N.Y.   10004
V. 1, 1962-   Quarterly, $123.95 per year

Standard & Poor's Stock Summary
Standard & Poor's Corporation
25 Broadway
New York, N.Y.   10004
Monthly, $56 per year

Stock Market Magazine
Wall Street Publishing Institute, Inc.
16 School Street
Yonkers, N.Y.   10701
V. 1, 1962-   Monthly.
Indexed in: *Reference Sources, Popular Magazine Review*

Trendline: Daily Action Stock Charts

Standard & Poor's Corporation
25 Broadway
New York, N.Y.   10004
V. 1, 1959-   Weekly, $520 per year

United & Babson Investment Report
Babson-United Investment Advisors, Inc.
101 Prescott Street
Wellesley Hills, Massachusetts   02131-3319
V. 1, 1919-   Weekly, $215 per year
Indexed in: *PROMT*

U.S. Securities and Exchange Commission. Annual Report
U.S. Securities and Exchange Commission
450 Fifth Street, N.W.
MISC-11
Washington, D.C.   20549
Orders to:
Superintendent of Documents
U.S. Government Printing Office
Washington, D.C.   20402
1935-   Annual, price varies

U.S. Securities and Exchange Commission. Decisions and Reports
U.S. Securities and Exchange Commission
450 Fifth Street, N.W.
MISC-11
Washington, D.C.   20549
Orders to:
Superintendent of Documents
U.S. Government Printing Office
Washington, D.C.   20402
1934-   irregular, price varies

*U.S. Securities and Exchange Commission. Official Summary of
Security Transactions and Holdings*

U.S. Securities and Exchange Commission
450 Fifth Street, N.W.
MISC-11
Washington, D.C.   20549
Orders to:
Superintendent of Documents
U.S. Government Printing Office
Washington, D.C.   20402
1935- monthly, $61.05 per year

Value Line Investment Survey
Value Line, Inc.
711 Third Avenue
New York, N.Y.   10017
V. 1, 1931-   Weekly, $495 per year.
Available in looseleaf and microfiche fomrats.
Indexed in: *PROMT*

Wall Street Computer Review
Dealers' Digest Inc.
2 World Trade Center
18th Floor
New York, N.Y.   10048
V. 1, 1983-   Monthly, $49 per year
Indexed in: *Science Abstracts, Computer Abstracts, Computer Database, Microcomputer Index, PC R2.* Indexed in ABI/INFORM.

Wall Street Journal
Dow Jones & Co., Inc.
200 Liberty Street
New York, N.Y.   10007
Subscriptions to:
Box 300
Princeton, New Jersey   08540
V. 1, 1899-   Daily (5/week)
Indexed: *Chemical Abstracts, PAIS, Book Review Index, Banking Literature Index, Children's Book Review Index, Fanatic Reader, Future*

Survey, Medical Care Review, Music Index, Personnel Literature.
Available online through DOW JONES/NEWS RETRIEVAL.

Wall Street Letter
Institutional Investor, Inc.
Circulation Department
488 Madison Avenue
15th Floor
New York, N.Y.   10022
V. 1, 1969- Weekly, $1,295 per year.

Wall Street Transcript: A Professional Publication for the Business and Financial Community
Wall Street Transcript Corp.
99 Wall Street
New York, N.Y.   10005
V. 1, 1963-   Weekly, $590 per year
Indexed in: *Predicasts Overview of Markets and Technologies (PROMT), Trade and Industry Index.* Available online through VU/TEXT Information Services.

APPENDIX V
ABSTRACTS AND INDEXES

The following are a selected list of abstracts and indexes with material on the New York Stock Exchange. Names and addresses and publication information have been included. If the material is also available in database format, it is noted in its description.

Accountants' Index
American Institute of Certified Public Accountants
1211 Avenue of the Americas
New York, N.Y.   10036
V. 1, 1920-   Quarterly, with annual cumulation. Indexes journal articles, accounting statements, and publications. Covers topics of finance and accounting. Available online through ORBIT Information Technologies.

America: History and Life: Articles Abstracts and Citations of Reviews and Dissertations Covering the United States and Canada
A B C-Clio
130 Cremona
Box 1911
Santa Barbara, California   93116-1911
V. 1, 1964-   4/yr. Indexes and abstracts U.S. and Canadian history sources. Also available online through Dialog.

American Statistics Index (ASI): A Comprehensive Guide and Index to

Statistical Publications of the U.S. Government
Congressional Information Service, Inc.
4520 East-West Highway
Bethesda, Maryland   10814
V. 1, 1974- Monthly, with quarterly and annual cumulations. Indexes statistics published by the Federal Government. Issued in two volumes, one an Index volume and the other an Abstracts volume. Also available online and on CD-ROM.

Bibliographic Index
H.W. Wilson Co.
950 University Avenue
Bronx, N.Y.   10452
V. 1, 1937/42-   Semiannual, with annual cumulations. Indexes bibliographies appearing in books, pamphlets, and periodicals. Also available online.

Biography Index
H.W. Wilson Co.
950 University Avenue
Bronx, N.Y.   10452
V. 1, 1905-   Quarterly, with annual cumulations. Indexes biographies appearing in books and journals. With a name index, an alphabetical listing of biographies, and an index to professions and occupations. Also available online and on CD-ROM.

Book Review Digest
H.W. Wilson Co.
950 University Avenue
Bronx, N.Y.   10452
V. 1, 1905-   Monthly, except February and July, with annual cumulations. Indexes book reviews appearing in journals with excerpts from the reviews. Also available online and on CD-ROM.

Book Review Index
Gale Research Co.

Book Tower
Detroit, Michigan   48226
V. 1, 1965-   Monthly, with quarterly and annual cumulations. Indexes
book reviews appearing in journals.

Business Index
Information Access Company
362 Lakeside Drive
Foster City, California   94404
Monthly microfilm reel. Accessed by microfilm viewer; indexes articles
from journals, plus the newspapers, *Barron's, Wall Street Journal,* and
The New York Times. Also available on CD-ROM.

Business Periodicals Index
H.W. Wilson Co.
950 University Avenue
Bronx, N.Y.   10452
V. 1, 1958-   Monthly, with quarterly and annual cumulations. Indexes
articles on business, finance, management, marketing, etc. Also
available online and on CD-ROM.

C I S Index
Congressional Information Service, Inc.
4520 East-West Highway
Bethesda, Maryland   20814
V. 1, 1970-   Monthly, with quarterly and annual cumulations. Indexes
Congressional documents, including committee hearings, reports,
publications of joint committees and subcommittees, etc. Issued in two
volumes, an Index and an Abstracts volume. Available online and on
CD-ROM.

Cumulative Book Review Index
H.W. Wilson Co.
950 University Avenue
Bronx, N.Y.   10452
V. 1, 1899-   Eleven monthly paperbound issues, including quarterly

cumulations in March, June, September, and December, plus an annual clothbound cumulation. Record of information on over 50,000 English-language books. With indexing by author, title, and subject. Also available online and on CD-ROM.

Index to Legal Periodicals
H.W. Wilson Co.
950 University Avenue
Bronx, N.Y.   10452
V. 1, 1908- Eleven monthly paperbound issues, including quarterly cumulations published in February, May, August, and November, plus a clothbound cumulation. Indexes legal periodicals published in the United States, Canada, Great Britain, Ireland, Australia, and New Zealand. Provides a Table of Cases arranged alphabetically by name of plaintiff and defendant; Table of Statutes, arranged by jurisdiction and listed alphabetically by name; and Book Reviews of current books related to law. Also available online and on CD-ROM.

Monthly Catalog of United States Government Publications
U.S. Government Printing Office
Superintendent of Documents
Washington, D.C.   20402
V. 1, 1885- Monthly. Indexes publications of Federal Government agencies by author, title, subject, series/report, stock number, and title keyword. Each entry includes author, title, subject headings, Superintendent of Documents call number, and item number. Also available online.

New York Times Index
University Microfilms International, Newspapers
c/o Deborah Harmer, Mgr.
300 N. Zeeb Road
Ann Arbor, Michigan   48106
V. 1, 1850-   semi-monthly, with three quarterly and an annual cumulation.

PAIS International In Print

521 W. 43rd Street
5th Floor
New York, N.Y.   10036-4396
V. 1, 1991 - Monthly. Formed by merger of *PAIS Bulletin* (1915-1990) and *PAIS Foreign Language Index*. Indexes periodical articles, books, pamphlets, government publications, and reports from public and private agencies. Indexes materials in English, French, Spanish, German, Italian, Portuguese. Also available online through BRS, Data-Star, and DIALOG and on CD-ROM through PAIS and SilverPlatter.

Readers' Guide to Periodical Literature
H.W. Wilson Co.
950 University Avenue
Bronx, N.Y.   10452
V. 1, 1901- Seventeen paperbound issues, plus an annual clothbound cumulation. Indexes selected United States general interest journals such as *Time, Newsweek, Business Week*, etc. Also available online and on CD-ROM.

Vertical File Index
H.W. Wilson Co.
950 University Avenue
Bronx, N.Y.   10452
V. 1, 1932/34-   Monthly, except August with annual cumulations. Indexes pamphlet material including selected government publications. Provides bibliographic information and ordering instructions. Also available online.

Wall Street Journal Index
University Microfilms International
300 N. Zeeb Road
Ann Arbor, Michigan   48106
V. 1, 1958-   Annual and monthly.
Indexes news about the New York Stock Exchange and the securities markets. Also available online and as part of CD-ROM product, NEWSPAPERS ONDISC.

ONLINE DATABASES AND CD-ROM PRODUCTS

The literature of the New York Stock Exchange and related subjects can be located by scanning online and CD-ROM databases. The following are descriptions of selected databases with article citations and abstracts as well as statistics. Databases are listed in alphabetical order, with names of their producers and vendors as well its format (i.e. online database, CD-ROM, or both).

ABI/INFORM. Source: UMI/Data Courier. Vendors: BRS, Data-Star, DIALOG Information Services, Inc., Mead Data Central, OCLC Online Computer Center, Inc.'s EPIC Service, ORBIT Search Service. Contains records from 1971 to present, available online and on CD-ROM. Provides bibliographic citations and abstracts for articles from over 800 business and management periodicals. BUSINESS PERIODICALS ONDISC (listed below), available through UMI/Data Courier, contains records of ABI/INFORM plus complete text in full-image of periodical article.

AP DATASTREAM BUSINESS NEWS WIRE. Source: Associated Press. Vendor: NewsNet. Provides up-to-the minute news reports on business and economic developments in governments and major corporations worldwide. Available to NewsNet subscribers with no time delays.

AP NEWS. Source: Associated Press. Vendor: DIALOG Information Services, Inc. Contains records from 1984 to present, available online. Covers full-text of articles concerning national, international, and business news; financial information, etc.

ASI (AMERICAN STATISTICS INDEX). Source: Congressional Information Service, Inc. Vendor: DIALOG Information Services, Inc. Contains records from 1973 to present. Available online and on CD-ROM through Congressional Information Services' STATISTICAL MASTERFILE (see entry below). Indexes and abstracts statistical publications from approximately 500 Federal offices or regional issuing agencies. Corresponds to print source of same title.

ACCOUNTANTS. Source: American Institute of Certified Public Accountants. Vendor: ORBIT Search Service. Contains records from 1974 to present; available online. Topics covered include: financial management, investments, taxation, etc. Indexes English language books, government documents, and journals.

AMERICA: HISTORY AND LIFE. Source: ABC-CLIO. Vendor: DIALOG Information Services, Inc. Contains records from 1964 to present; available online. Print equivalent is *America: History and Life.* Abstracts and indexes materials concerning United States and Canadian history. Source of information for economic and financial history, among other topics.

AMERICAN BANKER. Source: American Banker-Bond Buyer. Vendors: Data-Star, DIALOG Information Services, Inc., NewsNet, WESTLAW. Contains records from 1981 to present; available online. Corresponds to the print periodical publication, *American Banker.* Covers news concerning economic and financial services. Provides full-text of articles and speeches, current current regulations, and statistical data.

BNA DAILY NEWS. Source: Bureau of National Affairs. Vendor:

DIALOG Information Services, Inc. Contains information from January 1, 1990 to present; available online. Provides daily coverage of national and international government activities including the White House, Congress, Federal and state agencies, courts, etc. Contains full-text of publications which include: *Antitrust & Trade Regulation Daily, Securities Law Daily,* and *Washington Insider.*

BNA SECURITIES LAW DAILY. Source: Bureau of National Affairs. Vendors: Mead Data Central, WESTLAW. Available online. Provides daily documents from periodical, *BNA Securities Law Daily,* which covers legislative, judicial, and administrative activities at the Federal and state level that affect securities and commodities, mergers and acquisitions.

BNA SECURITIES REGULATION & LAW REPORT. Source: Bureau of National Affairs. Vendors: Mead Data Central, WESTLAW. Available online. Provides documents from periodical, *Securities Regulation & Law Report* which cover legislative, judicial, and administrative activities as well as those of professional organizations that affect the regulation of securities and commodities at the Federal and state level.

BIBLIOGRAPHIC INDEX. Source: H.W. Wilson. Available online through WILSONLINE. Indexes bibliographies appearing in books, pamphlets, and periodicals. Also available online.

BIOGRAPHY INDEX. Source: H.W. Wilson. Available online through WILSONLINE and on CD-ROM through WILSONDISC CD-ROM RETRIEVAL SYSTEM. Also available through OCLC's EPIC Service. Indexes biographies in books and periodicals.

BIOGRAPHY MASTER INDEX. Source: Gale Research Company. Vendor: DIALOG Information Services, Inc. Available online. Contains information on over 3,000,000 individuals. Indexes approximately 630 biographical dictionaries and directories.

BOND BUYER FULL TEXT. Source: American Banker-Bond Buyer. Vendors: DIALOG Information Services, Inc., Mead Data Central, WESTLAW. Contains records from November 1981 to present; available online.Corresponds to print publications: *The Bond Buyer* and *Credit Markets*. Provides current information on municipal bonds, corporate bonds, financial futures, etc.

BOOK REVIEW DIGEST. Source: H.W. Wilson. Available online through WILSONLINE and on CD-ROM through WILSONLINE CD-ROM RETRIEVAL SYSTEM. Also available through OCLC's EPIC Service and FirstSearch Catalog. Indexes book reviews and includes excerpts from selected reviews.

BOOK REVIEW INDEX. Source: Gale Research, Inc. Vendor: DIALOG Information Services, Inc. Contains records from 1969 to present. Indexes over 2,000,000 book reviews published in newspapers and periodicals. Print equivalent: *Book Review Index*.

BOOKS IN PRINT. Source: R.R. Bowker. Vendors: BRS, DIALOG Information Services, Inc. and on CD-ROM product, BOOKS IN PRINT PLUS, produced by R.R. Bowker. Contains bibliographic citations, publisher, and price information for currently in-print books in the United States. With lists of forthcoming books and books recently out-of-print. Corresponds to print publications: *Books in Print, Subject Guide to Books in Print, Forthcoming Books, Paperbound Books in Print*, etc.

BUREAU OF NATIONAL AFFAIRS, see under BNA

BUSINESS AND COMPANY PROFILE - Source: Information Access Company (IAC). Available through IAC's CD-ROM InfoTrac System. Combines its databases BUSINESS INDEX and COMPANY PROFILE, see entries below. Also available from IAC is the GENERAL BUSINESSFILE, combining its databases: BUSINESS INDEX, COMPANY PROFILE, and INVESTEXT.

BUSINESS AND FINANCIAL REPORT. Source. Dow Jones News/Retrieval. Available online. Provides continuously updated coverage of business and financial news from the Dow Jones News Service and other news items, plus the *Wall Street Journal.*

BUSINESS DATELINE. Source: UMI/Data Courier. Vendors: BRS, DIALOG Information Services, Inc., WESTLAW. Available on CD-ROM through UMI/Data Courier. Provides news releases from over 10,000 news sources among which are research institutes, government agencies, and universities.

BUSINESS INDEX. Source: Information Access Company (IAC). Available through IAC's CD-ROM InfoTrac System. Indexes approximately 800 business, management, and trade journals, plus newspapers including the *Wall Street Journal* and the *New York Times.* Also provides indexing coverage to business-related articles from over 3000 other magazines, newspapers, and journals. Approximately 150 of the periodical titles indexed contain abstracts. Available in combined format, BUSINESS AND COMPANY PROFILE, see entry above. Also produced by IAC is the GENERAL BUSINESS FILE, combining the databases, BUSINESS INDEX, COMPANY PROFILE, and INVESTEXT.

BUSINESS PERIODICALS INDEX. Source. H.W. Wilson. Available online through WILSONLINE and on CD-ROM through WILSONDISC. Also available through OCLC's EPIC Service and FirstSearch Catalog. Indexes articles, and abstracts of articles are available through WILSON BUSINESS ABSTRACTS (see below). Covers topics of economics, finance, management, marketing, etc. Equivalent to print index of same title.

BUSINESS PERIODICALS ONDISC (BPO). Source: UMI/Data Courier. Available on CD-ROM. Contains ABI/INFORM database plus full-page images of over 300 business periodicals abstracted by ABI/INFORM. Instead of ASCII full-text, provides full-images of all pages.

BUSINESS WEEK. Source: McGraw-Hill Publications Online. Vendors: DIALOG Information Services, Inc., Dow Jones News/Retrieval, Mead Data Central, NewsNet. Provides full-text coverage of BUSINESS WEEK from 1985 to present.

BUSINESSWIRE. Source: BusinessWire. Vendors: DIALOG Information Services, Inc., Mead Data Central. Contains records from 1986 to present; available online. Provides news releases from approximately 10,000 news sources among which are research institutes, government agencies, and universities. With name and telephone number of contact person within company.

CD/CORPORATE. Source: Lotus One Source. Available on CD-ROM combined with Lotus data access and retrieval software. Provides access to U.S. and international company information: mergers and acquisitions; stock price history; analyst reports on publicly traded companies, etc. Accessible through CD/CORPORATE are reports from Moody's, Thomson Financial Networks, Predicasts, and Macmillan. Optional online services may be selected and used with data from CD/CORPORATE. NEWSLINE provides direct access to Dow Jones News/Retrieval data and REPORTLINE is a source of the most current investment reports.

CD/INVESTMENT. Source: Lotus One Source. Available on CD-ROM, combined with Lotus data access and retrieval software. Comprised of data for the United States and international companies. Statistics presented include stock prices and dividend announcements; bond ratings, Value Line rankings and projections, etc.

CDA/SPECTRUM STOCK OWNERSHIP DATA. Source: Thomson Financial Networks. Available online. Through contract with the SEC, provides institutional filings and other ownership data.

CIS (CONGRESSIONAL INFORMATION SERVICE). Source: Congressional Information Service. Vendor: DIALOG Information

Services, Inc. Available on CD-ROM through Congressional Information Service's CONGRESSIONAL MASTERFILE 2, see below. Contains records from 1970 to present. Corresponds to print source: *CIS Index*. Indexes and abstracts Congressional working papers published by House, Senate, and Joint committees and subcommittees, including Hearings. Provides access to sections of Hearings, including transcripts of testimonies, exhibits, and statistical data.

CHARLES E. SIMON & COMPANY'S MERGERS AND ACQUISITIONS. See M & A FILINGS.

COMMODITY FUTURES TRADING COMMISSION (CFTC). Source: CFTC. Vendor: WESTLAW. Contains decisions from the CFTC or from an administrative law judge.

COMPACT D/SEC. Source: Disclosure, Inc. CD-ROM product provides access to over 12,000 public companies through searching by full company name, ticker symbol, subsidiary name, etc. as well as through an interactive DIALOG II emulation system. Records contain complete company profiles; annual (5-year comparative) balance sheets and income statements; annual cash flow statements (up to 3 years); quarterly financial reports; full-text of President's Letter; ratios and price/earnings data, etc.

COMPACT D/'33. Source: Disclosure, Inc. CD-ROM product offers access to data on securities registration including those reported in '33 Act registrations and certain '34 Act registrations.

COMPANY PROFILE - Source: Information Access Company (IAC). Available through IAC's InfoTrac on CD-ROM. Provides information, gathered from directory information and text of newswire releases, for over 100,000 private and public companies. Available in combined database format, BUSINESS AND COMPANY PROFILE, see entry above. Also produced by IAC is the GENERAL BUSINESS FILE, combining its databases BUSINESS INDEX, COMPANY PROFILE, and INVESTEXT.

CONGRESSIONAL RECORD COMBINED FILE. Source: Mead Data Central. Available online. Contains records of 99th through 102nd Congresses.

CONGRESSIONAL MASTERFILE 1. Source: Congressional Information Service, Inc. Available on CD-ROM. Provides access to *CIS U.S. Serial Set Index* (1789-1969); *CIS U.S. Congressional Committee Prints Index* (1830-1969); and *CIS Unpublished U.S. Senate Committee Hearings Index* (1823-1964). Available for purchase as a complete set, with a supplement consisting of four additional databases. The CIS Complete Set includes titles listed above, plus: *CIS U.S. Congressional Committee Hearings Index* (1833-1936); *CIS Index to Unpublished U.S. House of Representatives Committee Hearings* (1833-1936); *CIS Index to Unpublished U.S. House of Representatives Committee Hearings* (1937-1946); *CIS Index to Unpublished U.S. Senate Committee Hearings* (1965-1968); and *CIS Index to U.S. Senate Executive Documents and Reports* (1817-1969). CONGRESSIONAL MASTERFILE 1 Supplement Set includes: *CIS Index to Unpublished U.S. Senate Committee Hearings* (1833-1936); *CIS Index to Unpublished U.S. House of Representatives Committee Hearings* (1937-1946); and *CIS Index to U.S. Senate Executive Documents & Reports* (1817-1969).

CONGRESSIONAL MASTERFILE 2. Source: Congressional Information Service, Inc. Available on CD-ROM. Print equivalent is the *CIS/Index*. Contains records from 1970 to present. Printed, monthly *CIS/Index* updates are included with the subscription.

CONGRESSIONAL RECORD ABSTRACTS. Source: National Standards Association. Vendor: DIALOG Information Services, Inc. Contains records from 1981 to present; available online. Indexes and abstracts the periodical, *Congressional Record.* Covers Congressional activities concerning bills and resolutions; committee and subcommittee reports; public laws, etc.

CORPORATE AFFILIATIONS. Source: National Register Publishing Co. Vendor: DIALOG Information Services, Inc. Contains current records. Available online and on CD-ROM through DIALOG. Combines information from the print directories, *Directory of Corporate Affiliations* and *International Directory of Corporate Affiliations*. Provides data for parent companies and their affiliates. Each entry contains the company's: name, address, telephone number, business description, executive names, and corporate family hierarchy.

CORPORATE ANNUAL REPORTS. Source: Mead Data Central. Available online. Contains corporate annual reports from June 1989 to present.

CORPORATE OWNERSHIP WATCH. Source: Dow Jones/News Retrieval. Available online. Provides data on insider trading activity for over 8,000 publicly held companies and 80,000 individuals.

CUMULATIVE BOOK INDEX (CBI). Source: H.W. Wilson. Available online through WILSONLINE and on CD-ROM through WILSONDISC. Contains citations and prices for published books, with access by author, title, and subject.

DIALOG QUOTES AND TRADING. Source: Trade*Plus. Vendor: DIALOG Information services, Inc. Provides current (with daily updates--20 minutes delay) stock and options quotes from the New York Stock Exchange, the American Stock Exchange, NASDAQ, and the four major options exchanges. Also order entry provides option to purchase or sell any stock or option listed in the *Wall Street Journal*.

DISCLOSURE. Source: Disclosure, Inc. Vendors: BRS, Data-Star, DIALOG Information Services, Inc., Dow Jones News/Retrieval, Mead Data Central, WESTLAW. Available online and on CD-ROM through Disclosure's COMPACT D/SEC. Covers current financial records on more than 12,500 companies traded on the New York Stock Exchange, the American Stock Exchange, the Over-the-Counter Exchange, etc.

Information is from reports filed with the Securities and Exchange Commission by publicly traded companies.

DISCLOSURE COMPACT D/SEC see COMPACT D/SEC

DISCLOSURE COMPACT D/'33 see COMPACT D/'33

DISCLOSURE/HISTORY. Source: Disclosure, Inc. Vendor: BRS. Available online. Contains over ten years of historical financial and textual data from approximately 12,000 American and non-U.S. publicly traded companies.

DISCLOSURE LASER D/SEC see LASER D/SEC

DISCLOSURE/SPECTRUM OWNERSHIP - Source: Disclosure, Inc. Vendor: DIALOG Information Services, Inc. Available online. Current information on public corporate ownership. Specifies specific institutions and individuals, how they relate to the company, their holdings, and most recent trades.

DISCLOSURE WORLDSCOPE - Source: Disclosure, Inc. Available as a CD-ROM product from Disclosure. Provides corporate financial data for over 7,000 companies in over 25 companies. Available in formats: GLOBAL, WORLDSCOPE EUROPE, WORLDSCOPE SNAPSHOTS, and COMPANY PROFILES.

DISSERTATION ABSTRACTS - Source: University Microfilms International (UMI). Vendors: BRS, DIALOG Information Services, Inc., OCLC. Available online and on CD-ROM through UMI/Data Courier's DISSERTATION ABSTRACTS ONDISC. Provides citations and abstracts to American dissertations in every subject field, including business and finance. Records available from 1861 to present.

DOW JONES BUSINESS NEWSWIRES. Source: Dow Jones/News Retrieval. Available online. Provides current access to seven leading newswires: DOW JONES NEWS, comprised of stories from Dow Jones News Service, the *Wall Street Journal*, and *Barron's*; DOW JONES INTERNATIONAL NEWS, containing news from Dow Jones' international newswires, plus the *Wall Street Journal, Wall Street Journal Europe,* and the *Asian Wall Street Journal*; PROFESSIONAL INVESTOR REPORT, containing intraday trading activity on over 5,000 stocks traded on the NYSE and the American Stock Exchange and the OTC National Market System; DOW JONES CAPITAL MARKETS REPORT, containing coverage of world-wide fixed income and financial futures markets; FEDERAL FILINGS, real time coverage of M & A filings on approximately 18,000 companies.

DOW JONES ENHANCED CURRENT QUOTES. Source: Dow Jones/News Retrieval. Available online. Contains quotes on common and preferred stocks, with exclusive News Alert feature; corporate and foreign bond data; mutual funds, U.S. Treasury issues and options (15 minute delay).

DOW JONES FUTURES & INDEX QUOTES. Source Dow Jones/News Retrieval. Available online. Contains current, with 10-30 minute time delay, plus historical quotes for over 80 contracts from the major exchanges. With Dow Jones Industry Group & Equity Market Indexes.

DOW JONES HISTORICAL QUOTES. Source: Dow Jones/News Retrieval. Available online. Provides historical quotes for common and preferred stocks, with daily quote history for one year, monthly summaries back to 1979, and quarterly summaries back to 1978.

DOW JONES QUICKSEARCH. Source: Dow Jones/News Retrieval. Available online. Gathers information from 8 databases: current stock quotes, financial overviews, company vs. industry performance, latest news, etc.

DOW JONES REAL TIME QUOTES. Source: Dow Jones/News Retrieval. Available online. Provides real-time stock quotes.

DOW JONES TEXT-SEARCH SERVICES. See TEXT-SEARCH SERVICES

DUN'S FINANCIAL RECORDS PLUS. Source: Dun & Bradstreet. Vendor: Dow Jones/News Retrieval. Available online. Contains financial reports and business information from Dun & Bradstreet covering approximately 1.5 million private and public companies.

ECONLIT. Source: The American Economic Association. Vendor: SilverPlatter Information. Available on CD-ROM. Provides citations and selected abstracts of international literature in field of economics, finance, etc. Covers journal articles, books, and dissertations, as well as chapters and articles in books and conference proceedings. Print equivalents are: *Journal of Economic Literature* and *Index of Economic Articles.*

ECONOMIC LITERATURE INDEX. Source: The American Economic Association. Vendor: DIALOG Information Services, Inc. Available online. Indexes journal articles and book reviews from approximately 260 journals and over 200 monographs. Since June 1984, abstracts have been added to approximately 25% of records. Corresponds to the index section of the *Journal of Economic Literature* and to the annual, *Index of Economic Articles.*

FACTS ON FILE. Source: Facts on File, Inc. Vendor: DIALOG Information Services, Inc. Available online. Provides current news concerning business and the economy, politics, etc. Corresponds to printed publication, Facts on File.

FEDERAL INDEX. Source: Capitol Services International. Vendor: DIALOG Information Services, Inc. Available online. Contains records from October 1976 through November 1980. Covers: proposed rules, bill introductions, hearings, executive orders, roll calls, etc.

FEDERAL REGISTER. Source: U.S. Government Printing Office. Vendor: DIALOG Information Services, Inc., Mead Data Central. Available online. Available on CD-ROM through DIALOG OnDisc. Contains records from 1988 to present. Provides full-text coverage of the U.S. Government periodical, *Federal Register.* Includes: Presidential documents, rules and regulations, notices, proposed rules, etc.

FEDERAL REGISTER ABSTRACTS. Source: U.S. Government Printing Office. Vendors: BRS, DIALOG Information Services, Inc. Contains abstracts from the periodical, *Federal Register.* Covers: Federal regulatory actions, legal notices, proposed rules, public laws, etc.

FEDERAL SECURITIES LIBRARY. Source: West Publishing Co. Available as a CD-ROM product. Contains relevant statutes, regulations, judicial and agency decisions, and treatises. FEDERAL SECURITIES LIBRARY is comprised of: SELECTED UNITED STATES CODE SECTIONS; FEDERAL SECURITIES REGULATIONS; SEC RULES OF PRACTICE; SECURITIES CODE ANNOTATIONS; COMMODITY FUTURES TRADING COMMISSION DECISIONS; HAZEN, THE LAW OF SECURITIES REGULATION; SECURITIES TABLE OF CASES; NO-ACTION LETTERS; SECURITIES AND EXCHANGE COMMISSION RELEASES; and FEDERAL SECURITIES CASES.

FINIS: FINANCIAL INDUSTRY INFORMATION SERVICE. Source: Bank Marketing Association. Vendors: BRS, DIALOG Information Services, Inc., Mead Data Central. Contains records from 1982 to present. Indexes and abstracts approximately 250 journals, books, press releases, newsletters, etc. concerning the financial services industry.

FIRST CALL: REAL-TIME EQUITY RESEARCH. Source: Thomson Financial Networks. Available online. Electronic delivery system for real-time equity research, earnings estimates, and fundamental data on thousands of U.S. and international companies.

FORBES. Source: Forbes, Inc. Vendors: Dow Jones/News Retrieval, Mead Data Central. Available online. Full-text coverage of journal, *Forbes* which contains articles about the NYSE.

FORTUNE. Source: Time, Inc. Vendors: Dow Jones/News Retrieval, Mead Data Central. Available online. Full-text coverage of journal, *Fortune* which includes articles about the NYSE.

FUTURES: THE MAGAZINE OF COMMODITIES & OPTIONS. Source: Oster Communications, Inc. Vendor: Mead Data Central. Available online. Full-text coverage of the periodical from January 1989 to present.

GPO MONTHLY CATALOG. Source: U.S. Government Printing Office. Vendors: BRS, DIALOG Information Services, Inc., OCLC's EPIC Service, OCLC's FirstSearch Catalog, SilverPlatter Information. Available online and on CD-ROM through SilverPlatter. Contains records from 1976 to present for U.S. Government publications including: Senate and House hearings, reports, fact sheets, etc. Corresponds to print: *Monthly Catalog of United States Government Publications.* See also GOVERNMENT PUBLICATIONS INDEX.

GPO PUBLICATIONS REFERENCE FILE. Source: U.S. Government Printing Office. Vendor: DIALOG Information Services, Inc. Available online. Contains records from 1971 to present. Provides information on GPO publications currently for sale and lists forthcoming and recently out-of-print publications. See also GOVERNMENT PUBLICATIONS INDEX.

GENERAL BUSINESSFILE. Source: Information Access Company (IAC). Available on CD-ROM through IAC's InfoTrac system. Integration of Information contained in BUSINESS INDEX, COMPANY PROFILE, and INVESTEXT databases. Data accessible by subject, company, location, industry, SIC code, and product.

GENERAL PERIODICALS INDEX. Source: Information Access Company. Available on CD-ROM through IAC's InfoTrac system. Indexes approximately 1100 popular magazines and journals. Approximately 50 of the journal titles contain abstracts. Includes all titles indexed in MAGAZINE INDEX/PLUS and BUSINESS INDEX.

GOVERNMENT PUBLICATIONS INDEX. Source: Information Access Company (IAC). Available on CD-ROM through IAC. Indexes GPO's *Monthly Catalog*. Provides coverage of public documents generated by legislative and executive branches of the U.S. Government. See also entries under GPO.

HARVARD BUSINESS REVIEW. Source: John Wiley & Sons, Inc. Vendors: BRS, Data-Star, DIALOG Information Services, Inc., Mead Data Central. Available online. Contains records from 1971 to present, with full-text coverage from 1976 to present.

HISTORICAL DOW JONES AVERAGES. Source: Dow Jones/News Retrieval. Available online. Contains daily high, low, close, and volume for industrials, transportation, utilities, and 65-stock composite starting from May 1982.

HOUSE DEBATES AND PROCEEDINGS. Source: Mead Data Central. Available online. Contains House debates from 99th through 102nd Congresses, from January 1985.

IDD M & A TRANSACTIONS. Source: IDD Information Services. Vendor: DIALOG Information Services, Inc. Available online and on CD-ROM through DIALOG OnDisc. Contains records from 1984 to present for United States data; from January 1987 to present for United Kingdom data. Provides information on publicly announced merger and acquisitions transactions.

INDEX TO LEGAL PERIODICALS. Source: H.W. Wilson. Vendors:

Mead Data Central, OCLC's EPIC Service, OCLC's FirstSearch Catalog. Available online through WILSONLINE, plus vendors listed. Available on CD-ROM through WILSONDISC. Indexes legal publications from the U.S., Canada, Great Britain, Ireland, Australia, and New Zealand. With book reviews sections, table of cases, and table of statutes.

INNOVEST TECHNICAL ANALYSIS REPORTS. Source: Dow Jones/News Retrieval. Available online. Presents data based on price and volume analysis for over 4500 stocks traded on the NYSE, the American Stock Exchange, and the Over-the-Counter Exchange.

INSIDER TRADING MONITOR. Source: InvestNet, Inc. Vendors: DIALOG Information Services, Inc., WESTLAW. Available online. Provides transaction details of insider trading filings (ownership changes) received by the SEC since 1984. Includes insider name, insider's position, company name, SIC code, ticker symbol, CUSIP number, etc.

INSTITUTIONAL INVESTOR. Source: Institutional Investor, Inc. Vendor: Mead Data Central. Available online. Full-text coverage of periodical publication, *Institutional Investor*, a source of articles about the NYSE.

INVESTEXT. Source: Thomson Financial Networks. Vendors: Data-Star, DIALOG Information Services, Inc., Dow Jones/News Retrieval, Information Access Company, WESTLAW. Available online and on CD-ROM through IAC. Contains over 200,000 full-text reports, from 1982 to the present, written by analysts of investment banks and research firms. Reports analyze companies and industries.

INVESTOR'S BUSINESS DAILY. Source: Investor's Business Daily, Inc. Vendor: Mead Data Central. Full-text of newspaper, with articles and statistics about the NYSE.

KNIGHT-RIDDER FINANCIAL NEWS. Source: Knight-Ridder Financial Information, Inc. Vendor: DIALOG Information Services, Inc. Contains records from January 5, 1987 to present, with continuous updates. Provides full-text coverage of news stories concerning worldwide financial and commodity markets.

LC MARC - BOOKS. Source: U.S. Library of Congress. Vendor: DIALOG Information Services, Inc., WILSONLINE. Available online. Contains records from 1968 to present. Provides records for all books cataloged by the Library of Congress.

LASER D/SEC. Source: Disclosure, Inc. Available on CD-ROM through Disclosure. A document retrieval system for SEC documents. Materials may be retrieved by entering a compnay name or ticker symbol and selecting desired documents from a listing of available filings. The documents retrieved can be viewed on a large, high-resolution monitor or printed out on a high-performance printer. Materials include documents concerning companies listed on the NYSE, the American Stock Exchange, and NASDAQ. Other LASER D/SEC products are LASER D/INTERNATIONAL, consisting of over 7,000 foreign annual reports and LASER D/BANKING containing filings from over 500 banks, thrifts, and savings and loans. COMPACT D/SEC is available as an option on all LASER D/SEC systems.

LEGAL RESOURCE INDEX. Source. Information Access Company. Vendors: BRS, DIALOG Information Services, Inc, Mead Data Central. Available online. Contains records from 1980 to the present. Indexes approximately 750 law journals and 7 legal newspapers, plus legal monographs. Indexes: articles, book reviews, case notes, letters to the editors, etc. Additionally, provides listings of relevant law articles from databases, MAGAZINE INDEX, NATIONAL NEWSPAPER INDEX, and TRADE AND INDUSTRY INDEX.

LEGALTRAC. Source: Information Access Company. Available as a CD-ROM product through IAC's InfoTrac system. Indexes over 800 legal publications including all major law reviews, 7 legal newspapers, law specialty publications and bar association journals. Database is sponsored by the American Association of Law Libraries.

M & A FILINGS. Source: Charles E. Simon & Co. Vendors: DIALOG Information Services, Inc., WESTLAW. Available online. Contains records from April 1985 to present. Provides abstracts of all original and amended merger and acquisition documents released by the Securities and Exchange Commission. Information includes: company name, ticker symbol, CUSIP number, SIC code, etc. Called, CHARLES E. SIMON & COMPANY's MERGERS AND ACQUISITIONS in the WESTLAW system.

MCGRAW-HILL PUBLICATIONS ONLINE. Source: McGraw-Hill, Inc. Vendor: DIALOG Information Services, Inc. Available online. Full-text coverage of major McGraw-Hill publications among which are: *Business Week*, from 1985 to present and *Securities Week*, from 1986 to present.

MAGAZINE ASAP. Source: Information Access Co. Vendors: BRS, DIALOG Information Services, Inc. Available online. Provides full-text and indexing for more than 100 publications selected from the 500 publications covered in MAGAZINE INDEX. Contains records from 1983 to the present. Includes full-text of articles, editorials, columns, reviews, product evaluations, etc. Called MAGAZINE ASAP IIIin BRS system.

MAGAZINE ASAP III. see MAGAZINE ASAP.

MAGAZINE DATABASE. see MAGAZINE INDEX

MAGAZINE INDEX. Source: Information Access Co. Vendors: BRS, Data-Star, DIALOG Information Services, Inc. Available online. For CD-ROM coverage, see entry, MAGAZINE INDEX/PLUS. Contains records from approximately 500 popular magazines, including *Time,*

Newsweek, Business Week, Fortune, etc. Covers records from 1959 to March 1970 and 1973 to the present. MAGAZINE INDEX contains full-text of records from over 100 magazines from 1983 to present. Called, MAGAZINE DATABASE in Data-Star system.

MAGAZINE INDEX/PLUS. Source: Information Access Co. Available on CD-ROM through IAC's InfoTrac system. Indexes approximately 400 popular magazines and the *New York Times*. Covers current events, business, consumer information, etc.

MANAGEMENT CONTENTS. Source: Information Access Co. Vendors: BRS, Data-Star, DIALOG Information Services, Inc. Available online. Contains records from 1974 to present. Indexes and abstracts information from journals, conference proceedings, transactions, newsletters, and research reports. Covers areas of accounting, economics, finance, managerial economics, organizational behavior, etc.

MEDIA GENERAL FINANCIAL SERVICES. Source: Dow Jones/News Retrieval. Available online. Presents financial and statistical information for 6200 companies and 180 industries.

MUTUAL FUND PERFORMANCE REPORT. Source: Dow Jones/News Retrieval. Available online. Provides historical performance, assets, and background information for approximately 1500 mutual funds.

NATIONAL NEWSPAPER INDEX. Source: Information Access Company. Vendors: BRS, DIALOG Information Services, Inc. Available online and on CD-ROM through IAC's InfoTrac system. Indexes: the *New York Times,* the *Wall Street Journal, Christian Science Monitor, Washington Post,* and *Los Angeles Times.*

NEWSDAY & NEW YORK NEWSDAY. Source: Newsday. Vendor:

DIALOG Information Services, Inc. Available online through DIALOG's PAPERS database and on CD-ROM through DIALOG OnDisc. Covers news items concerning New York City government and business. Provides statistics on the securities markets. Coverage is from 1988 to present.

NEWSEARCH. Source: Information Access Company. Vendors: BRS, DIALOG Information Services, Inc. Available online for current month only. Indexes over 2000 news stories, information articles, and book reviews from approximately 1700 leading newspapers, magazines, and periodicals.

NEWSPAPER ABSTRACTS. Source: UMI. Vendor: DIALOG Information Services, Inc. Available online. Contains records from 1984-1988. Indexes and abstracts *American Banker, Atlanta Constitution, Chicago Tribune, Christian Science Monitor, New York Times, Pravda, St. Louis Post-Dispatch, USA Today, Wall Street Journal,* etc.

NEWSPAPER ABSTRACTS ONDISC. Source: UMI/Data Courier. Available on CD-ROM through UMI/Data Courier. Provides citations and abstracts for newspaper articles from *Atlanta Constitution, Atlanta Journal* (selected articles only), *Boston Globe, Chicago Tribune, Christian Science Monitor, Los Angeles Times, New York Times, Wall Street Journal,* and *Washington Post.* Updated monthly. Subscription options are flexible: each one includes the *New York Times* and subscribers can add any combination of the other newspapers.

NEWS/RETRIEVAL WORLD REPORTS. Source: Dow Jones/News Retrieval. Available online. Provides continuously updated major national and international news from the Associated Press, Dow Jones News Service and other broadcast media.

NEWSWIRE ASAP. Source: Information Access Company. Vendor: DIALOG Information Services, Inc. Available online. Contains records from PR NEWSWIRE (January 1985 to present), KYODO (July 1987 to present), and REUTERS (June 1987 to present). Full text coverage of news releases and wire stories with information on business and financial news, stock markets, commodities, world news, etc.

OASYS: ELECTRONIC ORDER ALLOCATION. Source: Thomson Financial Networks. Available online. Electronic network for sending and confirming trade order allocations.

OCLC EPIC Service. Source. OCLC Online Computer Center, Inc. Available online. Offers complete subject and keyword access to the OCLC Online Union Catalog as well as access to more than 450 databases from DIALOG Information Services, Inc., BRS, H.W. Wilson, VU/TEXT, and FT Information Online Ltd.

OCLC FirstSearch Catalog. Source: OCLC Online Computer Center, Inc. Available online. A reference service for patrons offering access to the OCLC Online Union Catalog and other databases. Includes a menu interface designed for library patrons. Provides access to databases from BRS, DIALOG Information Services, Inc., H.W. Wilson, etc.

OCLC Online Union Catalog. Source: OCLC Online Computer Center, Inc. Available online. Contains over 23 million bibliographic records with approximately 2 million added each year. Institutions represented include the Library of Congress as well as international research, public, special, and academic libraries. Provides records of books, serials, audiovisual materials, U.S. Government publications, etc. Location symbols of libraries owning Online Union Catalog materials are provided for each record.

PAIS INTERNATIONAL. Source: Public Affairs Information Service, Inc. Vendors: BRS, Data-Star, DIALOG Information Services, OCLC's EPIC system. Available online through the vendors listed. Available on CD-ROM through Public Affairs Information Service and through

SilverPlatter Information, Inc. Contains records from 1972 to present. Provides information on public policy literature of business, economics, government, political science, etc. Indexes periodicals, books, U.S. U.S. Government documents, state documents, pamphlets, etc.

PR NEWSWIRE. Source: PR Newswire Association, Inc. Vendors: DIALOG Information Services, Inc., NewsNet. Available online. Contains records from May 1, 1987 to present. Provides full-text of news releases of companies, public relations agencies, Federal government agencies, state and city government agencies, etc. Each release includes name and telephone number of a spokesperson to be contacted for further information.

PTS ANNUAL REPORTS ABSTRACTS. Source: Predicasts. Vendor: DIALOG Information Services, Inc. Available online. Presents current annual report information for over 4000 publicly held and selected international corporations.

PTS PROMT. Source: Predicasts. Vendors: BRS, DIALOG Information Services, Inc. Contains records from 1972 to present on DIALOG and from 1980 to present on BRS. Provides abstracts and full-text records from over 1000 business publications among which are trade journals, newspapers, newsletters, research studies, corporate news releases, investment analysts' reports, and corporate annual reports.

PAPERS. Source: Individual newspaper publishers. Vendor: DIALOG Information Services, Inc. Available online. Years of coverage vary for each file. Provides full-text coverage (excluding classified ads, sports statistics, fillers, and minor items) of the newspapers, *Boston Globe, Charlotte Observer, Chicago Tribune, Arizona Business Gazette, Houston Post, Newsday, New York Newsday, Philadelphia Inquirer, Sacramento Bee, San Francisco Chronicle, USA Today,* etc.

PERIODICALS ABSTRACTS ONDISC. Source: UMI/Data Courier.

Available on CD-ROM. Provides citations and abstracts from over 450 general-reference periodicals from 1988 to present. Also includes retrospective indexing and abstracting for a group of frequently cited titles back through 1986. Among topics covered are: consumer affairs, business, politics, the arts, etc.

POPULAR MAGAZINE REVIEW ONLINE. Source: EBSCO Industries, Inc. Vendor: BRS. Available online. Contains records from 1984 to present. Features abstracts of popular U.S. periodical literature.

RLIN. Source: RLIN Information Center, the Research Libraries Group, Inc. Available online. Database containing records of books, maps, periodicals, videotapes, scores, and photographs. Among the more than 100 institutions whose records are a part of the RLIN database are the Library of Congress, the National Library of Medicine, the U.S. Government Printing Office, the British Library, and the National Library of Canada. Records may be retrieved through personal name, title word, subject headings, or corporate or conference name. Searches may be broadened or narrowed with Boolean operators. Results of searches may be further limited by language, publication dates, country of publication, etc. Location symbols of libraries owning materials listed are included. Access to RLIN is available through Internet and Telenet. Subscribers may use RLIN as a search only automated system and libraries may subscribe to RLIN's cataloging, acquisitions, and interlibrary loan system.

READERS' GUIDE ABSTRACTS. Source: H.W. Wilson. Available online through WILSONLINE and OCLC's EPIC and FirstSearch Catalog Systems. Available on CD-ROM through WILSONDISC. Provides indexing and abstracting of approximately 200 general interest periodicals.

READERS' GUIDE TO PERIODICAL LITERATURE. Source: H.W. Wilson. Available online through WILSONLINE and OCLC's EPIC and FirstSearch Catalog Systems. Available on CD-ROM through WILSONDISC. Indexes general interest periodicals. Corresponds to printed source of same title.

REUTER FINANCIAL REPORT. Source: Reuters U.S., Inc. Vendor: Mead Data Central. Available online. Contains records from January 1987 to present. Provides full-text of financial news.

REUTERS. Source: Reuters U.S., Inc. Vendors: DIALOG Information Services, Inc., NewsNet. Available online. Contains records from January 1987 to the present. Provides full-text coverage from REUTER BUSINESS REPORT and REUTER LIBRARY SERVICE NEWSWIRES. Includes current information on stocks and commodities.

S & P. See Standard & Poor's

SEC DECISIONS AND REPORTS. Source: Securities and Exchange Commission. Vendor: WESTLAW. Available online. Covers adjudicative decisions of the SEC from 1934 to present.

SEC DOCKET. Source: Securities and Exchange Commission. Vendor: WESTLAW. Available online. Contains releases published in the SEC Docket from 1981 to present.

SEC INTERPRETIVE RELEASES. Source: Securities and Exchange Commission. Vendor: WESTLAW. Available online. Contains selected releases of the SEC from 1933 to present, including documents available in public files. New documents as they are published in the *Federal Register* are available from 1981 to present.

SEC NEWS DIGEST. Source: Securities and Exchange Commission. Vendors: Mead Data Central, WESTLAW. Available online. Contains SEC releases, announcements, and filings published in the *SEC News Digest* from July 1987 to present (WESTLAW) and June 1985 to present (Mead Data Central).

SEC NO-ACTION LETTERS. Source: Securities and Exchange Commission. Vendor: WESTLAW. Available online. Contains letters released by the SEC analyzing and responding to written requests that the SEC take no action regarding the securities transaction described in the letter.

SEC ONLINE. Source: SEC Online, Inc. Available online through vendors: DIALOG Information Services, Inc., Dow Jones/News Retrieval, Federal Filings, Information America, Mead Data Central, WESTLAW. Available on CD-ROM through: Lotus One Source, Standard & Poor's COMPUSTAT, and Silver Platter Information Services. Contains reports filed by publicly-held corporations with the SEC. Presents full-text coverage of all corporations listed on the NYSE, the American Stock Exchange, and NASDAQ. Types of documents available are: 10K, 20F, 10Q, Annual Report, Proxy Statement, and Company Resume. Contains records from July 1987 to the present.

SEC RELEASES, DOCKET FROM 1933: LITIGATION RELEASES; INTERPRETIVE RELEASES, INCLUDING SECURITIES ACT '33 RELEASES, SECURITIES EXCHANGE ACT '34 RELEASES, ETC. Source: Securities and Exchange Commission. Vendor: Mead Data Central. Available online. Provides full-text coverage of releases.

SIC STATE-OF-THE-ART PROTECTION. Source: Thomson Financial Networks. Available online. Securities Information or SIC is the sole operator of the SEC's Lost and Stolen Securities Program. Database system is used to identify lost and stolen securities.

SECURITIES WEEK. Source: McGraw-Hill, Inc. Vendors: DIALOG Information Services, Inc., Dow Jones/News Retrieval, Mead Data Central, NewsNet. Available online. Provides full-text coverage of the periodical, *Securities Week* from 1986 to present.

SENATE DEBATES AND PROCEEDINGS. Source: Mead Data Central. Available online. Covers 99th through 102nd Congresses, from January 1985.

STANDARD & POOR'S COMPUSTAT. Source: Standard & Poor's COMPUSTAT Services, Inc. Available on CD-ROM combined with COMPUSTAT's PC Plus Financial Analysis System. PC Plus offers users capabilities of downloading, combining items, customizing items and formats, and backtesting of investment theories. The COMPUSTAT database contains information for approximately 7100 publicly traded companies, including companies traded on the NYSE; 270 industry groups; 5700 inactive companies; 120 S & P Indexes; 20 years of annual data; 12 years of quarterly data; 7 years of business segments; and 20 years of monthly market data. COMPUSTAT also makes accessible data for: price-dividends-earnings; major indexes including the New York Stock Exchange Composite; monthly market information including high, low, and closing prices; and industry indexes. COMPUSTAT is appropriate for: securities analysis; investment portfolio management and oversight; competitive analysis; corporate planning; marketing; credit analysis; potential merger/acquistion strategies; and divestiture.

STANDARD & POOR'S COMSTOCK. Source: Standard & Poor's Corporation. Available online. Real-time financial information service with current data from over 50 markets and exchanges, domestic and international. Covers current information and statistics for equities, options, futures, commodities, foreign exchange, currency analysis, and news. Offers instantaneous global market coverage 24 hours a day.

STANDARD & POOR'S CORPORATE DESCRIPTIONS ONLINE. Source: Standard & Poor's Corporation. Vendor: DIALOG Information Services, Inc. Available online. A full-text database that provides strategic business and financial information for over 9,000 publicly-owned corporations. Company records consist of: name, state, city or country of headquarters; ticker symbol; primary SIC Code; bond descriptions; stock data, including shares authorized and outstanding, price and dividend history, and principal stockholders with holdings;

annual report data; capitalization summary, etc.

STANDARD & POOR'S CORPORATIONS. Source: Standard & Poor's Corporation. Available on CD-ROM product developed by Standard & Poor's and DIALOG Information Services, Inc. Provides data from printed Standard & Poor's sources, *Corporations Records; Standard & Poor's Register of Corporations, Directors, and Executives* as well as the COMPUSTAT Service. Presents data for both public and private companies. Information includes: name; ticker symbol; operating income; general business description; market territory; stock exchange; bond desciption; stock data, etc.

STANDARD & POOR'S DAILY NEWS ONLINE. Source: Standard & Poor's Corporation. Vendor: DIALOG Information Services, Inc. Available online. Contains business and financial news stories concerning over 12,000 publicly-owned companies.

STANDARD & POOR'S INDEX ALERT. Source: Standard & Poor's Corporation. Available online. Offers immediate access to S & P Index activity, notifying users of Index additions and deletions.

STANDARD & POOR'S MARKETSCOPE. Source: Standard & Poor's Corporation. An online, advisory information service that provides continuously updated information on over 5,000 corporations and mutual funds, with current analysis of stocks and bond market activity. S & P analysts rate stocks by assigning 1 to 5 STARS, the acronym for its Stock Appreciation Ranking System. Also presents commentary in MARKETSCOPE's Action Pages.

STANDARD & POOR'S MARKETSCOPE ALERT. Source: Standard & Poor's Corporation. Available online. A topic-based version of MARKETSCOPE, enabling users to conduct customized searches for all MARKETSCOPE articles on a given subject.

STANDARD & POOR'S ONLINE. Source: Standard & Poor's Corporation. Vendor: Dow Jones/News Retrieval. Available online. Provides 4700 company profiles containing current and historical earnings and estimates, dividend and market figures.

STANDARD & POOR'S REGISTER ONLINE. Source: Standard & Poor's Corporation. Vendor: DIALOG Information Services, Inc. Available online. Record of company information lists; company name, address, and telephone number; names of officers; primary and secondary SIC codes; year started; stock exchanges where company's stocks are traded; subsidiary status, etc.

STANDARD & POOR'S STOCK GUIDE/BOND GUIDE DATABASE. Source: Standard & Poor's Corporation. Available in flexible magnetic tape and electronic formats. Offers users ability to follow monthly trading activity, stock splits and dividends, bond rating histories, etc.

STATISTICAL MASTERFILE. Source: Congressional Information Service, Inc. Available on CD/ROM. Provides access to records from the printed, *American Statistics Index (ASI)*, *Statistical Reference Index (SRI)*, and *Index to International Statistics (IIS)*. Subscription includes a CD-ROM database disk (two disks are included for the retrospective service), with quarterly CD-ROM disk updates, plus monthly printed subscription.

TEXT-SEARCH SERVICES. Source: Dow Jones/News Retrieval. Available online. Searches approximately 550 sources in a menu driven or command edition. Provides full-text coverage of the *Wall Street Journal*, from January 1984 to present; the *Washington Post*, from January 1984 to the present; and full-text of selected articles from *Time, Economist, Forbes, Fortune*, and over 200 publications. Also Provides full-text of BUSINESS WIRE and PR NEWSWIRE press releases since July 1989.

TRADE & INDUSTRY INDEX. Source: Information Access Company. Vendors: Data-Star, DIALOG Information Services, Inc. Available online. Contains records from 1981 to present. Indexes and selectively abstracts journals and newspapers. Journals include: *Advertising Age, Tax Advisor,* etc. Newspapers include: the *Wall Street Journal, New York Times Financial Section, American Banker,* and *Barron's.* Database also contains records from the Area Business Databank which contains indexing and abstracts from more than 100 local and regional business publications, from January 1985 to the present. Indexing and abstracting for TRADE AND & INDUSTRY INDEX is also provided in NEWSEARCH for daily updating during the current month. Called TRADE & INDUSTRY DATABASE is Data-Star system.

TRADE & INDUSTRY ASAP. Source: Information Access Company. Vendors: BRS, DIALOG Information Services, Inc. Available online. Presents selective complete text and indexing for more than 200 journals chosen from the approximately 400 journals in TRADE & INDUSTRY INDEX. Coverage is from 1983 to present. Also contains news releases from PR NEWSWIRE. Called TRADE & INDUSTRY ASAP III in BRS system.

TRADELINE. Source: Dow Jones/News Retrieval. Available online. Provides up to 15 years of historical quotes on stocks, bonds, mutual funds, indexes, foreign exchange rates, etc. With option history back up to one year.

TRINET COMPANY DATABASE. Source: Trinet, Inc. Vendor: DIALOG Information Services, Inc. Available online. Provides current financial information on public and privately-held companies. Contains aggregate company information.

TRINET U.S. BUSINESSES. Source: Trinet, Inc. Vendor: DIALOG Information Services, Inc. Available online. Provides current financial information on public and privately-held companies. Contains share of market and top executive data for individual companies.

UPI BUSINESS & FINANCE WIRE. Source: United Press International. Vendor: NewsNet. Available online. Contains worldwide business and financial developments.

UPI NEWS. Source: United Press International. Vendor: DIALOG Information Services, Inc. Contains records from April 1983 to present. Provides full-text of news stories from United Press International wire service.

USA TODAY. Source: Gannett Satellite Information Network, Inc. Vendors: Data-Star, Mead Data Central. Available online. Contains records from 1988 to present (Data-Star); 1989 to present (Mead Data Central). Provides news items from the newspaper, *USA Today*. Covers subjects of business, investing, banking, etc.

USA TODAY DECISIONLINE. Source: Gannett News Media. Vendor: DIALOG Information Services, Inc. Available online. Contains records from 1990 to present. Offers top news stories in 18 categories including banking and economy, business law, personal investing, and international news.

VICKERS/ARGUS MARKET GUIDE ON-LINE. Source: Vickers Stock Research Corporation, an affiliate of Argus Research. Available online. Provides current financial information for companies traded on the NYSE, the American Stock Exchanges, and NASDAQ.

VICKERS INDUSTRY ON-LINE. Source: Vickers Stock Research Corporation, an affiliate of Argus Research. Available online. Provides data on institutional stock ownership by industry.

VICKERS ON-LINE. Source: Vickers Stock Research Corporation, an affiliate of Argus Research. Available online. Contains current information, with 24-hour access, concerning over 3500 institutional portfolios, summaries of merger and acquisition filings. Also includes trading activity and intention filings by insiders.

VU/QUOTE STOCK AND COMMODITY QUOTES. Source: NewsNet. Available online. Provides stock quotations for companies traded on the NYSE, AMEX, and NASDAQ, plus commodities. Stock quotes are delayed 20 minutes; commodities, ten minutes. Additionally, presents current market summaries: ten biggest gainers and losers, ten most active stocks, daily opening, daily high and low, latest quote, etc. With real-time Dow Jones Industrial Average.

WALL STREET COMPUTER REVIEW. Source: Dealers' Digest, Inc. Vendor: Mead Data Central. Available online. Full-text coverage of the periodical, *Wall Street Computer Review*, from 1988 to present.

WALL STREET S.O.S. Source: Security Objective Service. Vendor: NewsNet. Available online. Provides stock market data, analyzes the day's activity, offers trading recommendations, and forecasts the next three to five days using the Security Objective Service (SOS) Bull/Bear Index.

WALL STREET S.O.S. OPTIONS ALERT. Source: Security Objective Service. Vendor: NewsNet. Available online. Provides daily advice on Index Options.

WALL STREET WEEK ONLINE. Source: Dow Jones/News Retrieval. Available online. Comprised of transcripts of the PBS television program, "Wall Street Week."

WEEKLY MARKET ANALYSIS. Source: Dow Jones/News Retrieval. Available online. Presents U.S. money market and foreign exchange trends, with median forecasts indicators, equities, and debt market commentary.

WESTLAW FULL TEXT OF BILLS. Source: WESTLAW. Contains full text of bills from 101st and 102nd Congresses as part of WESTLAW's Legislation Library.

WESTLAW TOPICAL HIGHLIGHTS--CORPORATIONS AND SECURITIES. Source: WESTLAW. Available online. Contains documents that summarize recent developments in corporation and securities law.

WILSON BUSINESS ABSTRACTS. Source: H.W. Wilson. Available online through WILSONLINE, OCLC EPIC Service, and OCLC FirstSearch Catalog. Available on CD-ROM through WILSONDISC. Indexes and abstracts articles included in BUSINESS PERIODICALS INDEX database.

ZACKS CORPORATE EARNINGS ESTIMATOR. Source: Dow Jones/News Retrieval. Available online. Provides consensus earnings-per-share estimates and P/E ratio forecasts for 3500 companies and 100 industries.

AUTHOR INDEX
Numbers refer to entry numbers, not to page numbers.

323

TITLE INDEX
Numbers refer to entry numbers, not to page numbers.

SUBJECT INDEX

Numbers refer to entry numbers, not to page numbers.